MASTERING THE LAW

ATLANTIC CROSSINGS

Gabriel Paquette, Series Editor

MASTERING THE LAW

SLAVERY & FREEDOM
IN THE LEGAL ECOLOGY
OF THE SPANISH EMPIRE

RICARDO RAÚL SALAZAR REY

The University of Alabama Press
Tuscaloosa

The University of Alabama Press
Tuscaloosa, Alabama 35487-0380
uapress.ua.edu

Typeface: Perpetua

Cover image: Ramón Torres Méndez, *Champan en el rio Magdalena*, 1851
Cover design: Michele Myatt Quinn

Cataloging-in-Publication data is available from the Library of Congress.
ISBN: 978-0-8713-2066-9
E-ISBN: 978-0-8173-9316-8

To Juana de la Rosa, born in Africa and brought as a slave to Cartagena, where she eventually gained her freedom, an entitlement preserved by her daughters so that her grandchildren could be baptized and live as free *vecinos* of Cartagena

And when our time is eagerly reviewed by those not yet born, but who appear to arrive with kinder faces, it will transpire that the ones who suffered during past ordeals shall receive some approbation, in part because those of us who are a bit ahead of our time tend to suffer much.

—"Frente al balance, mañana," in *Vámonos patria a caminar*, by Otto René Castillo

CONTENTS

FIGURES

PREFACE

For three centuries, Iberoamerican customs, laws, and the institutions that enforced them—what I call here the legal ecology—provided Spanish subjects, including enslaved Afroiberians, freedpeople, and their descendants, with a common language and forum to resolve disputes. Looking to decipher the durability of the systems that produced the legal documents we find in the archives, I set out to trace back in time the ideas and the language that they embodied. Eventually, I found that the institutions governing the Spanish Empire were inseparable from the early medieval reception and Christianization of Roman law. Roman institutions were transmuted into medieval Iberian ones via the fires of the Reconquista. Carried in the minds of the Spanish conquistadors and the royal officials who followed them, they then spread across the Atlantic and Pacific to become the core components of the first global empire.

The narrative of decline that imbues the history of the Spanish Empire simply does not explain the legitimacy and competence demonstrated by its durability. Indeed, the Spanish managed to consolidate the unexpectedly vast military gains made during the Age of Exploration (1450–1550) while under increasing competitive pressure from other European powers. For the Spanish Hapsburg monarchs, projecting royal authority throughout their global domains required significant cooperation from the indigenous, African, and mestizo population they sought to rule. Throughout, Spain's medieval inheritance shaped the development of its empire in the Indies, in dialogue with the environment in which it operated.

In this book, I am guided by a few key questions. How did those ruled by the Spanish Empire and its institutions understand the latter? How did they participate in them, and how did they understand this participation? How did their engagement shape their everyday lives? How did it shape their understanding of their own place within the law? Conversely, how did they themselves shape the institutions of the Spanish Empire? On an interpersonal level, how did Africans, Amerindians, Europeans, and their mestizo descendants deal with their own multifaceted participation in this system? Finally, on the systemic level, how did the intelligentsia and ruling classes of the Spanish Empire reconcile, regulate, and even foment slave owning during a period of intense moral, ideological, and military competition?

My understanding of slavery, empire, and legal institutions has been shaped by insights and biases acquired growing up in Iberoamerica and immigrating to the United States. Attending public schools in Guatemala, I was exposed to an educational environment that traced all our ills to the Spanish Empire. At home, the dysfunctionality endured by those around me was casually blamed on the Iberian yoke. A favorite subject of adult conversation revolved around the constant balancing act required to avoid being victimized while attempting to benefit from pervasive bribery and corruption. Guatemalan self-understanding blames present ills on our Spanish colonial past, allowing us to absolve ourselves of responsibility with rueful gratitude.

The narratives underpinning the collective imaginary of my small town were thrown into sharp relief when I became an economic migrant. My arrival into California's precariat as an eighteen-year-old Guatemalan reinforced the importance of understanding the interplay between laws (local, state, federal), the institutions that enforce them, and the communities they regulate. Barred from lawful employment because of uncertain documentation, I quickly became an unsustainable burden on my aunt. After a communal crash course on what I needed from the Social Security Administration to unlock the labor system, I marched into a cavernous and chaotic federal office in downtown San Bernardino. In response to my pleas for help, a clerk pointed me to a massive book chained to the wall. This was not helpful. Trying to read impenetrable legal jargon on smudged and torn paper left me overwhelmed. Nevertheless, necessity is an engaging teacher, and with the persistence, kindness, and guidance of family, friends, and officials, I managed to grasp the legal procedure and ultimately resolve the issue. I would later find that this experience of dislocation and forced learning distantly echoed the experiences of enslaved Afroiberians under Spanish rule.

The view I had of the Spanish Empire remained largely unchallenged by the classes I took relating to Latin America in community college and at UCLA. California had been part of the viceroyalty of New Spain longer than it has been part of the United States, but collegiate surveys of that history introduced the Spanish as brutal yet brittle foils, easily swept aside by indomitable, if absentmindedly racist, American pioneers as they pursued their manifest destiny. Reinforcing my comfortable assumptions of Iberian perfidy, the rare class discussions of slavery in the Spanish Empire usually focused on plantation slavery in nineteenth century Cuba and in all cases portrayed it unambiguously as the epitome of black and white, a tale of victims and monsters.

My understanding of Iberoamerica was finally upended in graduate school, under the wise tutelage of John Womack Jr. and Vincent Brown. In a series of transformative research seminars, they helped me engage with records produced by the office of the Inquisition that was established in Cartagena at the beginning of the seventeenth century. What emerged was disorienting: there were no simple monsters and equally few heroic victims, only human beings of shifting races, empires, and nations collaborating in a great human tragedy. Learning about the Atlantic slave trade challenged my understanding of the capacity of our species for collective evil. While slavery is, to be sure, explicit oppression, as I examined the documents, the people in them came alive, rebuking me for reducing them to exploited ciphers or simplistic villains.

To my further surprise, I also discovered an empire whose rulers, despite operating in an almost continual state of crisis, generally attempted to provide Spanish Catholic *buen gobierno* (good governance) to their subjects. How they understood buen gobierno was shaped by Iberian history, the ideological justification of empire, and the need for cooperation from the subjects of the crown. At the same time, it operated within the context created by competing early modern European empires. Legalistic, profit-oriented, and ranging from the puritanical to the piratical, European arbitrage of the Atlantic world established an as-yet unending and violent series of negotiations between a kaleidoscope of patrons and clients, crafting explicitly unequal relationships.

As I show in this book, for Africans and their descendants in Spanish America, mastering the law was a key factor in how they became part of Iberoamerican society. Teaching *bozales* (new arrivals) the way that the legal ecology functioned was part of how the established Afroiberian communities protected their rights and customs. Slave owners preferred bozales and tried to keep them away from acculturated Afroiberians because they feared the limitations on their power that knowledge of the legal ecology provided. Access to the law for all subjects of the Spanish Crown, which explicitly included indigenous peoples, Afroiberians, and mestizos, was a cornerstone of the legitimacy that the Spanish Habsburgs wove into the fabric of their dominance in the Indies. For enslaved Afroiberians this social contract opened up spaces and opportunities for social mobility that encouraged them to become stakeholders in Iberoamerican society. None of this made enslavement anything less than exploitation enforced by violence, but mastering the law enabled Afroiberians to shape their lives and should be examined on that basis.

In my quest to understand the unexpectedly complex Spanish Empire, I gained an extensive appreciation for the capacious knowledge and cunning of the Afroiberians I encountered in the documents. My analytical choices respond to several factors. First, every surviving legal document we have is both mediated and a copy. The variations in the fidelity with which the testimonies of educated elites and acculturated Africans are recorded and preserved are at most matters of degree. Therefore, we can judge only approximately how accurately the content of the documents reflects the intentions and understanding of the named speakers. Second, my expectations of what is normal among marginalized migrant groups have been shaped by personal experiences like learning about the imminent launch of the euro in 1999 from my undocumented coworkers' musings on its possible effect on international exchange rates. Examples of sophisticated and multidirectional cross-border cultural diffusion driven by marginalized migrants abound, from the Tucanes de Tijuana singing about *Breaking Bad* to the policy proposals embedded in the Tamil-British artist M.I.A.'s highly popular music video "Borders."

Furthermore, my approach is influenced by the understanding that exploitation and inequality are universal in complex human societies; however, their severity and functionality, and the durability of the social systems they engender, are crucial to understanding power and its transformations. In some cases, social inequality may be perceived as legitimate enough to be endurable if existing disparities do not become so excessive as to overburden people's daily lives. The distortions caused by the institutions that produced the records available means that we must parse ambiguous evidence regarding how Iberoamericans perceived the legitimacy of the Spanish Empire. However, one-sided exploitation does not account for the complex human relationships found in the primary sources.

Finally, as I write this preface, we are well reminded that the law, institutions, and customs constitutive of the legal ecology operate interdependently, and that their capacity to restrain violence and exploitation by the powerful toward the vulnerable is contingent and seldom linear. Exploitative and unequal as it was, the Spanish Empire sustained itself through and found support among many of those whom we today do not perceive as its beneficiaries. On its own, condemnation of enslavement, patriarchy, exploitation, or imperialism is justifiable but does little to advance our comprehension of these phenomena. Accordingly, this work grapples with humanity's capacity to sustain and infuse legitimacy in contradictory ideas and behaviors, simultaneously kind and cruel, slave and free, lawful and lawless.

ACKNOWLEDGMENTS

I would like to acknowledge and salute the generosity and kindness of all the people who have helped me bring this project to fruition. In particular, the staff of the Archivo General de la Nación in Bogota (AGN), the Archivo General de Indias in Seville (AGI), and the Archivo Histórico Nacional in Madrid (AHN) were knowledgeable and helpful. My brilliant paleography teacher and unflagging collaborator Adriana Martinez Aguirre made the archives intelligible and helped me find and transcribe many of the cases I used. I am grateful to my students who read and discussed my work and listened to my struggle, especially Jenifer Rojas Orellana, Brian Bremmer, and Jeremy Timperanza. Special thanks to Manuel Arriola, *maestro de arte en la escuela Mesoamericano en Chimaltenango*, who raced against time to draw the maps which enliven these pages.

I gratefully recognize the work of the scholars who took on the responsibility to be readers, Nicole von Germeten and Michelle McKinley, both of whom provided rigorous and useful feedback. Deep thanks to Wendi Schnaufer, a senior acquisitions editor at the University of Alabama Press, for her patience and above-and-beyond efforts to make this project materialize in time to save my bacon. *Mi querido profe* Gabe Paquette gave me the opportunity to publish this book under his aegis and has been an inspirational mentor and a source of constant support. Editor extraordinaire Erna von de Walde injected her joyful sagacity at every level. What is good in this work owes much to her. And finally, to Mark Healey, the best jefe anyone could ask for, who carried me kicking and screaming across the finish line. Without him this book would not exist.

MASTERING THE LAW

INTRODUCTION

Slavery and the Law in Latin America

This book explores the legal praxis of Iberoamerican slavery and its consequences for the lives of enslaved Afroiberians and their descendants in the Spanish Empire during the long seventeenth century (1580–1714).[1] As such, I also examine the limits of coercive power and the unequal negotiations that formed the crux of early modern European imperial rule. For this purpose, I focus on a range of legal cases involving enslaved and freed Afroiberians in Spanish imperial courts, mostly in Cartagena de Indias. Throughout, I highlight the importance of African agency, the European context out of which the institution of slavery emerged, and the context of imperial competition that pervasively shaped its exercise.

Over the first two centuries of European colonization in the New World, particularities in the operationalization of slave law were sharpened by the development of competing imperial models. Intertwined and in dialogue with these meta-imperial forces were local individual and collective actions. Officials tasked with consolidating the bloody and uncertain territorial claims of the conquistadors carried with them a deep tradition of Mediterranean empire building. They understood that legitimacy is both theater and substance and that the Spanish Empire could exist only as long as enough people agreed that it did.[2] Therefore, the institutions they operated largely cooperated in maintaining the viability of the empire while simultaneously competing with each other for resources, authority, and the legitimacy arising from the dignity of their members and the equitability of their adjudications.[3]

Cartagena was a key site where institutionally mediated royal power shaped how Africans became part of Iberoamerican society. The social relationships animating the case studies at the heart of this work speak to the broader African experience in the Americas during the sixteenth and seventeenth centuries and the uncertain role of their mestizo children in the New World. In the vignettes presented here, Afroiberians face exploitation and inequality enforced through violence. Yet their stories also provide insights into how the individual and collective choices of the African diaspora shaped the architecture of Iberoamerican society, at times to the advantage of this community.

All these threads converge in the legal case initiated in 1706 by Francisco Copete Jr. after he arrived in Cartagena to reclaim his inheritance. Ten years after his mother's death, he petitioned for the property that she had supposedly left him in her will: two daughters of his families' onetime slave Juana de la Rosa. In his petitions to the court, Francisco presented little proof of his claims, explaining that his mother's will had burned in a 1697 attack by French privateers.[4] Instead he spoke at length about his social standing while denigrating that of the two women, petulantly telling the court that they only wanted to be free "so they could bum around the world making mischief."[5]

At first glance, the fact that a man with only marginal proof could show up a decade after the alleged fact and lay claim to two human beings based on the strength of his word seems like a straightforward account of law in the service of slavery. Yet the sisters, María Josefa Copete and Lorenza Elena, rebuffed Francisco Jr.'s petition and complicated this familiar narrative. They pointedly told the judge that, "having never allowed themselves to be abused or reduced to slavery, they had spent more than ten years in possession of their freedom" after the deaths of both their mother and their patron, Francisco's mother.[6] The sisters asserted that they were as free as Francisco, having been born after Juana earned her freedom through effective, loyal, and Christian service to his family. Over the next four years, in three separate court cases, María Josefa Copete and Lorenza Elena battled the scions of a wealthy creole family to a standstill. Francisco found, as have many others throughout history, that attempting to define people as property can be a treacherous endeavor.[7]

Unraveling the saga of Juana de la Rosa and her daughters, I found in the documents the practical manifestations of a global debate on legitimate imperial governance, the logic of the Caribbean economic zone, and the will of the traffickers, the trafficked, and their descendants. All of these actors influenced the emergent cultural norms surrounding slavery in Iberoamerica. The emphasis on culture is important here, because in the early modern period local and/or imperial cultural identities often collided with emergent and expansive state institutions. In the face of such resistance, the greatest of Renaissance princes—be it in Spain or elsewhere—understood the importance of crafting competitive cultural narratives as they sought to give the people who made up their polities some reason to stick together in the lion pit of imperial competition.[8] As the sociologist Ann Swindler explains, "in unsettled periods . . . cultural meanings are more highly articulated and explicit, because they model patterns of action that do not 'come naturally.' Belief and ritual practice directly shape action for the community that adheres to a given ideology. Such ideologies are, however, in competition with other sets of cultural assumptions. Ultimately, structural and historical opportunities determine which strategies, and thus which cultural systems, succeed."[9] The durability of Iberoamerica as a cultural zone gives testimony to the solidity of its creation.

The Spanish Empire and its residents navigated a ruthlessly competitive world, drawing upon a tradition of good governance unapologetically justified by its promotion of social stability.[10] *Las Siete Partidas*, a thirteenth-century Castilian legal code republished regularly after 1500, established the legal basis for slavery while encouraging slave owners and royal officials to manumit faithful Christian slaves to encourage good behavior.[11] The Spanish Crown developed and supported these legal mechanisms and Juana de la Rosa used them to acquire her freedom. María Josefa Copete and Lorenza Elena's claim to freedom was built explicitly upon the manumission of their mother, which was itself dependent upon narratives that ultimately reinforced the empire that enslaved her. Making sense of the Spanish American legal ecology and the choices people made within it requires sensitivity to the gravitational pull of risk—personal, regional, and imperial—which, like dark matter, invisibly yet pervasively shaped everyone's options.

When Juana de la Rosa disembarked in Cartagena in the 1670s, she found herself under the dominion of another pair of forced migrants, Manuela Cartagena de Leiva and her brother Francisco del Castillo, the mother and uncle of the persistent slaver Francisco Copete Jr. Arriving in Cartagena as refugees from the 1655 English takeover of Jamaica, del Castillo and Cartagena de Leiva used what they had salvaged to buy people and begin trading in tropical goods.[12] Over the next quarter century, the merchant siblings established a trading network centered in Cartagena that extended as far as the inland satellite towns of Mompós, Pamplona, and Ocaña. Through their business acumen and the labor of their slaves, they accumulated properties and married into two different creole families, establishing themselves as part of the regional elite by 1700.

Underpinning the family's prosperity, and visible to us because of a fortuitous future conflict, was Juana de la Rosa. Purchased by del Castillo after her arrival from Africa, she went on to earn the trust of the Copete/Castillo clan by proving herself a successful businesswoman and eventually became a factor in the family's commercial operations. She first appears in the historical record when Manuela Cartagena de Leiva and her husband Francisco Copete Sr. bought a *trapiche* (sugar plantation) named Tiquisama near the town of Ocaña.[13] Juana de la Rosa came along with the Copete household when it relocated from Cartagena to the plantation. While living at Tiquisama, she gave birth to her first daughter, baptized by a local priest as María Josefa Copete.[14] Because of the racial/cultural indicators that María Josefa later used to describe herself and her exclusive use of the Copete last name, it is very likely that she was the daughter of Francisco Copete Sr. This assumption is reinforced by witnesses who, unprompted, commented on the exaggerated antipathy that Manuela displayed toward the child.

Echoing a pattern common to slaveholding societies since antiquity, this involuntary triangle resulted in retaliation from the mistress of the house against Juana de la Rosa. Still, giving us a sense of her interpersonal and business skills, Juana somehow managed to keep her relationship with Manuela Cartagena de Leiva on enough of an even keel that when the latter left Francisco Sr. in Ocaña and returned to Cartagena, de la Rosa accompanied her. Back in Cartagena, Juana resumed her role as business agent of the Castillo/Copete clan. She also developed a relationship with an enslaved man, leading to the birth of her second daughter, Lorenza Elena. Emblematic of the complexity of these relationships, Manuela Cartagena de Leiva is reported by those same witnesses to have shown a great fondness for María Josefa's little sister.

Just as Juana de la Rosa became adept at business, she came to understand the possibilities of the law. Taking advantage of Spanish Catholic ideology encouraging owners to use manumission as a reward for model slaves, Juana leveraged her business and personal relationships to obtain a promise of liberation. The instrument of her freedom was a verbal agreement specifying that, after a period of service, Juana would be emancipated, with the option of remaining part of her former master's household. In the early 1680s, however, a local conflict forced Francisco del Castillo to leave Cartagena without documenting the agreement establishing Juana's freedom. Instead, as was customary, he promised to formalize it in his will. Del Castillo bought property and settled in the upriver town of Mompós, sending the products of his hacienda down the Magdalena River to be sold in Cartagena by de la Rosa, who remained in Manuela's household.[15]

By 1706, when Francisco Copete Jr. attempted his brotherly legal ambush, both his mother and uncle had been dead a decade; meanwhile, thanks to an overabundance of French pirates, both wills were missing.[16] Francisco tried to overcome the limited documentary evidence he presented by defining the sisters as "*negras*" (blacks), marking them as natural slaves undeserving of royal protection. His testimony is laced with the hardening racism of the time, as he attempted to use the "reality" of race to provide the certainty his case was lacking.[17]

María Josefa and Lorenza Elena countered that they were neither negras nor slaves. Instead, they referred to themselves in terms that signaled their acculturation and belonging, respectively as *parda* (half black, half white) and *morena criolla* (a black person born in the Indies), *residentes* (permanent residents), and later *vecinas* (legal residents of Cartagena) (figure I.1). Moreover, the sisters asserted that they had been born free and thus continued to be free, calling upon the royal protection of orphans and the presumption in favor of freedom in Spanish law. They closed by acidly noting that it was "beyond belief" that the members of the Copete/Castillo clan living in Cartagena would have kept their peace for ten years if they were in fact property.

In their declarations to the courts María Josefa and Lorenza Elena worked to diffuse their social and legal disadvantages while neutralizing the racial stigma that Francisco deployed against them by presenting themselves as acculturated, exemplary

Figure I.1. An eighteenth-century traveler's drawing of a mixed-race woman from Cartagena. *Mestiza de Cartagena de Indias*, by Antonio Rodríguez. Copper engraving, ca. 1799. From the Biblioteca Luis Ángel Arango, Banco de la República, Colombia.

subjects under the king's protection and deserving of royal justice. This language was available to them because, regardless of the lapses in its deliverance, Spanish Catholic buen gobierno was understood to be the rule and application of effective justice to all the subjects of the king according to their station and just deserts.

The judge found the sisters' arguments so persuasive that Francisco Copete Jr. was forced to hire a lawyer and search for further evidence in support of his claim. The resulting documents are polyphonic and mediated by the officials that produced them. However, it is clear that as the case progressed, each side called upon witnesses to legitimize their claims and contextualize the few relevant documents that had survived Manuela Cartagena de Leiva and Francisco del Castillo's deaths.[18] Triangulating the evidence, we get a sense of how Juana de la Rosa and her daughters tested and adapted strategies as well as tactics during their generational struggle for self-determination, navigating the routine, yet critical, interactions among enslaved Afroiberians, royal subjects, Iberian law, and imperial institutions. It is sadly unsurprising to discover that parda María Josefa Copete was likely the half-sister of Francisco Copete Jr. However, given how hostile the legal terrain is understood to have been for both enslaved people and women of any status it is surprising to learn how long and successfully the sisters held their own against an elite creole family.

Framing the case, Cartagena's stones and the people who laid them were a manifestation of Spanish Hapsburg governance, which sought to provide Catholic buen gobierno through an ecosystem of interdependent, yet mutually supervising institutions such as the *cabildos* (municipal councils), provincial governors, the *reales audiencias* (royal high courts), the Santa Hermandad (military order/rural constabulary), and the Holy Office of the Inquisition. Fitting these interlocking pieces together becomes easier if we follow Daniel Lord Smail's convincing call for a more "ecological understanding of the law." In Smail's conception, "we should treat the law as a coral reef" where "individual laws and statutes are ever so many calicle-forming polyps, gradually assembling a structure that is both living and dead." Law, then, functions as a reef, "a habitat for an extraordinary diversity of practices and unintended functions that grow up in its nooks and crannies."[19] Within the early modern Spanish Empire, the legal ecology became the essential platform upon which Africans and their descendants navigated, negotiated, and contested their enslavement and manumission. In doing so, an emergent "black majority" affirmed their humanity, established their membership in society, and pushed back against the dehumanizing tide of racialized slavery.[20]

This option was accessible to them because medieval Iberian law, although with many limitations, defined freedom as the natural state of man and theoretically placed the burden of proof on the enslaver.[21] Therefore, in the absence of definitive legal proof of enslavement, the sisters in this case were able to credibly argue that they had become free by their actions and the certainty of their arguments provided the proof. As the case dragged on, there were times when the sisters did not have legal representation; in those moments, we can hear their increasingly sophisticated voices, as they strategized, prepared legal arguments, and petitioned the courts. As this case demonstrates, opportunity and necessity made the law a key terrain in which Africans and their descendants forged socially legitimate spaces of freedom.

The legal victories achieved by Africans and their descendants in Cartagena were dependent upon the structure of Spanish imperialism. The narratives in the documents draw upon secular and canon laws, mediated through the institutions that enforced them, shaped by the demands of subaltern peoples, and bound by the exigencies of Spanish imperial governance. A working majority of metropolitan rulers and local elites in Cartagena understood, even if subconsciously, the trade-off between wealth extraction and community cohesion. Distant metropolitan authorities had to find an enforceable consensus around the rules through which Iberian conquerors, settlers, and administrators incorporated Africans into the expanding empire. Africans and their mestizo descendants, in turn, utilized and molded Spanish institutions to serve their interests. As a result, the archives of secular and religious courts are full of complex disputes, unexpected subversions, and tactical alliances among enslaved Afroiberians, freedpeople, and the crown, with and against each other and local elites.[22] Thus, María Josefa Copete *parda libre* and Lorenza Elena *morena criolla libre* used language that stressed Christianity just as much as fealty to the state while building deep and sincere relationships (unequal as they clearly were) that provided tangible support when they needed it.

By 1708, years of repeated failures by Francisco Copete Jr. to enslave his half-sister María Josefa Copete and her sister Lorenza Elena had involved supporters on both sides, including Francisco's sister Juana María de Copete, the "legitimate daughter of Manuela Cartagena de Leiva and her legitimate heiress." Responding to María Josefa and Lorenza Elena's increasingly sophisticated maneuvers, Copete Jr.'s lawyer, Sebastián Díaz, told the court that "badly advised and sponsored by José Moscoso, a local schoolteacher who died recently, [the sisters] say that they are free—a statement that they have never been able to justify; neither has their sponsor, nor their court appointed defender. And so, we have already spent three years in this conflict, and in such ways these and others disturb the case, and everything that has been said by the slaves and their defender has been fantastical and apocryphal. And they have been confounded in their injustice and malice because said slaves have been unable to be declared free."[23]

In the end, the tenacity of the sisters' defense prolonged this legal battle, allowing us to see social networks that are usually invisible to historians, relationships that were, in this case, developed by Juana de la Rosa and deepened by her daughters. The sisters' resistance required social capital that was probably unusual for the daughters of an enslaved African woman, but by no means impossible in the context of seventeenth-century Cartagena. Yet, the case of Juana de la Rosa's daughters is not unique; it is part of a deep and broad documentary base that scholars are increasingly mining to understand the role of the law in the creation, development, and endurance of Spanish dominion in the Americas. These three women's experiences reflect the tension between the paternalistic slavery established in the law—at least theoretically promoted by royal and ecclesiastical authorities—and the extractive interests of powerful slave-owning regional elites.[24] It is surely relevant that Francisco decided to pursue his claim during the War of Spanish Succession (1701–1714), which disrupted the importation of Africans into the region, raising the price of slaves. This contingency is reflected in the archives, as the possibility of a windfall gain saw some slave owners attempting to renege on previously agreed on paths to freedom, leading to legal pushback from enslaved Afroiberians.

The evidence left behind by Africans and their descendants challenges readers to acknowledge their agency and moral complexity, subverting simplified depictions of slaves as either victims or heroes. Instead, enslaved people emerge here as empowered participants in a system in which they played a multivalent role, mastering the legal spaces provided by the law. By making claims, Africans and their descendants became actors in the legal ecology, drawing on the webs of patronage that connected slaves, slave owners, and the imperial institutions charged with overseeing them. In the Spanish Caribbean, the ideological justification, legal structure, and social reception of slavery amalgamated into a resilient institution. This was possible because it enriched the slave-owning class while empowering enslaved Afroiberians and freedpeople to advocate for themselves, even as it proved a source of strength and cohesion for the Spanish Empire. The legal ecology represented all stakeholders as long as they played according to the rules—unequal and brutal as they often were.

THE DEBATABLE MAN

The imperial, institutional, and temporal focus of this monograph builds upon earlier scholarly attention to plantation slavery—most often focused on the United States, the Caribbean, and Brazil. Scholarship has tended to accumulate around the form slavery took at its height in the United States, namely, capitalist racialized chattel bondage. Despite this academic focus, which is reflected in the understanding of slavery among the broader public, over the four centuries of the Atlantic slave trade, 95 percent of enslaved Africans arrived, lived, worked, and died outside the borders of what is today the United States.[25] Scholarship on the first formative centuries of European colonization in the Americas is becoming increasingly aware of the historical importance of forced African migrants, who represented the preponderance of all migrants to the Americas before 1800. The emergent picture is one in which slavery and unfreedom—Amerindian, African, Asian, and European—was foundational for the Atlantic world and hence for global political and economic structures.[26]

The germ of my understanding of slavery in Latin America emerged from the frisson between Frank Tannenbaum's landmark 1947 book, *Slave and Citizen*, Alejandro de la Fuente's 2004 refinement of Tannenbaum's thesis, and my own immigrant experience. Tannenbaum posited that, "in contrast to the British colonies, slaves in Iberian American societies were endowed with a legal and moral personality. . . . These differences in the moral and legal settings of each slave system preconfigured or predetermined post-emancipation race relations in each area." As I tracked these ideas backward, it became evident that in late medieval Iberia, enslaved people were a vital part of society and always defined as legally human, never losing their "moral personality."[27] In northern Europe of the same time period, slavery disappeared and the legal structure supporting it atrophied. Later, as European powers began expanding their dominions into the Atlantic, the presence or absence of laws regulating slavery in medieval France, Britain, or Iberia precipitated different institutional orders in their respective empires. Unbound by previous legal tradition and keenly aware of the limitations faced by Spanish slave owners, Dutch, British, and French colonists increasingly sought to write slave codes that defined their captives as subhuman chattel.[28]

Tannenbaum's provocative thesis ushered in the systematic study of slavery in the Americas. His approach set up loaded comparative questions, asking how slavery in Portuguese and Spanish America differed from slavery in the French and English Empires.[29] Efforts to address these questions produced a wave of cliometric studies that in the aggregate seemed to contradict Tannenbaum's thesis, showing that the main determinant of a slave's living conditions was the work regime, not the imperial polity. The historical consensus then coalesced around the narrative that labor regime trumped law in the New World. In the words of Steven Mintz, "for a long time it was widely assumed that southern slavery was harsher and crueler than slavery in Latin America, where the Catholic Church insisted that slaves had a right to marry, to seek relief from a cruel master, and to purchase their freedom," yet closer study revealed that "in practice, neither the church nor the courts offered much protection to Latin American slaves."[30]

Reacting to this consensus, in 2004 Alejandro de la Fuente controversially reimagined the importance and functioning of the law in relation to the study of slavery. He argued that, while Tannenbaum's thesis contained some truth, he "gave laws a social agency that they did not have." Therefore, de la Fuente proposed examining "the notion of slaves' claims-making to bridge the gap between the law as an abstract declaration of rights and slaves as social actors with their own strategies and goals." However, for this intervention to gain traction scholars would need to uncover and explicate far more "claims-making" by slaves.[31]

Guided by the questions posed by de la Fuente and my own reading of the primary sources, I set out to explore how the letter of the law was implemented on the ground in Cartagena. I found many accounts portraying Spanish rule and the Catholic Church as predatory impositions on the enslaved and indigenous populations. Drawn to the abundantly documented plantation slavery, a historiographical current had developed that presented slaves as "socially dead" victims with limited agency.[32] However, I also discovered a growing body of scholarship that complemented the evidence I found, arguing that enslaved Africans and their descendants, as Catholic subjects of the crown, created for themselves significant opportunities to make and enforce claims through the law and the church. The result of this research led me to formulate the main argument of this book, which is that, as a fundamental part of Iberoamerican society, enslaved Afroiberians and freedpeople engaged with and molded a legal ecology that was hostile but not monolithic.[33]

To grasp the stakes, we need to appreciate the intersectionality of globalization, empire, identity, and slavery.[34] Their myriad connections are the essential, if generally unmentioned, context to what was taking place in the bedrooms, alleys, plazas, and government offices of seventeenth-century Cartagena. Indeed, European early modern imperial governance was designed for a world of patterned uncertainties and Africans featured heavily in the calculations of metropolitan authorities. Regardless of their individual trajectories, enslaved people were understood as international actors in their own right, whose decisions in the aggregate affected the functioning of the institution of slavery.

J. H. Elliott's *Empires of the Atlantic World* contrasts British and Spanish imperialism, ultimately highlighting the degree to which the history of the Indies was interconnected and contingent.[35] In his work he shows zones of imperial friction where different governments and forms of socioeconomic production competed militarily, religiously, and culturally. In the same vein, Joyce E. Chaplin argues compellingly that European imperialism was animated by the same competitive energy that drove early around-the-world voyages and that this shaped imperialism's impact on the peoples and places of the Americas, the Pacific Islands, Asia, and Europe.[36] At the continental, regional, or local analytical level, after the first and most consequential period of globalization, more and more of humanity was affected by exchange.[37]

The growth of unfree labor in European possessions—particularly the use of enslaved Africans—had consequences for the development of modern imperial ideologies, as people, goods, capital, and information moved along swelling trade routes with unexpected consequences.[38] In *Competing Visions of Empire: Labor, Slavery, and the Origins of the British Atlantic Empire*, Abigail Swingen lays out the overlapping and often competing agendas of planters, merchants, privateers, colonial officials, and imperial authorities in the seventeenth and eighteenth centuries.[39] As she clearly shows, each of these groups viewed comparatively their place within the growing British Empire. Her work is complemented by that of Trevor Burnard in *Planters, Merchants, and Slaves: Plantation Societies in British America, 1650–1820*, who shows the connections between the availability of demobilized soldiers from European wars and the growing supply of personnel to supervise the slaves in the tropical plantations spreading in the Caribbean basin.[40]

Slavery in the Americas lasted for four centuries and spread to every corner of the hemisphere.[41] However, it did not emerge from a tabula rasa. Deborah Blumenthal uses the rich archives of medieval Valencia to illustrate the importance and interconnectedness of slavery in the functioning of society in Mediterranean port cities. Blumenthal's portrayal of the intimacy of slavery in fifteenth-century Europe links medieval Iberian customary law to the "ordinary lives in the early Caribbean," as described by Kristen Block.[42] By comparing Block to Blumenthal we see the evolution of late medieval to early modern slavery. Socioeconomic competition in the Mediterranean paved the way for the Caribbean to become the site of intense slave-based protoindustrial production characteristic of the mature plantation complex.

Blumenthal's work on Valencia is especially relevant for understanding Cartagena, as both cities considered themselves, and were generally treated as, provincial capitals and not mere colonial outposts. Following the lead of scholars such as Pedro Cardim et al., my work moves away from hierarchical portrayals of the Iberian monarchies as arranged in a radial pattern around Madrid or Lisbon. Building on Blumenthal and Cardim et al., I reconceptualize these political entities as polycentric, allowing for the existence of many different centers that interacted and thus participated in the making of empire. The resulting political structure was complex and unstable, albeit with a general adhesion to the discourse of loyalty to God and crown.[43]

As Spanish American society emerged, all the stakeholders constantly negotiated the letter, meaning, and implementation of the law. This feedback loop transformed the identity and strategies of all parties. In explaining different aspects of Afro-Mexican life, Herman Bennett and Nicole von Germeten have led the way in uncovering the framework that shaped slavery in the Spanish Empire.[44] Bennett provides extensive evidence of the importance of Catholic sacraments, especially marriage, in molding the lives of Afroiberians in New Spain. Expanding on his work, von Germeten decenters the narrative that emerges from the archive, thinking critically about how the documents naturalize representations of the powerful as much as of the subaltern. She makes black *cofradías* (lay brotherhoods) the protagonists of their own story. Moving past the restrictive duality of resistance or collaboration, she shows how the cofradías acted as crucial mediators in the process of integration for newcomers. Learning from her groundbreaking work, my reading of legal cases flips the lens to explore how enslaved Afroiberians and their descendants used different avenues of engagement with the courts.

The work of Jane Landers and Barry Robinson, as well as that of Ben Vinson, Sherwin Bryant, and Rachel O'Toole, shows the centrality of African slavery in the formation and sustainability of the regional powers of the Americas.[45] The emergence of a multipolar geopolitical environment had a persistent effect on the lives of Africans and their descendants in the hemisphere. As different powers became established and laid out who, how, and why people could be enslaved or become free, they had to account for the general inefficiency of early modern systems of command and control that required the Atlantic empires to be overwhelmingly voluntary in their functioning. Because Africans were both forced migrants and the primary settlers of the Old World in the New, their loyalty was suspect, and in the work of these scholars we see the contested place they occupied in the competing imperial imaginations.[46]

Some of the ramifications of inter/intraimperial contact can be seen in Marisa Fuentes's *Dispossessed Lives: Enslaved Women, Violence, and the Archive*, in which she explores some of the connections between mainland North America and the British Caribbean.[47] The surviving records offer glimpses of royal officials drawn from around the British Empire interpreting and applying medieval law, both helped and hindered by a diversely socialized population of enslaved Africans and their descendants. Comparing the focus of court documents from the British colonies with those produced in Cartagena elucidates the functioning of the legal ecology in both contexts. Metropolitan authorities legislated with the awareness that local officials, through their allocation of limited resources, decided which laws gained traction and which became a dead letter. Contrasting the empty spaces in the archives of the different empires gives us some idea of the challenges Africans and their descendants faced in each region and the opportunities they carved out for themselves. One of the most salient differences between Spanish imperial jurisprudence and that of the British was that the latter increasingly defined slavery by race and placed the legal burden to prove manumission on freedpeople.[48] In contrast, under Spanish law slavery remained a legal condition tied to evangelization, not race, and, as Francisco Copete Jr. was to realize, the burden of proof was on the slave owners. In this same vein, Robert Cottrol's scholarship on the long-term consequences of racialized slavery makes clear the many ways the legal and social structures of competing European empires shaped, and were shaped by, this institution.[49]

Largely Afroiberian Atlantic hub cities like Cartagena were simultaneously threatened by foreign enemies and starved for resources, a tension that encouraged a consensual civil government, though still within the bounds of the exploitative relationships that powered the region. María del Carmen Borrego Plá's oeuvre in general and *Cartagena de Indias en el siglo XVI* in particular are essential resources in understanding the city in its local context.[50] Her work brings Cartagena and its administrative hinterland into sharper focus, especially when we take into consideration that, as imperial powers increasingly came to depend on African slavery, they used Atlantic port cities to process and control them. The praxis of Atlantic slavery necessitated and shaped the coastal urban centers of the seventeenth-century European empires, as they traded goods, people, and ideas between each other.

The second decade of the millennium saw the publication of several excellent monographs on different aspects of slavery and un-freedom in Spanish America, bringing out regional and temporal idiosyncrasies while emphasizing different pathways of accommodation or resistance available to enslaved Afroiberians and their descendants. My work is in close dialogue with three of these texts, specifically David Wheat's *Atlantic Africa and the Spanish Caribbean*, Michelle McKinley's *Fractional Freedoms*, and Sherwin Bryant's *Rivers of Gold*.[51] All of our monographs attempt to describe and explain a process that cannot be seen directly; the layering of our insights provides a more complete picture of how slavery functioned in Spanish America.

Of the three texts, *Atlantic Africa* has the broadest focus. In this book, Wheat "documents the story of sub-Saharan Africans becoming the colonists of the Spanish Caribbean,"[52] mapping out the connections between the Portuguese Empire in Africa and Spanish America. He reframes our understanding of the Caribbean as a majority-black region composed of overlapping Iberian and African worlds connected through imperialism and the slave trade. In the second half of the monograph, Wheat examines the participation of free and enslaved Africans in the colonial settlement of the Spanish Caribbean seaports and their hinterlands, pointing out that, in the Iberian Caribbean, "African forced migrants increasingly performed the basic functions of colonization."[53] For the European and mestizo elites ruling vast American territories populated largely by Africans and their descendants, the legal ecology supporting slavery became indivisible from legitimacy and good governance, key fronts in the hothouses of imperial competition developing in the echoing Mediterranean and Caribbean basins.[54]

Wheat's arguments emerge through the life of Juana de la Rosa. She survived the journey from Congo and became a leader among the businesswomen of Cartagena, eventually parlaying her expertise into what McKinley, in work described subsequently more fully, aptly describes as "fractional freedom." De la Rosa's daughters leveraged the Afroiberian community to defend and increase their liberties, laying open the mechanics of this creole society. Over the four years of the case, we see the transformation of María Josefa and Lorenza Elena from humble supplicants to *naturales de esta villa* (born in this town) onward to confident free *vecinas* of Cartagena.[55] The form and functioning of the institution of slavery was a focus of the Spanish monarchy, local elites, churchmen, and of course Afroiberians, all of whom shaped the legal ecology in pursuit of their interests.

While giving full weight to human agency, the legal ecology was a web of social constructs, partially outside the comprehension of those affected, which bound and roiled the lives of Indigenes, Africans, Europeans, and their descendants in the Spanish Caribbean. Reaching through slavery's legal dimension into its social practice gives us a fascinating window into the strategies of survival, resistance, and self-determination developed by Afroiberians and their increasingly diverse offspring as they became the foundation of Caribbean and American society.

Bryant's *Rivers of Gold* likewise situates slavery "as a fundamental aspect of colonial practice, sovereignty, and governance."[56] He makes a forceful case that slavery is much more than an economic system, however profitable, rightly demonstrating the brutally persistent attempts by a faction at the royal court allied with entrepreneurial local elites to profit from ordering society through slavery and the role of race among other early modern practices of differentiated rule. However, Bryant sometimes overvalues the most aggressive bids for control over enslaved bodies by extractive local elites in conjunction with likeminded imperial officials, obscuring the full picture. My work expands and complements Bryant's by examining evidence produced by different power brokers, including Afroiberians, created by a multivalent administration.

An example of what I call administrative multivalence is the largely undocumented role of Inquisition officials in cases involving Afroiberians. Despite inquisitors and church officials not having a defined legal role, they were consulted in all manner of civil, criminal, and religious disputes because of their legal training and social capital, as evidenced in the existing documents. Enslaved Africans and their descendants engaged both the personal and institutional interests of leaders in the Catholic Church, making the power relationships through which Afroiberians became part of society in the Spanish Caribbean more complex, diffused, and deeply rooted than schemes to exploit African labor might lead us to understand.[57]

The third monograph, and the one closest to my own in focus, is Michelle McKinley's *Fractional Freedoms*, which focuses on enslaved women and the law during the seventeenth century in the viceregal capital of Lima. She approaches enslaved litigants with an innovative sensitivity to social status and gender relations, paying attention to, for example, the ways enslaved women built alliances with church officials, naming and shaming slave owners who acted in socially unacceptable ways. McKinley's argument weaves together the dynamic relations between status and power among seventeenth-century Limeño society, complementing my own scholarship on the intersections between law, slavery, and empire. Her analysis of marriage, the central institution of imperial society, focuses on the way it was translated across every bracket of social and economic power. The better officials who populate our sources attempted to adapt procedures to local conditions, both punishing and protecting enslaved people as they understood their duty. Intertwined with this, both McKinley and I find traces of enslaved people leveraging communal knowledge to pursue their interests using unequal but broadly consensual narratives.

Finally, tying together my work and the three previous monographs is Gabriel Paquette's essential *European Seaborn Empires*.[58] Paquette's work lays out the functioning of global European imperialism and the regulation of forced labor that empire depends on. His work shows that Europe's early modern expansion was as much an intellectual as a military endeavor. *The European Seaborn Empires* provides the context necessary to understand the institutions of slavery and its consequences for the African diaspora in Iberoamerica by providing a concise overview of the financial, governmental, and cultural milieu that shaped the praxis of governance of the Spanish Empire. The self-conscious spirit of Catholic reform that animated Hapsburg governance was intimately tied to the violent fractures of the Protestant and Catholic Reformations. Christendom became aware of itself in a global framework even as it ferociously subdivided into competitive confessionalism. All of these factors came into play as Spanish officials translated the medieval Iberian legal ecology and its version of slavery to the Indies.[59]

Furthermore, the transmission of the Iberian legal structure to the New World was aided by the concentration of enslaved people in urban areas. Late medieval Iberian slavery comprised relatively small numbers of enslaved Africans and Moors mostly in towns and cities; in the early days of Spain's overseas empire, it was this form (albeit much expanded) that predominated in the Spanish Indies, facilitating the transfer of the existing legal ecology across the Atlantic. As a result, the Iberoamerican legal system took hold and maintained legitimacy for almost two centuries before the enormous pressures of managing the mature plantation complex were fully brought to bear on the Spanish metropolitan government.[60]

Overlaying secondary sources with evidence from the archives provides a basic understanding of a system in which European, African, and mestizo slave traders bonded Africans into Atlantic trade networks regulated by a legal and customary framework that could only function with the active collaboration of imperial officials, slave owners, and unfree people.[61] Africans and their descendants shaped and were shaped by the emerging imperial structures of the Atlantic, where they faced violence, exploitation, and systematic legal discrimination. At the same time, disrupting the schema of oppression, many Afroiberians became deeply intertwined with the lives of their owners or patrons and were thus privy to an intimate perspective on the empire's social and legal functioning. Afroiberians' engagement was facilitated by the Spanish Empire's system of overlapping secular and religious jurisdictions that combined executive and judicial functions along with comparatively low entry barriers for complainants. Leveraging this knowledge and the relationships that came with it, enslaved people developed social and legal strategies to improve their lives and protect themselves and their loved ones.[62]

OVERVIEW

This book draws on royal legislation, Inquisition records, and three broad groups of legal cases appealed to higher courts in Bogota and Spain. The first group are cases processed by the Cartagena branch of the Inquisition after its foundation in 1610.[63] The second group is comprised of cases from the Colombian National Archive in Bogota; this archive holds the majority of surviving civil and criminal cases from the region. The third group of cases is to be found in the Archivo General de Indias (AGI) in Seville and includes the civil and criminal cases appealed to the metropole. The AGI also holds the decrees and consultations regarding slavery between the crown, the Council of the Indies, and authorities in Cartagena.[64]

Sifting through the archival catalogs and laboriously reading through the (often incomplete) documents, I found it useful in navigating this ocean of fragments to overlay the social map onto the physical one, keeping in mind the interconnected and competing structures of the Province of Cartagena, the Caribbean basin, and global European imperialism. Even as it became clear that case outlines could be discerned from the initial petitions and judgments, the available full transcriptions led me to appreciate the complexity of the Spanish Empire's legal ecology. In these pages, I found granular evidence of the interplay between the law as an institution, officials' perception of the law, and subjects' perception of the latter. The colonial legal terrain was fertile ground for competition between institutional interests, for

reinforcing or challenging social hierarchies, and for disputing and asserting religious values.

This book is divided into four chapters. Each sets up and examines a different
aspect in the intersection of slavery and the legal ecology. The first chapter lays
out the geopolitical context of the early Spanish Empire and traces the medieval
background of slavery in the Americas, setting the stage upon which Africans and
their descendants were forcibly integrated into Iberoamerican society. These elements come together in the story of Domingo and Catalina Angola, two African-
born slaves. The Angolas, who each belonged to different households in the thriving inland town of Mompós, petitioned their parish priest for a marriage license
in 1629. This was not unusual, as the Spanish Empire's stated policy encouraged
and supported slave marriage and the Catholic Church obliged conjugal couples to
marry. When Catalina's owner forcibly removed her from the city to prevent the
marriage, a complex chain of events combining daring escapes and legal maneuvers
was set in motion. Catalina and Domingo engaged the church's defense of marriage
to affect their own destinies, conforming strategically to provisions of Spanish and
canon law in order to use the institutions that kept them enslaved to their advantage. I follow the secular and religious cases that ensued, introducing the legal and
institutional environment that enslaved people inhabited, showing the negotiated
boundaries within which enslaved subjects constructed their lives and elucidating
the formation and consolidation of their social networks.

This chapter also geopolitically anchors the vignettes that form the core of this
book. It introduces the Province of Cartagena and its importance to the development of the Spanish Empire—as well as its dependence on forced labor. Because
the institution of slavery was operational in the Iberian Peninsula prior to the conquest of the New World, intellectual, spiritual, and institutional continuity can be
found in the imperial understanding and regulation of slavery. This continuity became crucial with the collapse of the indigenous population of the Americas and
the union of the Spanish and Portuguese Crowns in 1580. The integration of Portuguese and Spanish commercial systems led to an exponential increase in the availability of enslaved Africans to provincial elites in the Indies, with far-reaching consequences for the Province of Cartagena.

In the second chapter, I examine the Holy Office of the Inquisition as it adapted
its role as protector of the faith to fit the rapidly changing Iberian empires. Exploration, trade, conquest, and imperial policy expanded the reach of the Inquisition globally at the same time that the enslaved population exploded in the Indies.
The large-scale migration of Africans posed difficult questions, both transcendent
and mundane, for metropolitan and regional church officials: What should be the
role of the Holy Office in the supervision of slaves? How should officials interact
with sometimes-pagan African slaves? How should they judge slaves' competency
to stand trial? Should there be different punishments for *bozales* (unacculturated

Africans) and *criollos* (those acculturated to or born in the Indies)? What levels of punishment were appropriate for which crimes, and to what extent was the general system of sanctioning transferrable to slaves?

Two witchcraft trials anchor chapter 2, those of Guiomar in 1565 and Felipa in 1641. A combination of secular and religious authorities handled the case against Guiomar prior to the establishment of a tribunal of the Inquisition in Cartagena in 1610. Her case occurs amid what appears to be a textbook case of popular hysteria. After being tortured by her owner and the governor, Guiomar confessed to fantastical crimes and implicated others; principally on the basis of her confession, provincial authorities condemned and executed her. Seventy-six years later, officials of the Inquisition handled Felipa's case in its entirety, leading to a very different result. Procedural safeguards and the sophistication of the personnel protected her from falling prey to anti-witch hysteria. The inquisitors deemed her confession, extracted through torture by her owner, to be false, and upon investigation, acquitted her of all charges. Furthermore, they ordered her master to cease retaliation against her.

Within the limitations of their legal status, how did enslaved subjects and freedpeople experience the presence of royal authority? The final two chapters use cases that were appealed to the Real Audiencia de Santafé (royal high court) in Bogota or to the Council of the Indies in Seville, illustrating the contested ways in which enslaved Afroiberians and their descendants exercised their legal personhood. By digging into the details of the cases, I show how local and regional officials saw their role in relation to unfree Spanish subjects. Examining how a freedwoman decided on which jurisdiction she should use to initiate a civil case in defense of her freedom, or under what conditions an aggrieved slave could use the courts to force a change of owner, I provide a picture of what strategies and narratives were available and when they could be used by enslaved Afroiberians to impose legal restrictions on the power of elites.

Specifically, chapter 3 considers claims-making through the multivalent participation of Afroiberians and their communities in civil suits. Africans and their descendants in Spanish America could achieve manumission through a combination of savvy, effort, and luck. Slavery, however, was not easily shaken off, and the specter of re-enslavement would haunt many freedpeople. Thus, one of the most common reasons for freedpeople and their children to engage with the law was to defend themselves against claims on their personhood by former owners or heirs thereof.

Chapter 3 also explores the role of the courts in interimperial competition. The Spanish, Dutch, French, and British Empires competed for the hearts, minds, and bodies of enslaved people. During times of war, Spanish propaganda promised that any slave deserting enemy polities and joining the Spanish would be freed and groups of former slaves could even achieve limited self-government if they organized into royally chartered towns. This promise had practical consequences: for example, many Africans held by the Dutch took the gamble of escaping from their captors in the hopes of finding better lives, founding villages that strengthened the Spanish while weakening the Dutch. Their willingness to heed the Spanish siren call depended on both the Atlantic imperial infrastructures and the perceived legitimacy of the Spanish legal ecology.

Finally, chapter 4 delves into Spanish royal justice as it pertained to the African diaspora in Iberoamerica. The courts patrolled the boundaries of socially and legally acceptable behavior. In the documents examined as the basis of this work, we see neighbors and acquaintances avidly gossiping over lawsuits, expanding the range of achievable results and trumpeting the parameters within which slaves and masters operated through the application of criminal law. Africans were disciplined by courts that guaranteed their owners' power while simultaneously benefiting from the checks on the latter enforced by said courts. For slaves vulnerable to abuse by social superiors, the ability to call upon royal justice provided a last line of defense. Disentangling the opportunities, benefits, and costs that royal courts presented to Afroiberians illuminates this morally complex and underexamined dynamic.

In my research, I found cases in which enslaved people were not only defendants but also accusers, and crucially, witnesses. Simultaneously, the cases presented in chapter 4 highlight the contradictory role of slave owners as both accusers and defenders of enslaved subjects. In general, the accretion of documents resulting from the successive judicial reviews of cases provides an extended view of the lives of both enslaved people and their owners. Overseeing both, in the panopticon of small towns, royal officials observed and were observed by the society that they regulated. As they negotiated the conflict embodied in criminal cases and implemented the law, these officials inevitably adapted to local circumstances. Stringing together these extended glimpses into everyday life in Iberoamerica shows how Africans and their descendants, sometimes coerced, sometimes willingly, but always as essential stakeholders, became part of the Spanish imperial enterprise.

1

EMPIRE, PROVINCE, LAW,
AND ENSLAVED AFROIBERIANS

Your Majesty is in need of a large number of judges in these kingdoms.
——The Cortes to the Empress Isabel (Cortes de los antiguos reinos
de León y de Castilla, 1532)

The port of Cartagena de Indias anchored the Spanish New Kingdom of Granada, an area roughly coterminous with present-day Colombia. An entrepôt, a military fortress, and an administrative nexus, Cartagena was archetypical of the port cities that integrated slavery into the Atlantic world.[1] Explorers moving down the coast of South America established the first tentative toeholds at the mouth of the Magdalena River during the 1510s, but these were largely destroyed by native counterattacks. It was not until 1533, during the second wave of exploration into the mainland, that Pedro de Heredia founded Cartagena.[2] Over the next fifty years, the city grew to become a regional powerhouse, a position it attained due to its secluded, easily defensible harbor and strategic location near the Isthmus of Panama, the main door to the Viceroyalty of Peru and its mountain of silver (figure 1.1). However, while the city and its hinterland became a lynchpin of trade, defense, and administration, semi-independent indigenous and maroon communities intermittently held sway outside of the areas controlled by the Spanish. In what follows, I explain the foundation and development of Cartagena as part of the Spanish efforts to consolidate their dominion of the Americas; situate the port and its administrative hinterland within the context of the global Spanish Empire under the Hapsburg dynasty (1514–1700); and overview the medieval background of African slavery and its functioning in the increasingly competitive Caribbean basin.

The rise and fall of the great port and fortress of Cartagena de Indias was tied to the rise and fall of the slave trade in the Iberian Atlantic. As the only legal port of entry for African slaves into Spanish South America from 1540 until 1776, Cartagena was a commercial nexus where people arriving from Africa were sold into forced labor. As the location of secular and religious courts and institutions, it was also where they became subjects of the Spanish Crown. At the same time, as a port

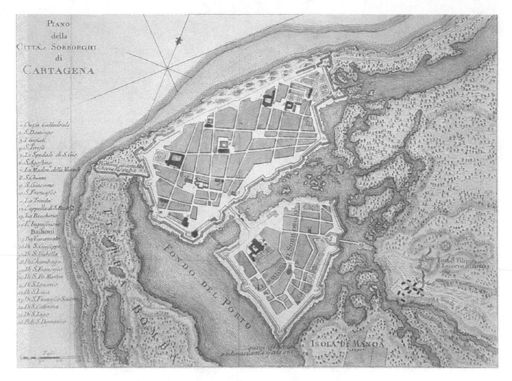

Figure 1.1. Eighteenth-century plan of the city of Cartagena and its suburbs. "Piano della citta, e sobborghi di Cartagena" by Violante Vanni. Print, 1777, Livorno, G. T. Masi e compagni. From the Biblioteca Luis Ángel Arango, Banco de la República, Colombia.

city largely run by Africans, it was where newly arrived slaves were incorporated into a growing creole population.

The indigenous demographic collapse was paced by increased Atlantic trade, as the proliferation of commercial connections within and between the Americas and Afro-Eurasia both accelerated and was accelerated by the need for labor in the most acutely depopulating regions of the Indies. The Columbian exchange and profound disruptions that accompanied European exploration and conquest of the Indies led to radical decreases in native population. In common with almost all early modern periods of dislocation, diseases did the majority of the damage, killing more European conquistadors than warfare and depopulating whole regions of natives who lacked foreigners' hard-earned immunities. Churchmen like Bartolomé de las Casas produced lurid polemics showcasing the worst abuses that labor-hungry *encomenderos* (recipients of grants of indigenous labor and collectors of tributes) inflicted on the conquered territories. Made aware of the wastage of their tax base and shamed by the Protestant sects for their barbarity, Spanish monarchs responded forcefully, passing repeated laws to protect their indigenous subjects and encouraging businesspeople to bring in other types of labor.[3] Concurrently, the integration of the Americas into the emerging global economy created the need and the capacity for the transatlantic transportation of forced labor.[4] After much experimentation, the various powerbrokers came to conclude that African captives best served their purposes, and the need for secure ports to manage human trafficking and the associated trade in tropical commodities drew people and goods through ports like Cartagena.[5]

The role of African forced labor was solidified by the 1580 dynastic union of Spain and Portugal, and mestizo Lusophone slavers came to dominate the trade. As Africans and their descendants achieved demographic preponderance in the region, ethnic and cultural mixing defined the coagulating cultural milieu, economy, and imperial governance.[6] In their urban strongholds, royal officials struggled to forge Amerindians, Africans, Europeans, and their mestizo descendants into loyal subjects.[7]

Enslaved residents of the Province of Cartagena experienced the constraints, but also the opportunities, created by their distance from the metropolis and their role as a node of Spanish imperial power embedded in a semifrontier region.[8] Despite the vitality of successful cities and towns, enemy raids, unpacified indigenous groups, *palenques* (communities made up of runaway slaves), and tropical diseases meant most coastal areas remained sparsely populated.[9] In the 1650s, Mompós and Tolú had less than a thousand inhabitants each, while Cartagena and Bogota barely reached five thousand. To put this in perspective, the contemporaneous population of Lima, the capital of the Viceroyalty of Peru, stood at over forty thousand.[10]

Over the course of the seventeenth century, forced African migrants and their descendants came to comprise the majority of the inhabitants of the Caribbean. They built the massive defenses that protected Cartagena, produced most of the food that fed the region, manned the iconic *bogas* (riverboat crews that grace the cover of this book) that carried regional trade on the riverine network, and ran the docks that linked the city to the rest of the empire.[11] Enslaved Afroiberians and freedpeople also dominated small-scale urban industries, services, and commerce.[12] As coastal settlements integrated their hinterlands into the Atlantic economy, commercial activity, and with it enslaved Afroiberians, spread along trade routes, solidifying slavery's urban character (figure 1.2).

The enormity of the territory that came under the control of the Iberian kingdoms required an intense and sustained increase in administrative capacity. Concentrated in strategic urban centers, significant imperial resources were devoted to maintaining the stability of Spanish rule.[13] Throughout the long seventeenth century, regional administrators who did not pay attention to local contexts ran the risk of finding their authority subverted and their subjects in rebellion.[14] The most successful, on the other hand, devised ways to convert potentially rebellious forced

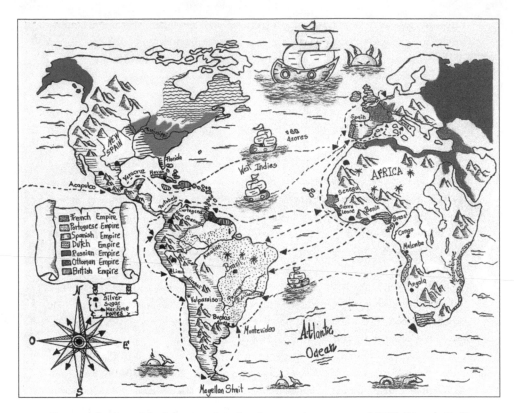

Figure 1.2. Map of the Atlantic political and economic zone around 1700. Ricardo Raúl Salazar Rey.

migrants into stakeholders in the establishment and consolidation of the empire.[15] Thus, the legal structure of slavery incentivized Africans and their descendants to work within the system to attain the benefits of playing by the rules. Reinforcing this, secular and ecclesiastical officials were directed to instruct enslaved people in their rights and responsibilities.[16]

The ability of enslaved Afroiberians and freedpeople to use the courts to seek redress and protection opened up opportunities for social and economic advancement, unusual in early modern history. Religious, civil, and criminal law, while not universally implemented, established opportunities and safeguards for an otherwise vulnerable population. We can see this in action by tracking Africans and their descendants as they partook in and enforced the sacraments, appealed to royal officials for protection, and petitioned the courts.

In its Promethean moment, Spanish dominion derived legitimacy and cohesion from the institutionalization of royal justice.[17] Foreign challenges to Spanish claims in the Indies quickly monopolized military resources. As conquest became empire, the crown buttressed regional stability by extending access to royal justice down the social ladder, necessitating greater administrative complexity. In the Province of Cartagena, overlapping imperial institutions, vibrant economic activity, and large numbers of enslaved people created a hothouse of interinstitutional maneuvering, which produced a rich precipitation of legal cases, local ordinances, and *cédulas reales* (royal decrees/charters). This material provides an unparalleled window into the foundational role of Africans and their descendants in the creation and endurance of the Spanish Atlantic.

CATALINA AND DOMINGO: BY ANY MEANS NECESSARY

On June 3, 1629, in the city of Mompós, Province of Cartagena, African-born slaves Catalina Angola and Domingo Angola petitioned their parish priest for a marriage license.[18] Their request was not unusual in the Spanish Empire, which, allied with the Catholic Church, encouraged and protected marriage, constricting slave owners' rights over those whom they considered their "property."[19] Building on extensive medieval precedents, Catholic high sacraments took precedence over kings, lords, and slave owners' rights, and marriage did not require consent from anybody but the couple and a priest.[20] Nevertheless, structural vulnerabilities pushed most unfree people wanting to get married to seek their owners' blessing.[21]

According to his later testimony to the vicar's court, during the first half of 1629 Bartolomé Moriano, Catalina Angola's owner, had been planning to move to Cartagena and take her with him. A valuable and trusted member of the Moriano household, Catalina likely knew early on that she faced separation from both her community and her beloved. Demonstrating their awareness of the options for resistance provided by the legal ecology, she and Domingo took steps to obtain ecclesiastical sanction of their union and thus prevent her relocation, as married couples could not be forcibly separated. Anticipating opposition from Catalina's choleric and authoritarian owner, the couple carefully and discreetly documented their preparations. However, before their marriage could be celebrated, Moriano became aware of their plans when his parish church published the wedding banns. Unable to legally block the marriage, he stormed home, "tied Catalina to a chair, beating her violently until she was covered in blood." Asserting his property rights above those of the Catholic Spanish monarchy, Moriano hired local roughs and had Catalina Angola dragged to a waiting ship and taken downriver to Cartagena.[22] The two cases that ensued, one secular and one religious, owe their existence to metropolitan recognition that military and economic power could not sustain their imperium without cultural legitimacy.[23]

Hearing of the abduction, Domingo Angola immediately denounced Moriano to the vicar general—a cleric trained in canon law who adjudicated religious cases acting under the authority of the bishop—invoking the protection of "*la Santa Madre Iglesia*" (Holy Mother Church) to counterbalance Moriano's power over

Catalina Angola. The crown had obtained control of the vicar general's office from the papacy in the Concordat of 1401, as the price of regularizing relations with a Holy See weakened by the chaos of the Avignon captivity.[24] In the Indies, royal support for canon law gave the vicar general's court broad jurisdiction and guaranteed interinstitutional cooperation.

In their time in the Indies, Catalina Angola and Domingo Angola had learned of the incentives offered to those who adhered to Spanish and Catholic practices and prepared accordingly.[25] Domingo petitioned the vicar's court against Moriano the day after the latter assaulted Catalina, framing his own and Catalina's actions in the language of Catholic piety and free will while contrasting their righteous vulnerability and desire to follow orthodoxy with the godless Moriano's cruelty and greed. He included in his petition their request for a marriage license and witnesses' declarations verifying their eligibility to marry.[26] In a particularly sophisticated flourish, Domingo closed by citing the Council of Trent's support for marriage as an individual and inviolable sacrament.[27] In response, the vicar general commanded Moriano to present Catalina Angola in court under threat of *excomunión mayor* (major excommunication).[28]

Meanwhile in Cartagena, Catalina had been deposited with a business associate of Moriano's to be sold.[29] Unaware of the fate of Domingo Angola's efforts, she took matters into her own hands, escaping together with Susana, another captive awaiting sale.[30] Making their way out of Cartagena, the women traveled down side roads toward Mompós. However, licensed slave catchers, who received rewards for recovering and returning slaves to their owners, monitored the roads and passes.[31] Catalina and Susana were captured by Antón del Río, a slave catcher responsible for an area known as La Balsa.[32] Putting them in chains, he wrote their owners to arrange for their return and the collection of his reward. While Antón waited for a response, Catalina and Susana convinced him of their docility, as a result of which he removed their chains and locked them in a small grain barn. The women then cut a breach in a wall and escaped once more.

In addition to using contractors like Antón, the Spanish Crown established that a bounty be given to anyone who caught a runaway and turned them in to local officials. As Catalina and Susana fled with Antón hot in pursuit, they were noticed and captured by a local foreman named Miguel Pérez and an unnamed slave accompanying him. Pérez tied them up and began escorting them toward the nearest town. At this point, a very grumpy Antón caught up with the group and demanded that the women be turned over to him. Pérez refused, sparking a confrontation during which Catalina and Susana escaped, again. All three men pursued them and managed to recapture Susana, but Catalina evaded them all and escaped, never to be recaptured.[33]

Catalina Angola's escapes created a problem for Antón del Río. When Moriano came to collect her and heard of the slave catcher's bungling, he sued for negligence, asking for Catalina's value of four hundred pesos and requesting Antón's incarceration. Moriano presented four witnesses in support of his case: First, Miguel Pérez told how he and an enslaved companion had come upon the fleeing women and captured them. He described the confrontation with an agitated del Río, who allegedly hurled insults and struck his companion, allowing the women to escape in the confusion. Two local residents testified after Pérez, corroborating his version of the events. Finally, Susana testified, telling of her and Catalina's flight from the merchant's house in Cartagena and their initial capture by del Río. Describing how they broke out of del Río's barn and were apprehended by the two other men, she confirmed that the confrontation between del Río and Pérez had enabled Catalina to escape. Susana had likely been punished for her rebellion and the records of her testimony are dry and to the point, but to my ear there is an unmistakable tone of satisfaction when she tells of their repeated evasions.[34]

On September 1, 1629, Cartagena's *alcalde* (councilman/mayor) Gregorio Vanquesel determined that the case had sufficient grounds to proceed and ordered del Río be imprisoned pending a full investigation and trial.[35] Del Río petitioned for bail, hired advocate Diego de Orozco, and began to establish his defense. They argued that del Río had performed his duties as the slave catcher of La Balsa in good faith, and therefore should not be punished for Catalina's escape. Orozco presented witnesses who testified to his client's good character and meritorious service; several witnesses mentioned that Catalina's original flight had been caused by Moriano's violent efforts to block her marriage.

As the extent of Moriano's abuse came to light, Orozco shifted his defense strategy to focus almost entirely on Catalina's maltreatment. Spanish officials generally considered violent interference in a marriage to be evidence of an owner's mistreatment of their slaves. Accordingly, if Orozco could prove Moriano had mistreated Catalina while violating canon law, he could argue that she had justifiably run away from an abusive owner's home, invalidating Moriano's claim against del Río.[36]

In October 1629, alcalde Vanquesel had a scribe send a copy of the evidence and testimony to a *letrado* (expert jurist) requesting he evaluate the file.[37] After consultation, Vanquesel pronounced his verdict, pushing the parties toward a settlement. He determined del Río bore responsibility for the loss of Catalina but provided him a chance to fix his mistake. Telling del Río to either find Catalina within six months and bring Moriano notice of her whereabouts "and in that way not create any cost for either side" or pay four hundred pesos, Vanquesel also instructed the parties to respect Catalina's right to decide her own marriage thereafter.[38]

For Moriano, this outcome, while not precisely what he had requested, represented a partial victory. He would eventually recover either Catalina or her value. Del Río's position, however, depended on his ability to catch Catalina and, considering the difficulties he had already experienced, it is unsurprising that he did not want to tangle with her again. Instead, del Río and Orozco used the six-month suspended sentence to prepare an appeal to the provincial governor, arguing that Moriano's actions preceding Catalina's escape warranted complete dismissal of the case.[39] Specifically, Orozco reformulated his defense around Moriano's and his wife's violent efforts to prevent Catalina and Domingo's marriage. The appeal contained a copy of all previous testimony and petitions, including Moriano's repeated denials of any wrongdoing. In a serious blow to Moriano's credibility, Orozco tracked down and included a certified copy of the ecclesiastical case started by Domingo Angola in the vicar's court.

Unbeknownst to the civil authorities, the religious case had developed concurrently with theirs from June to September 1629. Initially, the vicar general's court had issued a summary judgment ordering Moriano to bring Catalina back to Mompós within three days, on pain of excommunication. When Moriano failed to present Catalina after the allotted time, they declared him excommunicated. However, behind the scenes pressure was being applied, and on June 9, Domingo presented himself to his parish priest and declared that he wanted voluntarily to absolve Moriano from guilt and would never say anything against him again.[40]

However, Moriano's actions had aroused the opprobrium of his vecinos, who kept the case from being abandoned. Within two days of Domingo's withdrawal, several prominent members of the community came forward to testify against Moriano. These included a local deacon, an alcalde (officer) of the Santa Hermandad, and the lieutenant sheriff of the town. They testified to having seen Moriano beating Catalina to prevent her marriage, and furthermore that everyone in town knew of his cruelty in this matter.[41] This allowed the religious authorities to continue the case despite Domingo's statement, keeping Moriano on the defensive. After several months of further testimony, petitions, and counterpetitions, the case came before Francisco de Yarza, the impressively titled Dean of the Holy Church in Cartagena, Canon of the Cathedral, and Provisor and Vicar General throughout the bishopric of Cartagena. Yarza issued a final ruling on September 19, 1629. First, he affirmed the order of excommunication against Moriano until he present Catalina to the court and gave him a term of three days to comply. Second, he determined that Moriano should pay two hundred gold pesos for his repeated disobedience and his cruelty toward Catalina. Yarza closed by exhorting Moriano to repent and comply, "under penalty of major excommunication."[42]

Including the religious case, del Río's appeal worked about as well as he and Orozco could have hoped. On June 27, 1630, the governor of Cartagena repealed the previous sentence against del Río, exonerating him from financial or legal responsibility in Catalina Angola's escape and assigned Moriano both sides' legal costs, a penalty generally applied to cases brought in bad faith.[43] Moriano appealed this disastrous sentence to the highest court in the New Kingdom of Granada, the Real Audiencia de Santafé. The oidores (judges) of the Audiencia reviewed the file and on December 16, 1630, confirmed most of the governor's sentence. Moriano did receive some small relief, as the oidores assigned the court fees to del Río.[44]

Eighteen months after his intervention in Catalina's marriage, Moriano's actions had resulted in a cascade of negative consequences: Catalina ran away, he spent six months fighting an ecclesiastic case, he was excommunicated and fined two hundred pesos by the church, and also engaged in a futile sixteen-month legal battle with del Río. While he valued Catalina at four hundred pesos, a conservative estimate of his costs would place the latter around fifteen hundred pesos. The public proceedings had shamed him, degrading his honor. Furthermore, like other local elites, Moriano served as part of the imperial administration; excomunión mayor could cost him his position as treasurer of the Holy Crusade for Mompós. Indeed, we can see here how the fact that Spanish governance made public service attractive to local elites increased slave owners' susceptibility to pressure from the judicial apparatus.[45]

Moriano frequently asserted that Catalina was his property and, as such, it was his right to do with and dispose of her as he chose. Domingo's religious case, Catalina's escapes, and del Río's accusations, however, repeatedly proved the limitations of his power. Slave owners in the Spanish Empire did not possess untrammeled power over their slaves (i.e., *jus utendi, jus disponendi, et jus abutendi*). Ancient, medieval, and still entirely authoritative Spanish law endowed enslaved people with both legal and religious personhood, granting them legal standing before royal and ecclesiastical courts.

The legal condition of slavery and its concomitant social stigma disadvantaged unfree people in conflicts with social and economic superiors.[46] However, Africans and their descendants throughout Iberoamerica quickly learned to use the legal ecology to mediate or blunt negative actions against them. Claims-making allowed them to somewhat counterbalance the power of slave owners and other elites. During the long seventeenth century, the residents of New Granada voted with their actions by enmeshing themselves in the Iberoamerican legal ecology. Despite the well documented difficulties in the application of the law, its importance in the life of enslaved Afroiberians and freedpeople cannot be denied. To understand the social weight of the law we have to review the background from which the legal ecology derived its form and legitimacy.[47]

GUNS AND GOVERNANCE

Empire is as much an intellectual endeavor as a military one. Indeed, Christianizing and civilizing narratives were a key part of European imperialism.[48] As Iberians surged into the Atlantic, their ability to draw upon Christendom's deep well of collective learning on conquest, conversion, state formation, and imperial consolidation proved a decisive advantage.[49] A review of the history of the Caribbean basin throws up endless examples of scarce resources and attention directed toward

the creation and transmission of justifying stories.[50] However, within academia
and among the broader public, imperial competition has been lopsidedly understood using a military frame of reference, undervaluing (understandably) the mad-
deningly contradictory and inconsistently applied ideas that animated competing
empires.[51]

As a founding member of the first global order, the Spanish Empire pioneered
the adaptation of medieval precedents as it incessantly struggled to contain and
profit from increasing global complexity (figure 1.3).[52] However difficult to define,
in the *annus mirabilis* of 1492 Isabel and Ferdinand stood at an infliction point in European history as the stability of the Middle Ages was giving way to the accelerating
complexity of the early modern age. In her 1504 will, Isabel summed up her authoritative conception of Catholic buen gobierno. In a key passage, she admonishes
her heirs to "not consent that the *indios vecinos*, in our possession or still to be won,
receive any damage to their persons or goods; instead, you should command that
they be well and justly treated, and if they have suffered any damage, you should
remedy it, so as to not violate in any way the apostolic letters that commanded us
to take up this concession." One hundred seventy-seven years later, her instructions
had such legitimacy so as to be featured in the 1681 *Recopilación de Leyes de las Indias,*
which remained in force until the independence of Spanish America.[53]

In overseeing the spread of Iberian imperium in the Americas, the Catholic
monarchs self-consciously drew legitimacy from their medieval and ancient heritage, expressed by their relationship of authority over well-honed common identities. As they sought to maintain and expand Isabel and Ferdinand's achievements,
their heirs continued to draw upon medieval models to stabilize the growing complexity of their holdings. Identities woven into stories grouped under the rubric of
buen gobierno (with local variants) were adapted and reinforced by both church
and state through architecture, word, and deed. The grand narrative presented the
Hapsburg empires as *the* divinely guided force for global Christian civilization.[54]
The limited self-government faithful indigenous subjects could access as part of the
Republica de Indios and the hope of freedom for model Christian slaves are exemplary subsets of this narrative, deployed to address the constantly contested legitimacy of Atlantic imperial powers while taking advantage of the fluidity of human
identity.[55]

Medieval European kingship was defined in general by the struggle to reestab-
lish central control over the administrative fragmentation of the Dark Ages, and by
the late medieval period, the fractious Iberian monarchies were at the forefront
of state centralization.[56] The fluctuating borderlands of the Reconquista had fueled
the rise of a militarized landed aristocracy who usurped and resisted royal power,
necessitating a proactive response from the monarchies if they wished to avoid further fragmentation. Building on policies pioneered by the likes of Charlemagne
and Alfred the Great, successful Iberian kings like Alfonso X *el Sabio* (1252–1284)

Figure 1.3. Map of the world around 1700 with major empires and trade routes. Ricardo Raúl Salazar Rey.

encouraged trade, nurtured a pan-Iberian identity, sponsored education, and strengthened royal justice.[57] Importantly for our story in this book, the most durable achievement of Alfonso's reign was the creation of the *Book of Laws*, or as it became known from Cartagena de Indias to Manila, *Las Siete Partidas*.[58]

The stability of European society at the height of the medieval period was sorely tested during the crisis of the fourteenth century, precipitated by rapid climate change affecting Eurasia and the ravages of the Black Death. As Europe's population halved, warfare took on a new intensity exemplified by the ferociously expensive Hundred Years' War, which saw the kingdoms of Iberia and the British Isles pulled into a vicious civil war in France. Yet, despite all these pressures, the polities centered on the Mediterranean did not suffer widespread collapse, as effective governance managed the increasingly complex dialogues between royal justice, royal authority, military conquest, and aristocratic autonomy.[59]

Throughout Europe, royalists championed the application of a unified legal code, interpreted by justices who were appointed by the crown and served at the monarchs' pleasure.[60] Lowborn university-educated clerks staffed the chanceries putting into effect policies that reinforced royal justice by expanding its jurisdiction at the expense of feudal *fueros* (charters of privileges) and seignorial courts.[61] Institutionalization balanced the power of the traditional military elites by harnessing the abilities and ambitions of the *novis homines*. Still, the emergent central state was vulnerable to moments of weakness in royal power. Absent effective royal stewardship, the kingdoms of Iberia were liable to descend into a welter of private justice, lawlessness, and banditry.[62] Iberian examples abound, with the intermittent civil wars during the reign of Henry IV of Castile (1425–1474) and the War of the Castilian Succession (1470–1479) being particularly calamitous.

It is in this context that we can appreciate the accomplishments of Isabel I of Castile, who reigned from 1474 to 1504. A statesperson and innovator of European stature, she adapted medieval institutions and fused them with an expansive ideology underpinned by increased institutional capacity. Building on the achievements of her predecessors and aided by her marital alliance with Ferdinand of Aragon, Isabel strengthened royal power and justice. The Catholic Monarchs, as they came to be known, took measures against the nobility, destroying castles, repressing private wars between nobles, and reducing the power of the *adelantados* (conquering governors). By 1495, Isabel was even able to curtail the autonomy of Castile's wealthy and unruly military orders by incorporating them into the Consejo de las Órdenes (Counsel of Military Orders).[63]

Isabel consolidated her rule and pursued internal pacification through institutions that she forged as part of the union of Castile and Aragon and the completion of the Reconquista—the final incorporation of Muslim Al-Andalus into the kingdom of Castile and the subsequent expulsion of those Jewish and Moorish residents who refused to convert to Catholicism. These institutions included the cabildos, provincial governors, reales audiencias, the Santa Hermandad, and the Holy Office of the Inquisition. Future monarchs refined this governance toolbox, as they deployed its components to secure and consolidate the emergent global Spanish Empire.[64] For over three centuries, through two dynasties, countless wars, catastrophic population decline, forced migration, and the emergence of the global economy, these institutions held most of the empire together.[65]

At the heart of Spanish imperial power was an alliance with the Catholic Church.[66] The Catholic Monarchs and their successors carefully built a partnership with the papacy, leveraging their role in the Reconquista, the Reformations, and the Age of Exploration to negotiate a series of agreements with the Holy See known collectively as the Real Patronato Indiano (Royal Patronage of the Indies). Under the terms of these concordats the crown could nominate high church officials and manage church revenues throughout the empire. The joining of royal power and ecclesiastical patronage resulted in a mutually beneficial intermingling of trade, governance, and religion.[67]

The most notorious consequence of this alliance was the Spanish Inquisition, established in 1481 and given unprecedentedly broad jurisdiction to pursue the wicked. Spanish monarchs came quickly to depend on this institution to punish both moral failures and political enemies. In a fascinating parallel, the English Tudors established the hated Court of Star Chamber at Westminster around the same time period. Like the Inquisition, this court operated under Roman law—not English common law—and also most conveniently claimed jurisdiction over moral crimes. In the competitive and comparative early modern world, royal toolkits rhymed.

While the Catholic Church claimed universal jurisdiction, the basic units of government within the Spanish Empire were towns, represented by their cabildos. Notably, when Isabel took power, she had to quell the unruly cabildos of Castile. She was not the first Iberian monarch to face this challenge; medieval cabildos, many with fueros setting them partially outside of royal control, constituted one of the most troublesome institutional platforms hindering centralized rule.[68] Cabildos traced their origins to the Roman Empire's *municipium* and *civitas*.[69] Despite their diminished medieval reality, the idea of "cityness (*civilitas*), with all the undertones of civility and civilization which the Latin word still conveys to us," remained a key concept in the minds of Iberian settlers as they established settlements in the Indies.[70]

After the dissolution of central power accompanying the collapse of the Roman Empire, some town councils in Iberia continued to function, though much reduced in authority. Under decentralized Visigoth rule (500–711), surviving towns, along with a few new foundations, increased their power. The cabildos' accretion of administrative authority and independence accelerated as Al-Andalus began its long decline. During this period, borderlands suffered wastage and population loss under pressure from the intermittent military action accompanying the advancing Reconquista. To attract settlers to their new lands, Christian kings and great lords fortified and refounded towns, granting generous fueros to their cabildos.[71] The most coveted of the former were the right to self-rule, maintain fortifications, and administer justice within a particular cabildo's territory.

As Isabel consolidated her reign, ending the era of contested successions, the independence the cabildos had leveraged through their uncertain fealty diminished. During the Cortes of Toledo of 1480, the queen established the office of *corregidor* (royal representatives) henceforth to be embedded in the cabildos and began the long and painful process of destroying unauthorized fortifications. At the same time, Isabel faithfully respected Castilian law, under which towns maintained a large degree of self-governance vested in the cabildo. Indeed, most town charters allowed them to elect a cabildo capable of levying taxes and directing municipal government.[72] Representing a town's legal residents, the cabildo wrote local regulations and policed the vecinos, including enslaved people.[73] Finally, the cabildos were led by alcaldes, whose duties included adjudicating most legal disputes. Well aware of this tradition, conquistadors, adelantados, and the settlers who followed them chartered towns as they spread throughout the Indies.

As metropolitan power took hold in the New World, viceroys stood at the top of the royal hierarchy, with captain generals and governors reporting to this office. Major towns within each governorship were generally assigned lieutenant governors. The governor or his lieutenants could adjudicate cases brought before them and also heard appeals of cases handled by the alcaldes of the cabildos. Much of the energy needed to govern the Spanish Empire, and the form that this government took, was generated by the bringing of lawsuits, the adjudication of the same, and the control of channels for appeal.

Mechanisms of appeal allowed an outlet for discontent and bound the inhabitants of the empire to the monarchy. By seeking redress, claimants like Domingo Angola facilitated supervision of judicial officers, reinforcing a system of checks and balances. Both the Real Audiencia de Santafé in Bogota and the governor of Cartagena possessed judicial and executive responsibilities. They reviewed lower officials' decisions and served as counterweights to each other. The audiencias also possessed the legal faculty to communicate directly with the Council of Indies, and even the monarch, without receiving prior authorization from any other royal official. Furthermore, the audiencias oversaw the semiofficial contractors who provided what passed for cost-effective law and order in the sparsely populated backlands. Contractors like Antón del Río often operated within overlapping jurisdictions and their actions could result in contradictory legal claims. Judicial officials at all levels were regularly summoned to review the legality of disputed actions and adjudicate conflicts between contractors, royal subjects, and other imperial officials.[74] Accountability contributed to the legitimacy and durability of the Spanish legal ecology.

Patrolling the countryside, we find another royal institution adapted from medieval models. From the twelfth century onwards, men in Iberia organized *hermandades* (brotherhoods) based upon the crusading orders to patrol roads and rural areas of the peninsula. Often falling under the control of the regional nobility rather than royal officials, the hermandades acted as autonomous semiofficial police, drawing their authority from force while theoretically providing law and order. While suppressing alternate power bases in the countryside, Isabel established a kingdom-wide rural constabulary named the Santa Hermandad firmly under the crown's control, coopting local groups. As Spanish rule expanded into the New World, so did the institutional jurisdiction of the Santa Hermandad. Directed by alcaldes, the brotherhood was charged with patrolling, capturing, punishing, and returning escaped slaves to their owners.[75]

After the deaths of Isabel (1504) and Ferdinand (1516), the Spanish monarchies became part of the Hapsburg portfolio in the person of their grandson Charles V (1500–1558), Holy Roman Emperor. The Hapsburgs ruled over composite monarchies whose constituent parts had negotiated their political and legal submission. As we will explore further in chapter 2, the sixteenth and seventeenth centuries' wars of religion drove state formation in Europe; however, centralization was deliberately limited by the mind-bendingly complex structure of Hapsburg holdings.[76] The charters granted to the conquistadors operated in this framework, spreading Castile's basic legal framework throughout the Indies, modified and adjusted as circumstances and conditions warranted.[77]

Despite myriad challenges, by the 1580s the Spanish Empire was the first global superpower.[78] The apogee of Spanish Hapsburg power came with the union of the crowns of Castile and Portugal. In 1578, the House of Aviz, Portugal's ruling dynasty, went extinct. Charles V's son Philip II bid successfully for the throne, offering Portugal a charter that guaranteed Lisbon's administrative control over its empire while at the same time providing preferential commercial access to the vast Hapsburg possessions. After 1580, slaving *faetorias* (trading enclaves) pioneered by the Portuguese in Africa began shipping directly to the Spanish Indies.[79] The integration of the Spanish and Portuguese commercial systems allowed for an increasingly dependable flow of Africans to the Indies.[80]

The perceived need for African forced labor was central to the Union of Crowns and to global European imperialism in general. Emerging elites in the slave-importing regions of the Spanish, British, and Dutch Indies negotiated with their metropoles in shaping the legal framework of slavery.[81] But they all worked off the consensus that African slavery was needed to power the economy of the Caribbean basin.[82] As a counterweight to the rising power of other overseas slavocracies, Spanish metropolitan authorities promoted social stability in all aspects of governance from administrative boundaries to how judges dealt with cases involving enslaved people.[83] The legal ecology and the imperial institutions that grew from it served to contain and diffuse challenges to royal authority.[84] The legitimacy and durability of the Spanish Crown became inseparable from the way that its myriad subjects perceived themselves as participants and beneficiaries of royal justice, mercy, and Catholic good governance.[85]

PROVINCE AND LAW IN THE EMPIRE

Europeans exploring the coastline of what would become the New Kingdom of Granada described the area as "very rich, but abundant in bellicose Indians."[86] There appeared to be some gold in circulation among the indigenes and high-quality pearls were harvested in several bays along the coast. The region's long-term value was enhanced by the discovery of several well-suited ports that connected the Atlantic with navigable rivers from the interior. The combination of wealth and strategic location ensured a sustained imperial push inland. Spanish explorers/conquerors established settlements in locations with access to labor, mineral wealth, and transport (figure 1.4).[87]

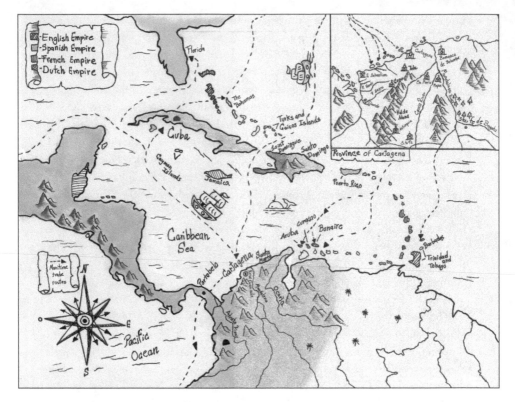

Figure 1.4. Map of the Province of Cartagena, Bogota, and local imperial outposts around 1700. Ricardo Raúl Salazar Rey.

Of the newly chartered towns, Cartagena de Indias, founded by adelantado Pedro de Heredia in 1533, emerged as the province's undisputed center.[88] Taking advantage of the city's secure position near the mouth of the Magdalena River system, merchants developed trade routes into the interior. Throughout the Caribbean, Spanish military and paramilitary forces were tested constantly by enemy scouts, pirates, and smugglers, and Cartagena's legendary wealth and strategic location made it particularly vulnerable to attacks by rapacious outsiders.[89] Responding to the threat, successive Spanish monarchs invested enormous sums in the city, tasking a steady stream of the best and brightest officials with developing and maintaining the forces stationed in Cartagena.[90]

Over the sixteenth and seventeenth centuries, the physical and human infrastructure of Cartagena became one of the linchpins holding together a sprawling global empire.[91] The great fortifications surrounding the city protected treasure ships and merchantmen alike.[92] The growing importance of the region allowed the merchant elite to negotiate trade concessions with the Consejo de Indias (royal council of the Indies) and solidified Cartagena's position as one of South America's major administrative and trade hubs.[93]

Land without people was considered wilderness and, after the conquest, the Spanish brutally solidified their control of the region by dividing among themselves the surviving indigenes in *encomienda* (religious tutelage in exchange for service). Unknowably and unstoppably, conquest and settlement brought with it the full suite of Eurasian and African diseases. Mosquitoes' effectiveness as a disease vector meant regions with a tropical climate suffered an accelerated demographic collapse.[94] By 1650, the indigenous populations of the Caribbean basin had declined by 95 to 99 percent.[95] Communities concentrated in highland areas suffered an only slightly less cataclysmic decline of 85 to 95 percent, largely due to the effects of colder temperatures on pathogens and their vectors.[96] Nevertheless, recurrent plagues, miscegenation, exploitation, and migration resulted in the transformation of most precontact indigenous cultures in a syncretic burst of ethnogenesis.[97]

Expectations set by contact population levels meant that, over the course of the sixteenth and seventeenth centuries, the demographic collapse left governments and settlers throughout the Caribbean basin with an unexpectedly vexing problem. As Peter Marzahl writes, "the most pressing problem the Spanish settlers faced was the lack of labor."[98] The legality of enslaving Amerindians was contested from the start. Returning from his first voyage, Christopher Columbus presented thirteen enslaved Native Americans to the queen at court. In response, Isabel publicly rebuked Columbus for enslaving her subjects and ordered him to free and return them to their land.[99]

Despite the metropolitan position on the subject, perceptions of increasing labor scarcity pushed European settlers in Iberoamerica to resist, subvert, or circumvent laws that sought to limit their access to Amerindian labor. Yet, in the face of determined opposition in the Indies, the Spanish Crown generally established, upheld, and applied laws prohibiting Amerindians' enslavement. In doing so, royal officials clarified and reinforced who could be enslaved and under what conditions. Complicating matters, the differences between the peninsular crowns on such fundamental matters as enslavement held even after the union of Spain and Portugal. These legal distinctions proved their relevance as Iberian slaving expeditions, which roamed freely in areas claimed by the Portuguese, would repeatedly be turned back from Spanish possessions.[100]

This combination of legal and demographic pressures led settlers and policy makers eventually to see forced African migration as the only realistic option for replenishing the regional labor pool.[101] Despite increasingly loud requests for more forced migrants, under Isabel and Ferdinand imperial authorities went no further than warily discussing the pros and cons of allowing recently converted heathens as slaves into the Spanish Indies. However, only two years after his accession to the throne, Charles V bowed to his subjects' pressure and opened the trans-Atlantic slave trade, granting a charter in 1518 to Lorenzo de Gorrevod permitting the transport of four thousand people directly from Africa to Spanish America. To be sure, even before the crown authorized direct transport of Africans to the Americas, Africans were essential in the creation of the New Kingdom of Granada and Cartagena de Indias.[102] In addition to Amerindian allies, Africans were an integral part of Spain's imperial expansion.[103] Slaves and their descendants comprised a significant portion of Spanish military forces in the region's conquest and subsequently helped organize, train, and supervise indigenous laborers. Successful conquistadors manumitted many of their surviving slaves and some were even rewarded with land, creating the nucleus of what would become a large free black population.

Transitioning from slave to freedperson, and—as the repeated attempts of Francisco Copete Jr. to enslave his half-sister shows—staying free, required legal framing, social acceptance, and institutional support. Spanish authorities extended and adapted medieval laws regulating slaves and freedpeople from the very earliest days of the empire.[104] The legal corpus governing the Spanish Indies came to be known as *Derecho Indiano* and was built upon the sturdy foundation of the *Siete Partidas*.[105] Deriving from Christianized Roman law, the *Siete Partidas* endowed slaves with both legal and spiritual personhood as children of God and subjects of the king.[106] Slavery was portrayed as evil and contrary to nature—a sad reality in a fallen world that should be regulated with Christian justice. In the view of the law, slaves were people; they were unfortunate people, but people, nonetheless. In unknowable proportions, the *humanitas* evident in the *Siete Partidas*'s framing of slavery responded to the zeitgeist of the twelfth century Renaissance and to the strategic reality facing medieval Iberia.[107]

Perhaps the most important, and least discussed, long-term constraining factor on the development of the institution of slavery in Iberia was the peninsula's geopolitical role as a borderland between Christendom and Islam. The Reconquista's seven hundred years of intermittent warfare, followed by the rise of Ottoman power, meant that Iberian slavery was codified and exported to the New World during a period when people on all sides (Muslims, Christians, and Jews) could and were enslaved. The dehumanization of captive Muslims could and would result in retaliation against Iberian Christians; Iberian rulers, therefore, had an interest in preserving some basic rights for enslaved people (for example, the right to self-purchase or redemption) to ensure the same rights for their own subjects and protect them from inhumane treatment by the other side.[108]

Furthermore, after the marriage of Isabel and Ferdinand, the Aragonese trading empire provided the unified monarchy with a cadre of administrators who could be deployed to the Indies and who were versed in Iberian slave law.[109] As the magnitude of the discoveries and challenges in the Indies became evident, Ferdinand of Aragon, acting as regent after the death of Isabel in 1504, convened noted jurists and theologians to write laws specifically for these new territories and peoples. The Laws of Burgos, issued in 1512, were the first major attempt by the Spanish Crown to regulate and protect the indigenous people of the Americas.[110] In 1542, Isabel and Ferdinand's grandson Emperor Charles V followed their precedent by issuing the so-called New Laws—officially titled "Laws and ordinances again made by his Majesty for the governance of the Indies and the good treatment and conservation of the Indians"—after much debate concluded that abuse by unscrupulous settlers was causing the continued collapse of the indigenous population.[111] The general thrust of these laws limited the control of local elites over pacified *indios* and prohibited outright their participation in some types of labor. One law went so far as to proscribe death for any Spaniard who used indigenous captives in the pearl fisheries.[112]

In addition to the law codes, *cédulas reales* were issued in response to petitions, requests for clarification, and jurisdictional disputes. One of the first to reference Cartagena dates to 1537, when an imperial *visitador* (inspector general) sent a report to Spain accusing the provincial governor of using "the fifty negroes that he had brought to despoil the burial mounds of the Cenú" instead of utilizing them on much needed public works.[113] Another oft-reissued directive prohibited the use of Africans as taskmasters for the encomenderos in the face of widespread reports of abuse.[114]

Cédulas reales directed to authorities in Cartagena addressed everything from the proper burial for slaves who drowned while working in the pearl fisheries[115] to administrative protection for a group of freedpeople living near labor-hungry ranches.[116] Another cédula prohibited indios from working as bogas transporting goods or people up and down the Magdalena, leading to the takeover by Africans and their descendants in this strategic sector of the economy.[117] Eventually almost all river traffic would be handled by enslaved bogas traveling under their own supervision.[118]

In letters to the king, local elites complained of the losses they suffered at the hands of runaways, the insolence and laziness of their slaves, and the constant impending rebellion they feared. Some described the enslaved Afroiberians in the Province of Cartagena as notoriously disobedient, to the point that the crown specifically addressed crime among the city's enslaved inhabitants in a royal cédula.[119] While some overwrought petitions portray a province in a state of constant apprehension regarding the enslaved population, a broader documentary survey, including royal instructions, legal proceedings, and religious policies, exposes a nuanced understanding of enslaved Afroiberians and freedpeople as part of society. In this mix, the crown positioned itself as a mediator between oppositional groups within legitimate boundaries as commonly understood. Fulfilling this function, we find a 1540 royal cédula that brokers peace by declaring forgiven "the *cimarrones cartageneros* who voluntarily lay down their arms and return to the service of their masters."[120]

To a degree, we are all captives of our sources and defending or debunking imperial propaganda provides the starting point for much historical writing. The present work wrestles with imperial propaganda on a moral and utilitarian level. The DNA of the Spanish Empire's moralizing bureaucracy can be traced to the organizing stories powerfully formulated by the scholars and statesmen of the Renaissance of the twelfth century, codified under the supervision of Alfonso X: the *Siete Partidas*. Self-righteous and oblivious at their worst, righteous agents of good governance at their best, royal officials and slave owners set the parameters which Africans engaged as they negotiated their captivity.[121]

For example, Cartagena elites regularly petitioned Madrid to be allowed to use harsher punishments to control their slaves. In their requests, they increasingly attempt to frame the "bad" behaviors of their slaves through the language of race. However, to what degree those appeals persuaded metropolitan authorities is unclear, considering that at the same time these provincial elites regularly and illegally armed their enslaved retainers, indicating that they did not (at least fully) believe their own racial rhetoric. Race and representation remain controversial ideas today, and as we seek to understand the past, they are one of the most fecund sources of confusion. Strong feelings cloud our ability to empathize with people in the past whom our current society would define as deplorable.

Keeping in mind the mutability of identity and its representation helps when evaluating the uses and social support of the narratives regarding Afroiberians we can recover from the documents produced during the long seventeenth century. Setting the tone of Iberoamerican social relations, forced labor came to underpin much of the growing wealth and power of regional elites, focusing their efforts to control the laws and regulations delimiting slavery. However, early structural choices set path dependencies limiting the range of possible downstream actions and establishing the expectations people had about what made their polity legitimate.[122] As Velleius Paterculus observed, "Precedents do not stop where they begin, but, however narrow the path upon which they enter, they create for themselves a highway whereon they may wander with the utmost latitude . . . no one thinks a course base for himself which has proven profitable to others."[123] The segmented benefits accruing to those who cooperated were expressed through the proliferation of categories like *parda criolla* (black born in the Indies), *morena libre* (free black), or *negro horro* (black freedman).

As the legal ecology was established, we can see Spanish authorities trying to figure out how to regulate the diffusion of European weaponry throughout the racially and culturally blended society that was emerging in Iberoamerica. In an ordinance from 1568, confirmed by the metropole in 1573, it is established that "no mulato, nor *zambaigo* (mixed Indigenous and African), should carry weapons, and those mestizos who live in the same places as do the Spanish and keep a home and grow crops can carry them with a license from whoever is the governor, and do not give them to others."[124] Terminology that is usually read as mixed race might more accurately be said to represent mixed culture with a racial dimension. Criollos and mestizas were ambiguous but vital intermediaries between Europeans, Africans, and indigenes.[125]

The Spanish legal and social framework allowed for manumission, incentivizing slaves to strategically join into social and economic life, thereby reinforcing imperial stability.[126] As subjects of the king, they could seek protection from royal and church officials, and in limited cases petition the courts to enforce agreements. Slaves also lived in a society deeply concerned with honor and righteousness, which shamed excessive cruelty toward one's dependents.[127] As Catalina Angola's odyssey shows, violence without legal, institutional, and societal support could be ineffective. Generally speaking, juridical, societal, religious, and economic structures in the early Spanish Empire demanded deference, obedience, and labor from enslaved Afroiberians while also nudging slaveowners toward a paternalistic relationship with their dependents.[128]

The tradeoffs between economic efficiency and popular legitimacy were at the forefront of the choices of Spanish leadership during the long seventeenth century. The structure of the Spanish Empire came under sustained pressure from European competitors after the collapse of the Union of Crowns in 1640. In 1665, the accession to the throne of the disabled three-year-old Charles II, last of the Hapsburgs, could have sounded the death knell of the empire. However, an extraordinary leader and stateswoman, the queen mother Mariana of Austria took up the regency and ably steered the ship of state under very difficult conditions until her death more than three decades later in 1696.[129] As part of her program to reinforce the legitimacy of the monarchy through the provision of good justice, Mariana supported a long-delayed project to organize and rationalize the laws of Indies. In 1681, the accumulation of ad hoc regulations was organized and made congruent in the nine-volume *Recopilación de Leyes de las Indias*. The *Recopilación* gives us a general outline of how Spanish law functioned for enslaved subjects. The compendium tempers or denies petitions in which local elites, usually through the cabildo, requested authority to establish stricter controls on the enslaved population, impose harsher punishments, or defang the protections contained in the law.[130] Scholars sometimes overestimate the power of local elites or the willingness of royal officials to ignore the law. This in no way minimizes the economic incentives encouraging slave owners to exploit as far as possible their human property; rather it shows a complex system in operation, one in which the long-term success of the Spanish Empire was inseparable from the effective application of royal justice tempered by the dispensation of royal mercy.

HEARTS, MINDS, AND BODIES

Slave owners and imperial powers alike sought to maintain possession while extracting the greatest possible value from the enslaved population. Motivating the latter, whether through punishments or rewards, required time and resources.

The kinds of incentives slave owners might offer were shaped by the constraints of scarcity, the physical environment, and the type of work performed.[131] Gang labor on sugar plantations, the classic example of effort-intensive low-skill regimented work, provided the maximum opportunity for slave owners to use physical coercion.[132] However, only a minority of slaves performed regimented plantation labor in the New Kingdom of Granada during the long seventeenth century.[133] Occupations that employed slave gangs in other areas of the empire developed differently in New Granada.[134] For example, slaves made up most placer mining crews but tracking the scattered and irregular gold deposits required skill and independence and gave enslaved workers access to sharp objects.[135] However, shaping everyone's frame of reference, Cartagena faced into the Caribbean basin, where during the long seventeenth century competing empires took over territory claimed by Spain and began to develop large-scale enterprises employing concentrated slave gangs.

In Cartagena, four variables broadly determined where a slave's occupation fell on the spectrum between labor-intensive and care-intensive: the individual's level of socialization, physical location, gender, and skill set.[136] The pricing structure of the slave market reflected these variables, with acculturated, skilled, urban slaves at the top of the value pyramid. Imperial and local authorities repeatedly sought to regulate slaves who lived and worked on their own, supporting themselves and paying a rent to their owners, who in turn treated them like an investment.[137]

High-skill care-intensive work was done by educated slaves as administrators, supervisors, and representatives. Whether in the storehouse, barn, or farmhouse, only able leadership could maintain profitability and keep chaos at bay. Despite the power differential between slave and master, a breakdown in this type of relationship would impose costs on both sides.[138] Skilled and trusted work was rife with opportunities for retaliation against vicious or violent masters. The capacity for effective resistance incentivized the use of positive rewards, with manumission as the ultimate prize. Enslaved men and women competed to earn a place in the occupations where they could self-purchase or otherwise negotiate for their freedom.

The social understanding of the responsibilities and obligations between slave and master in Cartagena was grounded in centuries of discussion, custom, and practice. If we look at the language used in court cases by all sides, it largely matches the observation of Keith Wrightson that "the most fundamental of all bonds in medieval society was that of mutual obligation."[139] Nonetheless, violence undergirded the rigors of labor and sudden sale loomed always as a possibility, depending on an owner's reaction to international politics, market conditions, and labor needs. Rural enterprises often preferred recently arrived Africans over those who had become acculturated, made connections within the community, and become aware of the institutional avenues of resistance against their masters. Fearing the *malos hábitos* (bad habits) synonymous with acculturation, masters tried to isolate new arrivals on their estates to prevent "contamination" by urban slaves.[140]

While Spanish policy posed well-studied dangers to those outside of the Catholic flock, it also established leverageable boons to those who engaged with it on its terms.[141] The Catholic Church, serving as the propaganda department of the empire, exhorted enslaved people to marry within the church and proclaimed the liberation of exemplary captives pleasing to God and king. Recently arrived Africans or bozales learned the moral justification for slavery and the paths to manumission simultaneously. Manumission, in fact, strengthened the system by providing aspirational examples, and marriage anchored slaves in towns surrounded by an accessible frontier. In Spanish America, enslaved families sanctioned by Catholic marriage received some protections from being sold separately. In contrast, in the expanding British colonies, normal practice evolved in the direction of breaking up black families at the discretion of the slave owner.[142] Consequently, slaves in the Spanish Indies could, and in many cases did, perceive the system that enslaved them as broadly legitimate. In this as in so many other ways, the needs of imperial administration and defense modulated the power of slave owners, without directly contradicting it.

As the population within the Caribbean basin became increasingly Afro-Creole, the legitimacy of Spanish governance validated narratives that framed the integration of Africans into imperial society.[143] The legitimacy of the empire also served to position communities of enslaved rebels as weapons of war. Finding it impossible to evict its competitors from the New World by military means, starting in 1528 the Spanish Empire leveraged its legitimacy by putting forth a credible offer to confirm the freedom of and provide some support for enslaved people who liberated themselves by absconding from rival empires.[144] Spanish policy self-servingly leveraged the human need for purpose by allowing escapees to build communities. The Spanish settled the refugees in towns strategically placed in regions where depopulation had opened breaches in imperial defenses. Royal officials could make binding agreements with formerly enslaved individuals or groups based on the legal principle that slavery was a temporary condition that could be left behind. This attitude stood in contrast to racialized chattel slavery prevalent in the domains of Spain's rivals, wherein the legal status was intrinsically attached to the people enslaved.

Because of the early and sustained dependence of the Spanish on forced African labor, every European invader from Drake onwards attempted to recruit from *cimarrón* (self-liberated) and palenque communities in service of their goals.[145] Jane Landers tells of the absorption by Spanish authorities of cimarrón villages, reestablishing their inhabitants as contractors charged with catching runaway slaves and defending peripheral areas from attack. More often than not, when the Spanish found that they could not defeat a particular band of runaways, they would negotiate to make them useful to the empire. Negotiations were carried out by Catholic priests acting as neutral parties, usually offering recognition and supplies in exchange for Christianization and service to the crown.[146]

In contrast, in the areas of the Americas wrested from Spain, competing European empires ruling over regions characterized by large-scale, slave-powered plantations increasingly viewed even "fractional freedoms" as problematic; this perception grew and hardened with the racialization of slavery.[147] The consensus in the non-Spanish Caribbean basin became that for slaves to understand the socioeconomic system in which they lived would represent an existential threat to the plantocracy.[148] Strategically taking advantage of these developments, from the sixteenth to the eighteenth centuries Spanish authorities extended an offer of freedom and land to enslaved people from rival empires, conditional upon their converting to Catholicism and becoming subjects of the crown.

Ironically, Dutch intraimperial trade/smuggling networks ensured that knowledge of the Spanish offer disseminated widely. Slaves fleeing to freedom shifted the cost of labor onto Spain's opponents, at the same time forcing them to expend resources policing the people they held in captivity. Responding to this challenge, British colonial courts and legislatures increasingly defined black people as subhuman, without rights under the law, erecting barriers to communication and manumission.[149] Similarly, the Dutch were reluctant to use slaves in positions that allowed independence or responsibility, placing legal restrictions on the ways that owners could deploy their enslaved workers.[150] However, due to the need for labor in Curaçao, Dutch authorities did allow enslaved people to work on merchant vessels, albeit with constraints.[151]

Among the burgeoning Afro-Caribbean population, the perceived legitimacy of the legal ecology served core imperial objectives, building trust in Spanish governance, and allowing forced migrants to become an economic engine for the region.[152] Legal incentives encouraged enslaved Afroiberians to enmesh themselves in imperial society to acquire resources and better their condition.[153] In Cartagena, enslaved people worked, drank, ran businesses, fought, saved money, became free, and even bought slaves of their own.[154] Newly arrived enslaved Afroiberians (bozales) depended on previous arrivals to teach them the pathways of integration and resistance to the imperial project. We can see this happening especially clearly whenever we examine surviving cases initiated by Afroiberians.

MARIA MONTERA GOES TO COURT

María Montera was an Atlantic merchant based out of Cartagena.[155] Likely the daughter of enslaved Africans, she bought her own freedom and then went on to achieve financial and social success. By the early 1630s, Montera ran a wholesale trading operation, owned at least three slaves, and confidently described herself as a vecina of Cartagena.[156] However, her success did not come without challenges, and the records indicate that she repeatedly turned to the courts to resolve conflicts in her business dealings.

Due to the loss of the notarial archives of Cartagena during the wars of Independence, only one case Montera initiated survives, thanks to a subsequent appeal to the Real Audiencia de Santafé in Bogota. In 1629, she appeared before a local magistrate, challenging Alonso Peralta's possession of two enslaved women, Francisca Angola and María Angola. Montera declared that she was the rightful owner of both slaves and had given them to Peralta as surety for a two hundred-peso loan. Charging that he continued to keep them despite the loan being repaid, Montera asked for the slaves to be returned and for Peralta to pay her lost *jornales* (wages).

The story of the dispute begins in late 1628, when Montera met Peralta at the office of the notary Francisco López Nieto in Cartagena's town center. They drafted, signed, and witnessed a contract in which Peralta lent Montera two hundred pesos so she could buy goods at the annual trade fair. Montera gave her slave Francisca Angola to Peralta as surety for the loan and agreed to pay him back by May 1629. Instead of interest, Peralta would have the right to Francisca's jornales until that time. Furthermore, Montera absolved Peralta of any legal liability if Francisca should die or fall ill while living and working with him, provided he treated her with due care. The contract also established that Montera would not sell or mortgage María Angola, another of her slaves, so that she could serve as a replacement in case anything should happen to Francisca.

However, things did not work out according to plan. When notified of the suit, Peralta responded with theatrical outrage and presented himself before the lieutenant governor to defend himself. According to his account, after their initial agreement, he had discovered that Montera was planning to sell María Angola, leading him to seek judicial remedies to prevent the sale and ultimately forcing Montera to negotiate a new deal. They agreed that Peralta would buy María Angola for 280 pesos and that Francisca Angola would become his property in exchange for canceling the original loan of 200 pesos. He concluded his writ to the court stating that Montera's declarations were "*siniestros y de malicia*" (malicious lies). Echoing a common strategy of elites dealing with freedpeople, Peralta laced his declarations with racial and cultural slurs toward Montera.[157]

In response Montera called upon her social network, neighbors, friends, and household members to back her, beginning with Antonio Báez (a free mulatto sailor), Bartolomé, and Juan García (a royal official). These three witnesses said that they knew the people involved in the case and estimated the value of Francisca Angola and María Angola between two to three hundred pesos each. Furthermore, to the best of their knowledge, Montera had received only eighty pesos from Peralta. In confirmation of this another of Montera's slaves, Jerónima Angola, declared that she had collected the eighty pesos from Peralta for the sale of María Angola. Finally, María Angola herself testified that Montera had sold her to Peralta for 280 pesos.

In response, Peralta presented his own witnesses: María Orellana (a small shop-keeper), Francisco Núñez (a *negro horro*), and Mariana Angola (Peralta's slave). They asserted that the original loan had been modified to include the sale of both slaves. Peralta then presented Francisca Angola, the other slave in question, as his star witness. She declared that to the best of her knowledge, Montera had agreed with Peralta to sell her, along with María, for 280 pesos in exchange for the cancellation of the debt.

Significantly, Peralta never presented any documentary evidence beyond the initial debt agreement to support his claims.[158] By contrast, Montera presented documentation for all transactions, refuting Peralta's declarations. The care with which María Montera set up the contract and then documented every subsequent change in their business dealings paid off in her petitions to the courts. On October 15, 1629, *teniente de gobernador* Francisco de Betancourt sent notice to both parties to appear and to hear the sentence from the *gobernador y capitán general* of Cartagena, Francisco de Murga. The governor declared that Montera had proven her claims while Peralta had failed to prove his and ordered Peralta to return Francisca Angola along with her *jornales* to Montera.[159]

Unsurprisingly, Alonso Peralta did not accept the ruling handed down by the governor. On February 20, 1630, he presented an appeal to the Real Audiencia de Santafé in Bogota. His appeal forced both sides to produce a certified copy of the original case file and reiterate their arguments. Nevertheless, the preponderance of evidence continued to favor Montera, and the oidores affirmed the governor's sentence, adding only that each side should pay for its own legal costs.[160]

CONCLUSION

The stories that we have examined are about more than just disputes and transactions; these case studies distill the delicate balance between power and legitimacy that maintained social complexity in the Spanish Empire. The surviving documents provide glimpses into relationships suffused with control, resistance, and accommodation. María Montera overcame her enslavement and became a slave owner while dealing with discrimination. Simultaneously, Alonso Peralta sought to operationalize his privilege by denigrating Montera and to discredit her arguments by highlighting her race and status as a freedperson to the court. In contrast, Montera never addressed Peralta negatively and instead repeatedly expressed her faith in the law and royal justice. The motivation behind Peralta's attempt to keep both slaves from Montera is hard to determine, but considering the result, he miscalculated. Montera's preparation and the strength of her arguments overcame Peralta's advantages, preventing him from effectively impugning her in their business dealings. Nonetheless, it is significant that he thought it was possible.

In the Spanish Empire, governance and the legal ecology functioned through interdependent and mutually supervising institutions within, and comparatively with surrounding polities without. As with all states, limited resources encouraged selective prosecutions; however, without perceptible enforcement the law risked becoming a dead letter. Metropolitan policy counted on targeted exemplary enforcement to maintain respect for legal norms. Without the protections and boundaries established by the law and enforced by royal officials, the costs borne by enslaved Afroiberians, freedpeople, and their descendants would have been prohibitive. Generally predictable (if unequal) rule of law allowed Africans and their descendants to act as a regional economic engine, the importance of which is hard to overstate as they constituted the majority of the population.[161] Additionally, as the empire coped with myriad military threats, the credibility of Spanish offers of manumission allowed for the recruitment of enslaved soldiers from within while drawing in escaping slaves from without.

Comparing and contrasting how enslaved Africans engaged with the legal ecology of the various European empires operating in the Caribbean can give us insights into how the latter approached governance and its consequences.[162] Temporal, economic, and social variations make it difficult to find perfect matches; however, keeping the differences in mind, some elements can be compared usefully. For example, a 1788 criminal case in the French colony of Saint-Domingue (Haiti) affords an interesting contrast. The case involved a slave owner who tortured two women, Zabeth and Marie-Rose, on suspicion of conspiring to poison him along with other members of his household.[163] The egregiousness of the slaveowner's conduct led to him being taken to court and, despite his protestations that the case would encourage rebellion among the unfree population, condemned for cruelty under French law. Both the colony's governor and *Intendant* (chief military officer) noted the prosecution's exceptionality, writing that it provided a "unique opportunity to arrest, by means of a single example, the course of so many cruelties."[164] By applying the law to a brutal owner, French colonial authorities might have provided some redress for the many instances of unpunished abuse; however, their claims overstate the impact of this one case.

In comparison, in the Spanish Empire, both religious and secular courts enforced the law with much greater regularity to the benefit of enslaved subjects. As royal and ecclesiastical officials applied the law, they relied on the cooperation of the subjects within their purview.[165] Effective Spanish governance depended on institutional actors providing incentives for royal subjects to help enforce the law.[166] As seen in the next chapter, the Inquisition's ability to carry out its mission largely depended on the voluntary confessions and denouncements of ordinary churchgoers, a dynamic we have already discovered through the case of Catalina and Domingo Angola. When their plan to marry resulted in Moriano assaulting Catalina and shipping her down the river, Domingo denounced him to the vicar general. In his petition Domingo presented himself as a faithful son of the church, reinforcing the legitimacy of canon law. When enslaved people, or any imperial subjects,

engaged with royal or religious institutions, they effectively pledged their alle-
giance to the ideology of Iberian imperialism, bolstering its overall legal structure.

In the face of Moriano's interference, Catalina and Domingo chose different, yet
equally important, forms of resistance. Scholars have relatively thoroughly investigated active and violent rebellion, like the *petit marronage* Catalina chose. Resistance
that utilized imperial ideology to access institutional channels is less studied. Yet, as
this chapter has demonstrated, Africans and their descendants, as Catholic subjects
of the crown, could avail themselves of claim-making opportunities by engaging
with the church and other imperial institutions.[167]

Domingo's maneuvering through the religious channels to resolve a dispute
was an intentional outcome encouraged and supported by some local elites and the
Spanish Crown.[168] This case highlights the ambiguous social consensus and support
for legal and religious strictures on slave owners. By partaking in and enforcing the
sacraments, and by appealing to royal officials for protection with the use of the
court system, slaves and freedpeople became stakeholders in the establishment and
consolidation of the Spanish Empire.

2

CASES of FAITH

Thou shalt not suffer a witch to live.
—Exodus 22:18

For the Spanish Empire, the separation of church and state was anathema. The legitimacy of conquest, slavery, and royal rule itself were deeply rooted in Catholic Christianity. As Spaniards and their descendants built the structures of empire, they sought to "serve God, and to get rich."[1] While today we might consider religion and government as ill-suited partners just as much as we would consider science and astrology separate subjects, from the medieval and early modern world view there were no hard and fast boundaries between the two spheres. In fact, Spanish subjects of the long seventeenth century would consider our certainty in their separateness a sign of mental illness.

This chapter situates the Holy Office of the Inquisition in the human geography of the Spanish Empire. After reviewing the Inquisition's medieval foundations, we examine two witch trials set in Cartagena, one before and one after the establishment of that city's inquisitorial branch in 1610. Further, via the entanglements of the slaves with the Inquisition, the chapter explores how the unfree in Spanish America interacted with their environment using the categories with which they presented and understood themselves. Within the larger imperial context, the circumstances and beliefs of individuals shaped the opportunities available to them and the choices they made. Essential to understanding the Inquisition's institutional ethos and praxis in the New World is its foundation in the Old, as a thoroughly medieval response to religious and political heterogeneity.

THE HOLY OFFICE

The foundation of the Spanish Inquisition occurred during a burst of institutional innovation directed toward consolidating the gains of the reconquista as the Age of Exploration spun up.[2] Complicating a common understanding of the Inquisition as an obscurantist tool of repression, the Spanish version was a Renaissance project that reconceptualized the Papal Inquisition as a tool to concretize the monarchy's

military and political gains while disciplining a violent, religiously fervent population.[3] Spanish monarchs modulated the role that the Inquisition played in the legal
ecology in response to the challenges of governing an emergent global empire and
the wars of religion unleashed by the Reformations.[4]

However, to understand the Catholicism that the Spanish Empire spread around
the world, we have to go back to the early Middle Ages when Christianity confronted another monotheistic religion. Christian supremacy on the Iberian Peninsula was shattered with the initial wave of Muslim conquests that crested at Tours in
732 CE, leaving a few beleaguered semi-Christian kingdoms huddled in the mountain fastness of the Pyrenees and contemplating an uncertain future.[5] For the re-
mainder of the medieval period, Iberia was a house divided, rent along religious,
political, and cultural lines. The process of reasserting Christian religious and political control came to be known as the Reconquista, an idea and a process that waxed
and waned for almost eight hundred years.

For medieval Iberians the Reconquista offered a simple future alongside a complex reality. It provided comfort to a Christian minority after it became obvious to
both Christians and Muslims that at least in the short term they would be unable
to defeat each other militarily. Endlessly yearned for and imagined, the completion
of the Reconquista came to mean the liberation of Christians from the yoke of the
Saracen and the conversion or expulsion of all nonbelievers and "foreigners" from
Iberia. Consistent yet perennially shifting borderlands led to both sides practicing
convivencia (pragmatic toleration), as structurally intolerant societies and ideologies adapted reluctantly to forced cohabitation. Muslim controlled regions of Iberia were generally wealthier and more sophisticated than their Christian counterparts, leading to lucrative cross-border trade while drawing in a steady stream of
scholars who wanted to learn in the Muslim centers and mercenary knights from
across Christendom seeking to reap the spoils of holy war. Both Arab and Gothic
rulers struggled to achieve internal cohesion and governability while dealing with
intermittent bouts of armed conflict, an unstable amalgam that proved culturally
and economically dynamic. For example, it was in this environment that Alfonso X
oversaw the creation of the *Siete Partidas*.

As a result of these factors, during the medieval period, the Iberian Peninsula
was at the forefront of Europe's intellectual, technological, political, and religious
development.[6] Convivencia agitated the orthodox of all three faiths, complicating
the job of secular and religious leaders but providing a legacy of cosmopolitan governance that proved key to the intellectual architecture that enabled the Age of Exploration.[7] Royal officials, military, religious, and judicial personnel spread across
the world charged with what seemed to be an absolute mandate to establish universal Catholic monarchy. However, these orders were leavened by the understanding
that pragmatic toleration and effective governance were essential to sustaining the
gains of conquest.

As long as Muslims controlled significant Christian populations—and vice versa—each side generally respected the religious and cultural integrity of the other.[8] However, as the military power of Muslim polities in Iberia went into terminal decline, a large population of Jews and Muslims was transferred to Christian control, culminating in the completion of the Reconquista in 1492 and the consolidation of the nominal hegemony of the Catholic Monarchs. This shift changed the long-standing balance of power, presenting the new overlords with difficult choices, with none as intractable as those regarding taxation and religion. Under the leadership of Isabel and Ferdinand, the victorious Christians had to innovate to consolidate their newly acquired temporal and spiritual power.

In common with other late medieval European rulers, Ferdinand and Isabel conceived of the preservation of religious homogeneity and orthodoxy as a crucial matter of state.[9] Church and state understood overt religious toleration as a fundamental challenge to their legitimacy.[10] In this context, the Inquisition existed since the thirteenth century as a Vatican-appointed tribunal aligned with secular authorities and dedicated to combatting heresy. In 1478, presaging future challenges, and based on suspicions of disloyalty and popular violence toward new converts, Isabel and Ferdinand petitioned Pope Sixtus IV to grant them authority to establish and control a branch of this institution in Spain.[11] In this way, the Tribunal del Santo Oficio de la Inquisición became the primary Spanish institution charged with policing the beliefs and practices of *conversos* (converts and their descendants).

The Holy Office supervised new converts while simultaneously protecting them from mob violence. Without such an institutional guardrail, unscrupulous actors could harness white-hot popular religiosity to attack and to dispossess vulnerable populations on the flimsiest of pretexts.[12] Indeed, in the lead-up to and after the fall of Granada, popular religiosity among Old Christians pushed the Catholic Monarchs to adopt increasingly aggressive conversion policies toward their Muslim and Jewish subjects, even though this meant forfeiting the additional taxes non-Christians paid. Furthermore, recalcitrant Muslim and Jewish communities became a concern to the crown due to their shared religious and political connections with North Africa and perceived ability to appeal for outside intervention. In the face of these challenges, Isabel and Ferdinand issued two royal decrees (1492 and 1501) ordering their Muslim and Jewish subjects to convert, depart, or die. This forced homogenization reduced social tensions and protected the realm from the dangers, real and perceived, of insurgent activity. Modern revulsion at the iconic fate of the Jewish and Muslim communities in Iberia risks obviating the reality within which Isabel and Ferdinand maneuvered.[13]

The choices that Isabel and Ferdinand made were in the context of the renewed Muslim menace in the form of the Ottoman Empire; their immediate successor Charles V had to deal with the twin existential challenges of the Ottomans advancing on the borders of his eastern and western European possessions and the spread of Protestantism.[14] In 1517, after Martin Luther opened the Pandora's box of the Reformation, religious unity and the prevention of heresy became increasingly central to the Inquisition's mission. Luther's challenge found a receptive audience among the many who had grown disgusted by the corruption and venality common among the upper echelons of the Catholic Church. In areas that came under Protestant domination, the stability and unity fostered by a millennium of Catholic institutional knowledge were destroyed.[15] Flanked by Reformation in England and France, the Spanish monarchs witnessed a surfeit of examples of the chaos and atrocities that resulted from sectarian conflict as different factions sought to impose themselves outside the Roman Catholic order.[16]

Isabel and her successors came to rely on the Santo Oficio's uniquely universal jurisdiction to consolidate their authority over kingdoms where local privileges and exceptions to royal authority were aggressively guarded. Inquisition procedure established that the property of the accused should be seized and only returned at the conclusion of the process, after the deduction of any financial penalties. This meant that the mere threat of an inquisitorial investigation and concomitant property seizure was enough to deter most members of the upper class from challenging the monarchy. Building on its success in Iberia, the new Hapsburg monarchs established branches of the Inquisition in other kingdoms of their empire.

As the Inquisition spread, the monarchy expanded Holy Office's mandate, charging it with controlling entry into the empire, specifically to prevent the immigration of Protestants, Jews, and Muslims. It also policed the fraught world of ideas and the emergent republic of letters, preventing the entrance or spread of any material that did not conform to orthodoxy. Although the Holy Office adjudicated only a few hundred cases per year, the power of the Inquisition resonated throughout life under Hapsburg rule. Throughout, the need for popular legitimacy pushed inquisitors to balance rigor and mercy in order to protect the faith and reconcile those who strayed from the Catholic flock.[17]

Due to the intertwined ideological and religious justifications for Spanish conquest, the crown exempted Amerindians from the jurisdiction of the Holy Office.[18] However, the Inquisition kept watch over all other inhabitants of the Spanish Americas, establishing its first offshoot in the New World in Lima in 1570, followed in 1571 by an office in Mexico City. Forty years later, in 1610, the importance of the Caribbean basin led to the foundation of a branch in Cartagena, where Africans and their descendants became the primary demographic under the jurisdiction of that tribunal.[19]

Cartagena, along with Veracruz and Havana, was one of only three legal ports of entry for slaves into the Indies. That privileged position intersected with the proximity of the Inquisition to foster a climate of intimate interactions between the enslaved population and religious personnel (figure 2.1).[20] The intersection of

Figure 2.1. Palace of the Inquisition in Cartagena de Indias (construction completed ca. 1770). Ricardo Raúl Salazar Rey.

imperial functions makes the study of Cartagena fruitful in comprehending the interaction between enslaved Afroiberians and the Inquisition.[21]

Along with the rest of the Caribbean basin, Cartagena developed without significant Amerindian labor. Moreover, European immigrants seldom came to the province with the intention of doing heavy manual labor. In response to labor shortages caused by the depletion of indigenous people discussed in chapter 1 and the perceived benefits of slave labor, over one hundred and thirty-five thousand enslaved Africans came through Cartagena between 1595 and 1640, making them by far the largest group of settlers to arrive prior to Colombia's independence.[22] The Spanish Empire's policy of limiting European immigration reinforced the primacy of African labor. Recent scholarship has determined that two-thirds of the more than two million enslaved Africans arriving in the Spanish Americas landed before 1810, predating large-scale plantation agriculture in Cuba and Puerto Rico.[23]

As the demographic weight of Africans and their descendants comes into focus, historians have begun to appreciate the form and significance of the interactions between the enslaved population and the Inquisition.[24] Classic studies using Inquisition records sometimes agglomerated slaves with other lower-class subjects or used inquisitorial sources without critically analyzing how and why they were produced.[25] The legal condition of slaves as property complicated the dynamic between them and the Inquisition. Afroiberians' interactions with the Inquisition were seldom straightforward, as risks and opportunities hung over every encounter between enslaved subject and inquisitor.[26]

An expansive reading of the Holy Office's records provides a glimpse of slaves' social and institutional relationships. In many cases, slaves, masters, and inquisitorial functionaries formed a triangular relationship. Inquisitors interrogated slaves to learn of their masters' thoughts and actions, and, conversely, called on masters to testify against their slaves. However, a significant number of cases involving slaves resulted from conflicts unrelated to the master-slave relationship. In these cases, the Inquisition only minimally involved the slaves' masters.

Cartagena and its hinterlands were not a slave society, but a society with slaves. In a slave society, the domination and exploitation of enslaved people proceed without outside restrictions.[27] In contrast, embedded as they were within the composite monarchy of the Spanish Empire, local elites' efforts to cement their control over the enslaved population did not reign supreme.[28] The cases examined in this chapter show the mediating effect the institutional objectives of the Inquisition had on the lived reality of masters and slaves.[29] To get a sense of the environment that the branch of the Inquisition grafted itself onto in 1610, we first examine a case that occurred forty-five years earlier.

WITCH HUNT

One evening in September 1565, the wealthy vecino Diego Polo presented himself before the governor of Cartagena, licenciado (lawyer) Antonio de Salazar, warning of witchcraft among some slaves in his home and in the city.[30] As Polo told it, he had overheard an argument between two enslaved individuals he owned, Antón and Guoimar. As he approached, he heard Antón pleading with Guiomar to get off of him and accusing her of paralyzing him. Provoked by Antón's shouting, Polo barged in and confronted a frightened Guiomar, who confessed that she had used special yerbas (herbs) to paralyze Antón. Polo commanded Guiomar to fetch a sample of these herbs and demonstrate their effects on a young girl. After imbibing the mixture, the girl collapsed, appearing dead. Horrified, Polo accused Guiomar of killing her, yelling, "Whore! You are a whore!" The young woman recovered, but Polo continued to beat and question Guiomar, pressuring her to confess to witchcraft. She resisted and claimed to have only knowledge of some harmless yerbas. She did, however, tell of negros brujos (Afroiberian witches) whose souls left their bodies to roam the town and who possessed the ability to turn into dogs and tigers, claiming that they had killed "una india y un moreno" and two children.[31]

Polo took the battered Guiomar to the governor's home as proof of his accusations. Under questioning from the governor, Guiomar testified that she had received the yerbas from Bartolomé, an enslaved man belonging to Juan Rodríguez, a resident of the Getsemaní neighborhood. Based on this information, the governor ordered the interrogation of Bartolomé, who strongly denied either using yerbas or practicing witchcraft. Disbelieving Bartolomé's testimony, the governor ordered him to undress and supervised his torture on the *potro de madera* (rack). This torment elicited a limited confession from Bartolomé, who claimed that the herbs served as a love potion that enslaved women and *indias* (female Indians) only used "to play."[32]

Falling prey to the fear pervading the city and unwilling to accept Bartolomé's confession, the governor ordered a second and more brutal round of torture. In agony, Bartolomé broke, begged for forgiveness, and confessed to giving the herbs to Guiomar so she could kill children and enslaved people. He admitted to speaking with the devil, who appeared in the *"forma de negro"* (the form of a black man); that the devil had given him the power to turn himself into a snake; and that Guiomar had the ability to turn into a tiger. Bartolomé described how the devil had come, taken their hands, and told them they could only live as witches by drinking the blood of children. Then, he confessed that he sucked children's blood and ate their flesh and that the witches gathered at a bridge to call on the devil, who let their souls fly in the air while their bodies stayed on the ground. After Bartolomé confessed all of this and more, the governor finally ordered his men to untie him.[33]

Subsequently, the governor ordered another round of torture be applied to Guiomar, which extracted from her a new declaration similar to Bartolomé's. Both tormented individuals implicated other enslaved subjects in their confessions. As more enslaved people were implicated by coerced testimony, the governor brought them in for questioning and torture. The tales of *brujería* (witchcraft) among the enslaved population provoked a wave of fear and paranoia through Cartagena. Responding to the rising tension in the city, the governor ordered all of the implicated individuals imprisoned, hired four new guards to ensure that they were isolated in the city jail, and subjected them to enhanced interrogations.[34] The torture inflicted on the prisoners included being undressed, having an iron collar placed around their neck, being thrown on the rack, having their arms and legs stretched back, and being beaten about their body with a *garrote* (club).[35] Of the fourteen slaves named, seven were tortured and compelled to confess. Six accused people for whom there was only marginal evidence of participation in witchcraft were eventually released. Only one brave soul endured torture but continued to deny any involvement in the alleged coven.

The brutal methods used by gubernatorial authorities to extract confessions from the slaves accused of witchcraft ceased once the cases came under the purview of judicial officers. These officials engaged standard procedure, formally charged four of the enslaved subjects, notified their owners, and named the *procurador* (defense attorney) Bartolomé de Vega to defend the accused. At this point, it appears that all torture of the prisoners ceased. Unsurprisingly, after formal charges were brought, none of those being interrogated confessed to having any knowledge of witchcraft.[36]

Proper procedure established that royal officials investigate and gather evidence to confirm a *denuncia* (accusation) before initiating criminal procedures. Furthermore, the law provided that interrogation by torture should only be used as a last resort. In this case, Governor Salazar clearly failed to follow these prescriptions. In light of this, procurador de Vega immediately presented a series of petitions arguing that all charges against the enslaved individuals under his care should be dismissed. In his brief, he first attacked the case's origins, calling into question the veracity of the initial allegations and arguing that Diego Polo's *incierta denuncia* (unfounded denouncement) was uncorroborated by any other evidence and certainly did not reach the standard to justify judicial torture.

Additionally, during court proceedings, de Vega reminded the court that no record existed of the many deaths that the accused brujos claimed to have caused. He also argued that torture weakened the legal value of the confessions, as "slaves always confess what torturers want to hear when subjected to those punishments."[37] Finally, he declared that the charges as a whole were absurd, as the yerba supposedly used to kill people did not even touch them. As he wielded the law as an intellectual shield against an emotional, fear-based response from the town's population, de Vega's calm, rational, and legalistic approach counterpoised the town's hysteria.

During this time, the accused *yerbatero* (herbalist) and *brujo* (witch) Bartolomé died of his wounds in the governor's jail, which ultimately accelerated the adjudication of de Vega's case. The governor placed a statement by *alguacil* (sheriff) Juan de Herrera on the record, declaring that despite his best efforts, Bartolomé collapsed and died from his wounds while being carried to the jail from the governor's house. Ruling it a legal death, Governor Salazar declared a postmortem judgment. The sentence convicted Bartolomé of being a yerbatero and *hechicero* (sorcerer) who communed with the devil and turned into a witch. The governor ordered that Bartolomé's body be lifted onto a mule and carried through the streets while a *pregonero* (town crier) announced his sentence, and that his body be burned at the stake in the central plaza with an iron collar about his neck. Finally, the sentence assigned Bartolomé's owner all the costs incurred during his trial and execution.[38]

Meanwhile, the case against the surviving accused individuals progressed. De Vega called many enslaved and freed witnesses who testified that they had no knowledge of witchcraft practiced in the community or of the participation of the accused in the supposed demonic arts. Several vecinos testified to the prisoners' good character. In October 1565, Governor Salazar, "after carefully evaluating the case documents and the merits of this process," passed judgment on Guiomar, Catalina, and "the other Catalina," who belonged to Diego Polo, Beatriz de Quintanilla, and Diego de León, respectively. Despite the defense's voluminous testimony and petitions, the governor found the enslaved women guilty of all the alleged crimes. He ordered them to be taken to the beach on mules and burned to death while having their sentences read. He also applied the costs of the judicial process to their owners.

Given the persistence with which her owner, Diego Polo, was agitating for her execution based on the "strength" of the evidence against her and her repeated confessions, procurador de Vega chose to not challenge Guiomar's sentence, which was carried out in October 1565. Her dying declaration was witnessed and attached to the case file sent to the Real Audiencia in Bogota. Before being executed, she upheld her previous confessions and reaffirmed her guilt and that of her codefendants.

However, de Vega requested permission from the governor to appeal the sentences of both Catalinas to the Real Audiencia de Santafé.[39] In January 1566, he presented a memorial to the Audiencia, reiterating and expanding his earlier statements, arguing that Guiomar and Bartolomé had only confessed and accused others to make the torture stop. Furthermore, he highlighted that the first Catalina maintained her innocence despite repeated torture. De Vega argued that Bartolomé's testimony did not constitute enough evidence to convict either woman of witchcraft, especially given the positive testimony on their behalf by other enslaved witnesses, freedpeople, and vecinos.

Nevertheless, on July 19, 1566, the oidores of the Real Audiencia upheld the guilt of the accused women. However, the court modified the kind of executions that they would endure, ordering them hanged rather than burned. This was a mercy considering the horror of death by fire. Because this was a capital case, de Vega and Beatriz de Quintanilla requested, and were granted, a final desperate appeal for the first Catalina. However, the oidores again reaffirmed the sentence and ordered it be carried out forthwith.[40]

Throughout the proceedings, royal officials attempted to control the hysteria gripping the city and struggled to follow procedure during the investigation, trials, and judgments. Like all early modern polities, the Spanish legal system sanctioned the use of torture. While the long and carefully chronicled torture did not technically constitute a breach of official imperial procedure, it skirted very close to the line of permissibility. Peripheral outposts in the mid-1500s, such as Cartagena, lacked the trained personnel who were usually assigned to torture details. Group hysteria and inexperience drove officials in Cartagena to the excesses that Bartolomé de Vega denounced at various points in the trial and which resulted in the deaths of four innocents.[41]

Partially as a result of similar witchcraft cases, it became apparent that local officials were ill prepared to handle the explosive passions aroused by religious crimes. A remedy appeared in the guise of the Inquisition, which, since its foundation in the late fifteenth century, had trained its personnel in adjudicating all types of religious cases. As already mentioned, the Catholic Monarchs supported the strategic spread of the Holy Office as part of their program of centralization, and upon their deaths future imperial authorities established branches of the Inquisition throughout the empire, where they served as an essential part of the administrative and regulatory apparatus. In 1610, royal officials inaugurated the Cartagena branch of the Inquisition in the Indies. To understand how the creation of this institution affected the treatment of enslaved Afroiberians in religious matters, I examine and contrast the preceding case with one that occurred eighty years later.

WITCH HUNT, REDUX

In 1641, Felipa, an African woman described by the evaluators as bozal, who lived and worked on a *hacienda* (a large, mostly self-sufficient, polycultural farm) near the town of Zaragoza in the Province of Cartagena, was taken into custody in the secret prisons of the Inquisition. Her owner's accusation against Felipa, and Felipa's subsequent confession, bore a remarkable resemblance to the accusation against Guiomar and her confession eighty years earlier. The summary, sent to Spain for review and approval, gives us a sense of her travails and the difference that the establishment of the Cartagena branch of the Inquisition in 1610 made in the lives of those accused of religious crimes.

As with Guiomar, it all began with a death. After a trusted and strict enslaved overseer on the hacienda died of unknown causes, her master accused Felipa of causing his death through witchcraft.[42] Under duress, while being beaten, she confessed her guilt to the *familiar* (local lay officer) of the Inquisition who resided in Zaragoza. The story she told closely mirrored the witch narratives that the Inquisition officers encountered in other jurisdictions throughout the empire.

Felipa described participating in witches' sabbaths, during which she (and other women on the plantation) had carnal knowledge of the devil. She also confessed to preparing a potion that allowed her to fly all over the countryside. Most damningly, she confessed to using her satanic powers to kill the overseer of her master's hacienda. Considering the testimony against her and her detailed confession, the case, thus far, appeared an open-and-shut case of witchcraft. Notably, the narratives in Felipa's case fall squarely within the spectrum of concurrent European witch trials. Even if Felipa was only repeating what she had heard from others it shows Atlantic flows of information shaping the understanding of the supernatural held by residents of Cartagena.[43]

In stark contrast to the secular courts' handling of Guiomar's case, the Inquisition, generally immune to the type of hysteria that had gripped Cartagena in 1565, easily dismantled Felipa's confession and the accusations against her. The sophistication and experience of its trained officers benefited this particular female slave. The Spanish Holy Office, with over two hundred years of institutional memory, trained and supervised its *calificadores* (evaluators) well, ensuring their due diligence in examining an accusation against a slave.[44]

The Inquisition taught its officers to view accusations of witchcraft with particular skepticism. After their initial evaluation of Felipa, the calificadores began to
doubt her culpability. They repeatedly described her as "*muy bozal*" (very unacculturated), especially after ascertaining that her grasp of Spanish was rudimentary at
best. They called on the large Jesuit mission dedicated to ministering to newly arriving slaves to obtain a translator. The Jesuits assigned Domingo, a native Folupa
speaker, who had lived in Cartagena for many years, as her interpreter. In four interviews carried out with Domingo's help, the calificadores determined that she
was incapable of committing her accused crimes because of her "*demasiada rudeza y
bozalidad* (excessive lack of acculturation)"[45] and concluded that Felipa had merely
parroted a script beaten into her by her master. The calificadores gathered with the
other inquisitorial staff to consult on the case, decided to exonerate Felipa completely, and warned her master not to retaliate against her for any reason. They
further instructed a local priest to supervise her catechization and encouraged her
integration into the community of believers.

This case highlights how the institutional depth embodied in the officers of the
Holy Office could limit a master's power. As in the case eighty years earlier, Felipa's owner, angry because of the mysterious death of a favorite, had suspected Felipa killed him. As with Guiomar, he then whipped his slave, forcing her to confess.
Upon the transferal of the case to Cartagena, the slave master reiterated his accusation of witchcraft and demanded she be put to death. During the early part of this
trial, he beat Felipa, causing her pain, terror, and despair. The case records clearly
reflect the owner's anger and bloodlust. In a crucial difference, however, the beat-
ings finally stopped when she was transferred into the custody of the Inquisition.
Unlike the Real Audiencia in Guiomar's case, the Inquisitors viewed a confession
obtained through torture as problematic.

Considering the rage evident in the testimony of Felipa's owner, it is clear he re-
strained himself from personally carrying out the biblical injunction "to not suffer
a witch to live" because he knew the Inquisition jealously guarded its jurisdiction in
these matters.[46] In the eyes of the law and the Inquisition, killing any slave was considered murder, and perpetrators were prosecuted and punished.[47] Felipa's owner
wisely decided to involve the Inquisition instead of acting against her himself. To
his chagrin, the Inquisition did not always favor the desire of slave owners, and the
judgment acquitted Felipa. Professionally skeptical canon lawyers heard her case,
determined that the accusations against her were baseless, and warned her owner
not to punish her further on pain of confiscation of his ward. While the conditions
of Felipa's enslavement and the relationship with her owner involved great risks
and difficulties for her, the institutional pragmatism of the Inquisition served as a
mitigating force in her life.

Paradoxically, the accusations against Felipa (who was exonerated in 1641)
seemed to have a much more solid foundation than those against Catalina (who was

executed in 1567). Not only did Felipa's master and others testify against her but she also confessed to the crime. However, the Inquisitors, constantly dealing with cases involving accusations of witchcraft, had a good sense of the type of person who had the level of acculturation necessary to commit this kind of heresy. They ascertained that Felipa, due to her low level of socialization, likely did not commit the crimes alleged against her. In cases of witchcraft, the inquisitors generally held a skeptical and sophisticated attitude—unfounded accusations seldom swayed them.[48]

LOCATION AND SOCIALIZATION

In my first foray into the history of Cartagena de Indias I set out to reconstruct the interactions between slaves and the Inquisition.[49] The heterogeneity of the picture that emerged seemed to make it impossible to schematize these interactions in an intelligible way. Eventually I realized that the seeming contradictions were the result of assuming a monolithic and unchanging group of slaves who interacted with an equally static Holy Office.[50] While many of the full case files were lost during the South American wars for independence, fortunately, the regime of checks and balances that characterized the Spanish Empire in general, and the Holy Office in particular, ensured that not all was lost. The case reports sent back to Europe with the treasure fleets remained in the vaults of the Supreme Inquisition headquarters, La Suprema, in Madrid. These reports summarized opened, in-process, and closed cases, allowing the staff at headquarters to monitor the performance of their junior colleagues. Comparing these case reports allows for a differentiation and analysis of Inquisition cases involving enslaved people along the two most critical variables: location and socialization.[51]

In Felipa's case, the inquisitors clearly considered her level of socialization when determining her guilt and verdict. Knowledge of and participation in the institutions of Spanish society, both religious and secular, set the tone of the interactions between Africans and their descendants and the Inquisition in Cartagena. Knowledge about Catholic doctrine and practices was especially important. Accepting, learning, and performing Catholic doctrine served as a passport to the community of believers and the official protections it bestowed.[52] The inquisitorial manuals directed officials to give weight to the condition and socialization of slaves when investigating and passing sentences, acknowledging the complexity and demographic diversity of their flock. The foundational instructions of the Cartagena Inquisition stated that the inquisitors should have "softness and mercy in the cases of idolatry," especially for slaves not completely educated in the Christian faith and for those who "rebelled and fortified themselves in palenques."[53]

Inquisitors were also instructed to consider age, motive, circumstances, and intention as modifiers to socialization, as the following case exemplifies. Procedure established that minors, regardless of their legal status, should always be assigned a *procurador ad litem* (advocate for the duration of the case) to defend them. In 1685, the Inquisition in Cartagena dealt with the fallout of a swordfight that resulted in the death of Manuel Melgarejo and the serious injury of Domingo Martínez de León, the Inquisition *receptor* (forfeiture administrator). The pair had a longstanding feud that resulted in an argument early on a Sunday; later that day Melgarejo waited for Martínez de León in the central plaza armed with his sword to resolve their disagreement. According to several witnesses, Melgarejo attacked Martínez de León and Juan Domingo, the young slave carrying his parasol. During the melee, Juan Domingo attempted to aid Martínez de León and eventually fled to seek help. As the fight progressed, several other people joined in, making it difficult to determine who threw which blows and who killed Melgarejo.[54]

In the days following the incident, Melgarejo's father brought charges against Martínez de León and Juan Domingo, accusing the boy of throwing the rock that dealt the final fatal blow. The Inquisition assigned the young slave a procurador ad litem, Alonso de Vargas, to defend him against the charges. De Vargas quickly established that Melgarejo had attacked first, chasing Juan and attempting to kill him with his blade, and that the youth had barely escaped with his life. Alonso even presented evidence that, despite Melgarejo having collapsed during the fight, Juan had chosen not to finish him off. He then argued that even if Juan Domingo had indeed harmed Melgarejo, he was only performing his duty to defend his owner, positing that "according to all relevant legal traditions and by the authority of the classical authors, a slave must always come to the defense and care of his master in both words and actions." Lastly, he reminded the court that for minors of less than fourteen years of age, the law established a higher evidentiary bar in determining criminal guilt.[55]

At first glance, this case confounds expectations. The case is processed through the Inquisition's court and it is well established that institutional courts favor members of the institution. Yet the Inquisition staff member is found guilty. Melgarejo's father is powerful enough to get Martínez de León fired and punished but Juan Domingo is comprehensively absolved. At the end of the yearlong case, the Inquisition suspended Martínez de León from his position as receptor, banished him from Cartagena for two years, and fined him two thousand pieces of eight. However, they absolved Juan Domingo, concurring with his defender's arguments. In their decision, it seems the inquisitors considered Juan's age, the chaos of the situation, and the duties inherent in his condition as a slave.

The Inquisition's response to religious crimes in New Granada was inseparable from the social and demographic reality of the region. In 1610, Cartagena had approximately one creole slave for every two newly arrived bozales, and the challenge of catechizing and educating the enslaved community strained the capacity of religious authorities. Despite the predominant number of bozales, the majority of the enslaved individuals who directly engaged the Inquisition exhibited a fair degree of socialization. While a greater level of institutional understanding put slaves at greater risk for punishment for heresy and other religious crimes, it also provided them with opportunities to employ ecclesiastical institutions for their own ends. Overall, as the church endeavored to convert and catechize new arrivals, Afroiberians taught each other about the Inquisition as one among other Spanish methods of societal control.

The inquisitorial records reveal the presence of syncretized modes of thought and understanding in acculturated Africans and their children. The social imaginary that they built as they were integrated into the province bore little resemblance to the official version and norms of Christianity set forth by the Catholic Church. Enslaved Afroiberians, both bozales and criollos, lived a much more complex reality. Afroiberian culture, rather than standing in opposition to official Spanish culture and Catholic doctrine, reflected a constant two-way interaction. For example, records abound of the establishment of Catholic shrines in palenques around Cartagena and throughout the rest of the Indies.[56]

The physical location of enslaved people, connected to their socialization in origin and result, also shaped their exchanges with the Holy Office.[57] A bozal sent to work in a city would have greater opportunities to learn how the Inquisition, its familiars, and related Catholic institutions worked as part of Spanish imperial society than a slave sent to a more sparsely populated area. Furthermore, greater distances from cities and towns reduced slaves' contact with and information about all aspects of royal rule. For example, the Inquisition in Spanish America, despite its fearsome reputation, was not omnipresent or even particularly present in some places. The difficulties of policing its vast jurisdiction were remedied in part by its ability to use local agents to extend institutional presence into outlying areas. These were the familiars, whom royal orders required in every town of over two hundred vecinos. They were charged with reporting any local deviations that they believed merited follow-up to the central office in Cartagena. At the end of the day, when the Inquisition focused its attention and authority on a particular case or area, it could prove a very powerful institution indeed.

To understand the view slaves and freedpeople had of the Inquisition, and their perception of role in the legal ecology, we have to be sensitive to the layers of motivations that were at play. As members of Christendom, slaves could serve as witnesses against harsh administrators or strategically blaspheme to force their owners to stop punishing them. Reading the records against the grain shows that, depending on circumstances, slaves could manipulate this bastion of imperial administration to protect their interests.

Slaves' socialization and physical location determined much more than their experiences with the Inquisition. It extended to their interactions with almost all branches of imperial institutions, as noted by Frederick Bowser in Peru. Bowser analyzed Lima slave marriage licenses issued between 1600 and 1650, showing acculturated urban slaves' ability to negotiate the legal ecology of the Spanish Empire.[58] Moreover, these licenses suggest that slaves with marriages sanctioned and protected by the church tended to be urban and acculturated. Bennett confirms this pattern for seventeenth-century Mexico City.[59] Finally, Javier Villa-Flores, in *Dangerous Speech: A Social History of Blasphemy in Colonial Mexico,* shows the inventive and adaptable ways Africans used rhetoric in leveraging their knowledge of Spanish imperial governance, confirming that the patterns described here for Cartagena were replicated in other parts of the Spanish Empire.[60]

CARROTS AND STICKS

Contrary to popular representation, the risks of engaging the Inquisition were substantial but should not be overestimated. The Inquisition was a prestigious institutional actor that followed clear, well-known protocols and procedures. As in most transnational institutions, the majority of its members were career men who owed their livelihood and promotion to adherence to protocol, rules, and regulations. Zealous avengers were rare.[61] The response of different members of the institution to a bureaucratic snafu during an investigation in 1627 in Cartagena shows this functionality in action. When *fiscal* (prosecutor) Juan Ortiz discovered that the original accusation and the witness statements against Pedro Angola, a slave being held in the Inquisition's prison, had been misplaced, he brought the case to a halt. The fiscal then called on all the witnesses to return and resubmit their declarations.[62]

The original evidence of Pedro Angola's guilt had been overwhelming, and the accusations against him grave, making Ortíz's actions all the more remarkable. On September 1, 1627, inquisitorial officers had arrested Pedro and interned him in secret prisons of the Inquisition. The charge against him was that he had severely harmed an old man, Diego, who belonged to the widow of one of the tribunal's officers. Five eyewitnesses confirmed the accusations, and a doctor certified that a wide, sharp weapon caused Diego wounds between his kidneys, on his face, and on his arm. As a result of his wounds, Diego nearly died while choking on his own blood. He survived but suffered permanent damage to the nerves in his face and legs.

On September 13, the imprisoned Pedro Angola aggravated his situation by hitting Rodrigo Pereira, the alcalde in charge of the Inquisition's prison, with a stick. After the incident, Pedro tried to escape but was caught and returned to the prison. That same day, the Inquisition took testimony from Pereira, three of his slaves, and a vecino, confirming the alleged misdeeds. Moving quickly, the inquisitors interviewed Pedro Angola the next day, during which time he admitted partial responsibility for the altercation. He told the fiscal that, while trying to castigate some of the bothersome slaves working in the jail, he had accidentally hit the alcalde. Overreacting to this misunderstanding, Pereira then began to beat him severely with his *bastón* (staff), forcing Pedro to hit him again to stop the blows and escape. The jailer and the slaves who worked in the prison contradicted Pedro's story. They provided evidence against him, telling the fiscal that Pedro had hit Pereira *de mala fe* (in bad faith).[63]

A few days later, when the inquisitors went to review and evaluate the evidence, they realized someone had misplaced all the files prior to September 13, the date Pedro attacked the alcalde. Instead of adjudicating based upon the remaining evidence, they recalled all the earlier witnesses and ordered "all proper procedure be followed."[64] Because of Pedro's clear guilt in both instances, adherence to proper procedure did not benefit him. However, the case shows inquisitors' willingness to expend the necessary resources to abide by protocols, even when it would seem unnecessary. This created an environment that tended to protect the innocent from both arbitrary punishment and the whims and passions of royal and other officials and private parties.

In the case analyzed here, pursuant to the inquisitors' order, the original witnesses reconfirmed their testimony regarding the altercation between Diego and Pedro; similarly, the doctor confirmed the severity of Diego's wounds. Both the depositions and medical certification were expeditiously completed on September 17. Now armed with the full case, the inquisitors could consider all the evidence and sentence Pedro Angola. On September 20, only nineteen days after Pedro's initial arrest, the inquisitorial court delivered its verdict. It condemned Pedro Angola to be paraded around the streets and given two hundred lashes while a pregonero announced his sentence to the public. After this punishment, Pedro was to labor in the royal galleys for ten years and (if he survived) to serve the monks in the monastery of San Sebastián in Cartagena for the rest of his life.

The Inquisition speedily adjudicated this case along established jurisprudence. The sentence it imposed contrasts with Roman precedents and contemporaneous Dutch law, in which striking an imperial official was punishable by death. The Inquisition, however, sent Pedro to serve the crown, the church, and the poor. Even in a case in which the Inquisition condemned a slave for physically assaulting one of its members, the sentence emphasized rehabilitation and service. This cannot be attributed simply to Christian charity but must be understood in the light of the institutional objectives of the Holy Office. It was counterproductive to alienate the community within which inquisitors operated.

Indeed, the Inquisition depended on the communities that it was embedded in to carry out its charge of investigating and resolving cases of heresy and crimes against canon law. Scholars have estimated the institution's Spanish iteration executed between three to five thousand people throughout the empire from its inception under Isabel and Ferdinand until 1713. In contrast, the great witchcraft trials in Protestant Europe during the same period resulted in an estimated forty to one hundred thousand deaths.[65] Inquisitional investigations were a regulated legal process that sought to determine the validity of the charges. To view the actions of the Holy Office as primarily repressive ignores the ideological basis upon which it acted. Rather than punishment, the Holy Office's goal was to secure the repentance and reintegration of the condemned while fortifying the authority of state and church.[66]

The significance of the Inquisition rested not only on the limited number of faith-centered cases that it prosecuted but also on the exemplary nature of its punishments, acquittals, and dictums.[67] It enforced royally and ecclesiastically approved moral, social, and religious norms within the Spanish Empire, supported by a widespread and consistent effort by the Catholic Church and the Spanish Crown to indoctrinate the people in these precepts. This imperial ideological cooperation gave the pronouncements of the Inquisition significant social and moral heft. Inquisitors declared their verdicts and carried out their punishments in the most public manner possible, creating maximum impact. In a classic reverse psychology move, the Holy Office worked hard to foster a reputation for secrecy in its investigations, which magnified the effect of its dramatically public verdicts and punishments.[68]

Additionally, in common with medieval guilds, the Inquisition served as a criminal and civil court for legal cases involving its own staff and associates. Vecinos sought the honor of being associated with the Inquisition, largely as familiars, to gain the social prestige and legal validation it offered. Before recruiting and naming members and familiars, the Inquisition certified a candidate's *pureza de sangre* (purity of blood), good reputation, and honorable character. While it afforded social capital, association with the Holy Office also placed the chosen under the jurisdiction of the exacting gaze of the inquisitorial court.

During the long seventeenth century, the Inquisition, at its best, held its members to a high standard of personal and legal responsibility, extending through cases involving those of lower socioeconomic status. For example, in 1668, *capitán* Juan López de Medina, a familiar of the Inquisition in Cartagena, was arrested and incarcerated, being accused of the *homicidio voluntario* (murder) of the slave Domingo Folupo. The Inquisition gave Medina no special treatment; it investigated Domingo's death as homicide instead of as a property dispute, recognizing his condition as a subject of the king, not just chattel.

On April 6, 1668, Domingo Folupo had an altercation with Juan Arara, one of Medina's slaves. After they had spent the day working together, Domingo, a senior riverboat pilot, had an argument with Juan over the ownership of an oar, a dispute that quickly became physical. Juan did not fare well in this contest and fled back to his master's house to report the aggression. Medina, seeing the damage done to his slave, mounted his horse and sped off to confront the aggressor. Several bystanders warned Domingo to run as Medina approached, but he refused, saying, "Let him come. I want to talk to him." Feeling himself in the right, he waited with the oar in question to confront Medina.[69] The slave of an elite owner, and a respected river pilot, Domingo felt himself a member of society in which he owed unrighteous deference to nobody. However, when Medina arrived at the dock, he attacked Domingo, cutting him twice with his sword.

Domingo Folupo's owner, *capitán* Gregorio Vanquesel, knew Medina served as a familiar of the Inquisition and immediately sought redress from the inquisitorial court for the wounding of his slave. Vanquesel could have taken his accusations to a different jurisdiction, but instead chose the more efficient tribunal of the Holy Office, trusting its institutional integrity not to favor one of its own. In response to this formal accusation, the inquisitors opened an investigation to determine whether sufficient evidence existed to proceed with civil and criminal charges against Medina.

The legal case centered on ascertaining Medina's motives and intentions and the series of events that led him to wound Domingo.[70] On April 11, doctors examined and certified the nature and gravity of Domingo's wounds, and on April 14, Domingo and three eyewitnesses gave sworn testimony describing the incident. On April 16, Domingo Folupo began convulsing and died, increasing the charge in the case from assault to murder.[71]

Proceeding with the case, the inquisitors ordered precautionary house arrest for Medina until they could decide if the mounting evidence against him warranted formal charges. They interviewed four more people and took Medina's confession. The accused submitted several petitions asking for temporary release, including one to perform his duties as the *hermano mayor* (older brother) at the annual celebration of the saint's day of his *cofradía* (lay brotherhood), but the investigators denied them all. His wealth, religious leadership, military rank, and service to the Inquisition were insufficient to let him escape procedural rigors during the adjudication of the case.

After three months of investigation, on July 2, the Inquisition brought murder charges against Medina. The tribunal's secretary recertified the original interviews to be considered in the judgment and gave each party ten days to submit new evidence and testimony. Vanquesel accused Medina of murdering Domingo *adrede* (deliberately) without provocation and requested criminal punishment. He also demanded the payment of six hundred pesos as compensation for his loss, as well as reimbursement for Domingo's medical care, burial, and all legal costs.

Medina defended himself, accusing Domingo of threatening him, such that he had no choice but to use force to defend himself. Furthermore, he argued that he had used proportional force in defending himself. Medina estimated that Domingo's original wounds were not fatal but had suppurated due to botched medical treatment, a product of his owner's negligence. In his defense Medina presented nine witnesses, including three doctors, four soldiers, and two military officers. Vanquesel presented seven witnesses, including two doctors, two slaves, and one freedperson. All the witnesses from both sides who knew Domingo Folupo testified to his good character and exemplary work as a riverboat pilot.[72]

On September 27, 1668, after hearing all the testimony, the judges met, and, in their deliberations, two opposing factions formed. One side, headed by licenciado Sánchez, a letrado of the Inquisition, argued that Medina should be absolved, based on the classical legal tradition that prohibited enslaved people from attacking enslavers. Inquisitor Matías Guerra championed the opposing view that, upon consideration of the evidence and testimony, it was clear Medina had overreacted to any perceived threat and therefore bore some responsibility for Domingo's death. The college of judges decided that while the crime did not rise to the level of homicidio voluntario, Medina should be punished for confronting Domingo and taking the law into his own hands. They sentenced him to pay two hundred pesos to Vanquesel and ordered each side to pay its own legal costs.

Medina did not suffer the full penalty prescribed by law for murder, but, considering his claims of self-defense, the fine that the tribunal imposed on him was substantial, although the costs he incurred during the six months the case lasted were probably greater. He spent months under house arrest and was unable to participate in regular economic, social, or religious activities, including leading his cofradia's yearly celebration. He also suffered public humiliation, which was substantial due to his high social status. The justice provided was moot for Domingo, who died at the start of the case. Nonetheless, it reinforced the rule of law and, in so doing, promoted slaves' ability to live with some measure of safety and security. The Inquisition completed the entire legal process, from accusation to sentence, in a period of less than six months, an efficiency that would be envied by many modern litigants. (In the US in 2005 the average criminal case took over two years).[73] Among some part of the public at least, the perception was that inquisitorial justice could be expeditious, thorough, and evenhanded.

LUIS MÉNDEZ, *MAYORDOMO*

In 1650, some of the enslaved workers on Sebastián de Ponte's plantation on the outskirts of Caracas conspired to end the tenure of the abusive and strict *mayordomo* (administrator) Luis Méndez. Their physical location afforded them access to the familiar of the Inquisition in Caracas. Among them, those with higher levels of socialization used their knowledge of church law and inquisitorial procedure to denounce Méndez to their owner, Sebastián de Ponte, accusing him of practicing black magic. This forced the former to report the accusation to the familiar, initiating a chain of events during which the slaves leveraged the institution to their benefit.

Upon receiving the report from the familiar in Caracas, the Holy Office brought Méndez, a self-described "free mulatto," into the Cartagena office for questioning.[74] According to the testimony, Méndez, a strict disciplinarian, "kept the slaves on their toes."[75] In his efforts to reduce persistent pilfering, the mayordomo periodically gathered together all the slaves of the plantation into a circle, inserted a pair of scissors into an empty *almud* (barrel-shaped grain container), and, calling out the name of each slave, asked, "By Saint Peter and Saint Paul, who stole such and such a product?" The almud would spin and stop, pointing at the thief. Witnesses indicated that Méndez's sorcery generally correctly identified the culprit, who would then receive a beating for his misdeeds.[76]

The *fiscal receptor* (initial prosecutor) submitted the witchcraft accusations to the calificadores (evaluators). Because of the multitude of witnesses and the social position of the plantation owners, the calificadores handled the allegations carefully. They ordered Méndez's arrest and brought him to one of the tribunal's secret prisons. In his initial statement, Méndez acknowledged playing to the superstitions of the slaves in hopes of dissuading any further stealing by using a *chanza* (useful trick) with the almud, telling interrogators how he had learned while working in Brazil the effectiveness of tricking enslaved workers into believing he could ascertain the identity of any thief.[77] He denied any supernatural source for the accuracy of his almud by explaining he manipulated the scissors in the almud to point at someone whom he had already observed stealing.

After arguing against the charges, Méndez then tried to discredit the witnesses against him by claiming they were hostile. He told the inquisitors his accusers were his enemies, seeking his downfall through treacherous testimony.[78] Despite his multilayered defense, the case against him proceeded at a deliberate pace. As the months passed, Méndez grew anxious and agitated; the Inquisition was notorious for dealing harshly with practitioners of supernatural stratagems.[79] In December 1650, a despondent Méndez committed suicide in the dungeons of the Inquisition.[80]

Although Méndez had performed his unmagical trick to protect his employer's property, Sebastián de Ponte did very little to defend his mayordomo. On the contrary, Ponte, his wife, and his sister-in-law all testified against their star administrator. At first glance, their testimonies could be read as pious submission, but the fiscal structure of the Inquisition put enormous pressure on them to turn against Méndez once a coherent group of enslaved workers of their hacienda made a credible accusation. If they did not, anybody from this group, who regularly interacted with the clergy, could denounce them as complicit in Méndez's acts. Ponte and his family would have then been at the mercy of the Inquisition for aiding and abetting Méndez—a terrifying prospect, because once an accusation was deemed credible and a case opened, the property of those awaiting trial could be confiscated.

In Méndez's case, a group of enslaved workers, through the savvy utilization of the rules and procedures, made common cause with the Inquisition. The enslaved accusers leveraged Spanish Catholic ideology and institutions to get rid of an abusive mayordomo. They took advantage of the confluence of proscriptions against witchcraft, inquisitorial investigational procedures, the financial interests of the institution, their knowledge of how to frame their grievances, and finally, their legal and ecclesiastical personhood within the church, to protect their traditional right to measured pilfering from their master.

THE COSMOPOLITAN ATLANTIC

Part of what made the Inquisition so powerful was that almost anybody, if carefully questioned, could be found to have violated some level of Catholic strictures. Perfect morality, especially for the powerful, was as hard to achieve in the past as it is today. This applied to the powerful at all levels of society, and within the Afroiberian community, Africans and their descendants used the Inquisition to settle scores among themselves. In the case of Manuel, an arrogant cosmopolitan Atlantic creole, rival factions struggling to get the upper hand on a plantation inserted the Inquisition into their dispute. Their proximity to Cartagena provided another tool in his enemies' efforts to abase Manuel.

Born in Cape Verde and raised in Portugal as the property of ship *capitán* Diego de la Torre, Manuel traveled between the ports of the peninsula, Africa, and the Indies as the right hand of his master. In 1648, he lived and worked on the plantation of de la Torre in the outskirts of Cartagena. Manuel enjoyed a position as one of the elite skilled slaves of the plantation and as a leader among the community. He was very proud of his upbringing in Iberia and used it to boost his prestige among the residents of the plantation, carelessly boasting to his workmates "how poor are the Masses of your land, I swear that if they were the ones of Portugal, I would go hear them."[81]

The rival faction, headed by Marcos and Esteban, denounced him to the Inquisition, charging that Manuel never attended Mass or confessed, and that he had a small statue of the Virgin Mary in his room that he beat in anger. They accused him of lording it over his fellow slaves, disparaging their religious beliefs and ridiculing local church ceremonies. In consideration of the number of witnesses and the public nature of his actions, the authorities arrested Manuel, interning him in the secret prisons of the Inquisition.

After his imprisonment, Manuel, with the help of his advocate, mounted a spirited two-pronged defense. First, responding to the Inquisition's practice of not informing the accused of the charges against them, the identity of the plaintiffs, or their testimony, Manuel and his procurator tried to impugn the testimony of his accusers by identifying them and telling of their prior enmity toward him. In this, they succeeded. Manuel correctly identified most of his accusers, declaring that, motivated by envy and hatred, they had interposed the denuncia to discredit him with his master and force his sale. Unbeknownst to Manuel and his lawyer, several of the initial depositions by hostile witnesses supported his claim. Marcos, one of the leaders of the opposing faction, declared that Manuel had spread malicious rumors to convince his owner to sell him; *capitán* de la Torre testified that during an altercation, Esteban and a gang of slaves tried to kill Manuel. To confound things further, the plantation's overseer told the inquisitors that Manuel had an affair with Esteban's wife. The luxuriant, if conflictive, social life of the plantation was accepted as a matter of course by all parties.

Secondly, the defense showed that Manuel had indeed gone to Mass and confessed himself during the period in question. Manuel and his advocate called several fellow enslaved people and freedpeople from his parish to testify they regularly saw him at church and taking communion. However, outside politics continued to play out, as some of his witnesses failed to appear. Despite the effort he put into his defense, the balance of the testimony eventually led to Manuel's conviction, although the inquisitors gave him a relatively light punishment.[82]

The animosity in the testimony of Manuel's accusers arose from the factional enmities on the divided plantation of Diego de la Torre. Socialized slaves knew accusing Manuel of failure to participate in Mass would be hard to disprove. The group led by Esteban was not simply oppressed or controlled by the Inquisition; rather, they leveraged their socialization into Spanish imperial society to turn the Holy Office into an ally to further their vendetta against Manuel.

Conversely, Manuel used his awareness of Inquisition procedure, especially in disqualifying witnesses, to bolster his defense. This case illustrates not only the institutional praxis of the Inquisition but also some Afroiberians' knowledge of these procedures and their willingness to use them for their own purposes. Far from being passive victims of the Inquisition, in many cases slaves actively participated in the inquisitorial process, reinforcing the authority and effectiveness of the Inquisition through their actions.

MATEO THE *MOHAN*

This next case hinges on the ways that distance to and visibility from nodes of inquisitorial power influenced the strategies enslaved Afroiberians used when navigating their status as property. Mateo Arará, a *mohan* (a master healer or shaman), expertly took advantage of the gaps in the Inquisition's reach around the peripheries of Spanish American society. Operating over a wide region for years, Mateo maintained a thriving medical practice, using methods of questionable religious orthodoxy without any objections from the Holy Office.[83] However, on September 6, 1651, inquisitorial officials arrested him and brought him to their secret prisons: he had been accused by sixteen witnesses of being an evil mohan.[84] The gravity and complexity of the accusation he faced led the inquisitors to depose Mateo in depth. In his testimony, Mateo constructed a multilayered defense, probably prepared beforehand in anticipation of a denunciation. As an acculturated subject, Mateo knew the risk of this charge and the most effective methods of defense.

During the first of the three hearings included in the case file, he carefully portrayed himself as a healer with no connections to the demonic arts. He also argued that, by providing medical services to both slaves and free, he worked for the benefit of the realm. His initial defense proclaimed his innocence as a simple healer who used natural medicines to cure snakebites and other sicknesses. He buttressed these claims by displaying a detailed pharmacological knowledge of the "many herbs and roots that he used to cure."[85] However, his accusers provided the inquisitors with a detailed description of Mateo's powers, including his use of an *escobilla* (ceremonial broom) that could, when activated by incantations, detect healing herbs, find and banish sickness, and unmask evil shamans. Inquisitors found this escobilla in Mateo's possession at the time of his arrest, complicating his efforts to present himself in an acceptable light.[86]

In his second hearing, the inquisitors confronted Mateo, who had no idea of the extent of the accusations against him, with the escobilla, and demanded he explain its existence and purpose. Mateo reaffirmed and tried to strengthen his original position that he was a healer who worked by his own arts with no demonic assistance. He described the escobilla as an innocent talisman used in his work. To bolster his case, Mateo told a story of his usefulness to the imperial order. Four years before his arrest, one Lieutenant Saavedra, in charge of the town of Mompós, had specifically requested Mateo's services as a healer. He wrote a letter to Mateo's master indicating that the town had "many sick blacks."[87] At the behest of royal officials, Mateo was sent to Mompós, curing many Afroiberians and two priests with herbs, prayers, and his escobilla.[88] Not only did he cure the sickness in the gold mines and haciendas of the town but he also used his escobilla with "great trust in the Virgin Mary and our Lord Jesus Christ" to discover the evil yerbatero causing the affliction.[89]

Mateo's beliefs and practices had strong indications of African origin but had clearly been transformed by contact with the Catholic religion.[90] During his trial, he emphasized this transformation and incorporation of Christianity to appeal to his customers, both enslaved and free. Still, Mateo's contortions as he adapted his story when confronted with the initial report's information trapped him into several admissions of questionable practices and impermissible syncretism. During his third interrogation, he effectively sealed his fate by admitting he cured a very sick boy by tricking the devil into taking a small chicken in his stead. According to his testimony, he placed the chicken next to the boy's head; while praying, he intoned, "I want the boy you take chicken."[91] His own account of this story confirmed engagement with demonic forces in his healing practices.

Under pressure magnified by this admission, Mateo confessed he had learned his arts in Africa from his uncle, a healer in the court of a king. He told the inquisitors that in Africa "they did not know God" and that he used his skills only for good and in the service of helping those in need. He placed emphasis on his herbal remedies, probably due to his knowledge of Catholic distinctions between permitted herbal healing and prohibited magical rituals.[92]

Inquisition policy allowed for inquisitors faced with consistent obfuscation to use gradated judicial torture to elicit a truthful confession. With this possibility probably on his mind, after repeatedly failing to convince the inquisitors of his innocence, Mateo gave a fuller confession and threw himself upon the mercy of the court. The inquisitorial officers carefully probed and tested his stories using the information they had received from the accusers to find weaknesses and contradictions that showed Mateo transgressing the acceptable limits of his practice. At the same time, Mateo calibrated his answers and admissions to minimize his exposure to punishment. This strategy paid off: Mateo received a relatively lenient sentence of two hundred lashes, ten years of service, and religious education in the convent of Santo Domingo in Cartagena.[93]

The Inquisition's familiars could not be everywhere. A vibrant syncretic market for the wares and services of shamans and healers existed in the penumbra between nodes of inquisitorial power. In the Spanish Empire the legal category of slave was understood capaciously enough that some of the most successful practitioners in this marketplace were enslaved women and men. His understanding of Spanish institutions long kept Mateo Arará outside the gaze of ecclesiastical authorities, allowing him to enjoy the lifestyle of prestige, power, and risk that accompanied his practice as a successful healer/shaman. It was only once a group of his peers allied against him and collectively denounced him that the Holy Office's agents managed to bring him to ecclesiastical justice.

CONCLUSION

The Spanish Inquisition was a remarkably versatile institution that endured and adapted for almost 350 years, inspiring respect, fear, and hatred among friends and foes alike. Despite colonizing the imagination of Spain's enemies, during most of its existence the Inquisition maintained both popular legitimacy and royal favor, without which the institution would have collapsed.[94] In an interesting example of the pervasive role of the institution, inquisitors subjected Ignatius Loyola himself to extreme vetting twice in the run up to his founding of the Jesuits, without losing his support. The limited number of cases that it heard and the minute number of executions it supervised starkly contrasts with its fearsome reputation.

Perhaps the Inquisition's greatest asset was the carefully crafted image it projected, leveraging its own narrative to reinforce itself. The fear and respect it inspired attracted regional elites into its service, as familiars. These force multipliers allowed the institution to project power further afield than the relatively limited number of the staff it employed would suggest. A good metric to evaluate the effectiveness of the Holy Office is the almost complete lack of religious conflict throughout the Spanish Empire at a time when sectarian battles ravaged much of Europe. In combination, universities and printing presses were indispensable to the great administrative complexity of the Spanish Empire; without the Inquisition as custodian, it would have been unimaginable to permit multiple universities with printing presses to operate throughout Spanish America in the age of Luther. Spain's imperial governance counted on the legitimacy of the Inquisition.

Enslaved Africans—the only large group brought to the Indies from non-Catholic or so-called pagan regions—challenged the institutional culture of the Inquisition. Isabel and Ferdinand had instituted the Holy Office in Iberia to safeguard the kingdom and the faith from backsliding New Christians. However, as the empire expanded into the Indies and Africa, the Inquisition developed the complementary role of supervising the Christianization of new subjects, mostly enslaved populations, and their compliance with Catholic orthodoxy. This frame of analysis balances the outside weight of the Spanish Inquisition in our historical imagination, clarifying its relationship with enslaved people as an imperial institution that provincial subjects could engage to curtail the power of regional elites.

The expanding portfolio assigned by the crown to the Holy Office enmeshed it in Spanish America's legal ecology. The multipolar institutional environment required the support of regional elites while simultaneously curbing their ability to pursue their interests when they diverged from wider imperial objectives and ideology. Prestige and wealth did not confer immunity from royal justice or untrammeled power over lower classes. The crown's need to maintain control and to discipline those who challenged its authority created multiple institutional avenues of cooptation and cooperation for its subjects. Because enslaved people under Spanish rule were members of the religious and political community of the Spanish Empire, intermittent misalignment of the interests of local elites and imperial authorities produced opportunities that enslaved Afroiberians exploited. Given their ubiquitous presence in their owners' homes, slaves were uniquely positioned to aid the Inquisition's efforts to supervise and draw resources from slave-owning elites. The fate of Luis Méndez is a poignant example of how enslaved people could maneuver their enslavers into acting against their own apparent interests.

Spanish institutions agglomerated into a legal ecology that differentiated slavery in the Hapsburg Empire from other early modern Atlantic empires. Socialization allowed enslaved Afroiberians to understand the legal ecology, and physical location dictated their ability to access it. The Inquisition case that caused the cosmopolitan creole Manuel's downfall depended on his rivals being able to access a familiar. In these cases, urban slaves' greater institutional knowledge augmented their opportunities to utilize imperial institutions. While people on the peripheries of metropolitan centers had less access to the Inquisition, some slaves, like Mateo Arará, took advantage of the diminished institutional presence to surreptitiously evade the Holy Office's scrutiny.

A higher level of socialization and understanding of Catholic society, therefore, increased a person's responsibility to adhere to its norms. The first thing that an organism or empire needs if it is going to survive instead of just melting into the surrounding medium is a boundary defining who is in and who is out. The Inquisition policed the boundaries and expected Afroiberians like Mateo Arará, Luis Méndez, and Manuel, who understood Catholic doctrine and religious strictures, to comply with the dictums of theology. Concurrently, the institution considered factors that hindered a slave's full understanding of his or her offense when adjudicating, such as youth or short length of time spent acculturating in the province. The Inquisition found neither Felipa nor young Juan guilty, citing elements that left them unable to fully understand or be responsible for their actions.

The Inquisition's moral foundations were built on its role as protector of the universal church, which included enslaved Afroiberians among its membership.[95] The maximum expression of this was the Catholic project of global evangelization.[96] At the forefront of this endeavor were the Inquisition and the Jesuits allied with the Spanish and Portuguese empires, global in their vision, idealistic in their rhetoric, and pragmatic in their actions.[97] At the local level, we see the Holy Office engaged in a symbiotic relationship with the enslaved people and freedpeople under their charge.[98] This was embedded in inquisitors' training and institutional memory, preparing officials to engage with enslaved subjects as claimants, prisoners, and witnesses. Inquisitors used both positive and negative incentives to further their objectives of inspecting, molding, and controlling the beliefs and actions of the faithful. Concurrently, the ideological and legal underpinning of Spanish slavery encouraged enslaved Afroiberians to participate in policing the faith. Through this, enslaved subjects became a source of strength and cohesion for the empire.

3

SLAVES and the COURTS

We order our high courts that if any black, or whosoever, held as a
slave, declare themselves free, they should hear them, and do justice,
ensuring that because of this they are not mistreated by their masters.
—Holy Roman Emperor Charles V, King of Spain, and his
Cardinals (promulgated in 1540; republished in 1681)

In Iberoamerica, enslaved Africans and freedpeople had both need of and access to
the courts. This chapter follows lofty imperial mission statements as they were op-
erationalized by the institutions based in Cartagena de Indias. The tension between
principle and the possible grounded the opportunities Africans and their descendants had as they maneuvered through the legal ecology. Defined within the Spanish Empire as children of God, human beings, and subjects of the king, on these
terms enslaved people could interact as equals with other members of society.

In regulating the institution of slavery in the Spanish Empire, judicial officials
drew heavily upon the work of late classical and medieval legal scholars who had
Christianized Roman slave law.[1] Of course, the legal framework was not constructed for predominantly humanitarian reasons; it also served important social
control functions. The legal ecology evolved not only to enforce the law but also to
ensure social cohesion and participation. Therefore, to engage it effectively it was
not sufficient for Africans and their descendants to argue rationally for their personhood. For their arguments to be effective, they had to find ways to incorporate
themselves indelibly in the Spanish imperial project—not as disposable robots on
the great sugar plantations but as the primary constituency of the Caribbean basin.
By containing the power of slave owners, reinforcing the legitimacy of the crown,
and encouraging slaves to remain loyal, royal justice, if effectively delivered by the
courts, made the empire stronger.

Obviously, enslaved Afroiberians did not have unlimited, automatic, or uncontested access to the courts, but neither did other Spanish subjects. Iberoamerica was
structured hierarchically, with top-down domination complicated by the mutuality of honor and social privilege.[2] Wealth and status conferred advantages as well

as responsibilities and all members of society, from elites to plebeians, especially the unfree, were keenly aware of this.[3] At the same time, all Spanish law, including that which pertained to enslaved subjects, derived legitimacy through the pursuit of Christian justice. Courts in the Spanish Empire, in common with most sociomoral regulators, framed their environment through exchange, reciprocity, and debt.

Within this system, slavery was justified as a righteous alternative to death as a pagan, a mechanism for incorporating defeated enemies into an expansionist Christian society. In this spirit, for example, the *Siete Partidas* permitted enslaving prisoners of war or rebels against their legitimate rulers. Both the Portuguese and the Spanish used this legal reasoning to justify buying or capturing Africans as they explored the Atlantic.

The narrative that permitted the obvious injustice of enslavement in a self-consciously Christian world vision would have consequences for enslaved Afro-iberians. For most Africans brought into Iberoamerica, Christianization was intertwined with enslavement. Civil and religious officials portrayed this contradictory process either as a just punishment or as saving the life and, more importantly, the immortal soul of those enslaved. Even an enthusiastic slaver like Christopher Columbus felt compelled to deploy this justificatory fig leaf in a 1494 letter to the Spanish monarchs in which he argued that "slaves as many as they shall order to be shipped, and these shall be from idolaters."[4] While the righteousness of this logic was attacked by contemporaries, it retained broad legitimacy among the people of the Spanish Mediterranean and American port cities. It is largely within those parameters that legitimate regulation of slavery was built. This system did not produce the concentrated, coercive state power that would be necessary to deliver the efficiencies of scale in the production of slave-powered, tropical goods that the British and the Dutch would achieve on their generally smaller, insular possessions.[5]

Meanwhile in the Caribbean basin, early modern imperial ideologies were unsettled, changing in dialogue with the cumulative choices of all the participants in the messy business of competitive empire building.[6] During the long seventeenth century, as the metropoles reacted to each other's policies, we see reflective differences developing in the legal ecologies of competing European empires. This motility is evident in the ways that English and Spanish imperialism incorporated racial thinking, giving us some idea of the costs and opportunities, each empire responded to and the day-to-day implications for the people held as slaves.[7] At a structural level, the move from cultural to racial thinking deeply affected how the Dutch, British, and French Empires and their successor states absorbed people along with the cohesion of the societies that developed. Depending on the conditions of their entry, there were different tracks through which both forced and voluntary migrants could earn membership in society. The intellectual mechanics of absorption were such that a wealthy German merchant's path to full citizenship would be short. Slaves were at the opposite end of that spectrum, and for most Africans in the Indies ruthless exploitation was a daily reality. However, depending on what empire they found themselves in, their race, and especially that of their children, played a different role in determining their range of probable opportunities.[8]

In its fully developed form, the ideology justifying racialized chattel slavery argued that nonwhites were intrinsically inferior to whites and therefore only fit to serve. It did not focus on barbarians versus civilized people or Christianity versus paganism. Rather, it imagined certain humans as being subhuman. Thus, over time it became theoretically impossible for Africans and their descendants under English control to become "white," or civilized.[9] Within the Spanish Empire, by contrast, written law, imperial institutions, and the praxis of justice set the parameters for the integration of enslaved Afroiberians into social and economic life.[10] For example, from the 1540s onward there are detailed instructions for the taxation of freedpeople in the Spanish Indies, issued repeatedly and included in the *Recopilación de Leyes de las Indias* in 1681.[11] While the taxation of someone who has overcome enslavement is certainly exploitative, being taxed was also a defining criterion for inclusion into civic life. How worthwhile would a freedperson find paying taxes if to do so was accompanied by the explicit right to access the courts and enjoy good governance from the king?

In their efforts to provide effective justice, Spanish monarchs dealt with the immensity of their realms by drawing on the Roman, Gothic, and medieval inheritance of Iberian legal and constitutional traditions. Although today we conceive of judges as bound by the law with limited discretion, judges in the Hapsburg Empire were allowed broad flexibility in how they adjudicated cases, with both justice and the good of the empire as their highest considerations.[12] Laws were understood as guidelines that judges and other royal officials should reference in mediating disputes and dispensing justice, as royal officials stitched together diverse populations within the limitations imposed by early modern systems of communications, command, and control.

The scarcity of trained personnel and the vastness of Iberoamerica meant that most judicial officials also served as administrators carrying out a broad set of responsibilities. A trained jurist would be expected to have a sense of late medieval laws, primarily the high point of medieval legal humanism *Las Siete Partidas* (1256–1265), the codes issued after the conquest, and the *cédulas reales* promulgated in response to specific questions or problems. Due to the expanding and changing nature of the empire, its laws were riddled with exceptions, expansions, and explanations.[13] Aware of all this, the crown instructed judges to consider local customs, expectations, and the lived reality of their jurisdiction in making their rulings. Inheriting the standard medieval legal morass, the Spanish Hapsburg monarchs embarked on a sustained push to rationalize, codify, and disseminate the law. Making a virtue of necessity, they drew legitimacy for this process by building upon the most suitable parts of Iberia's well-developed legal tradition, culminating in the 1681

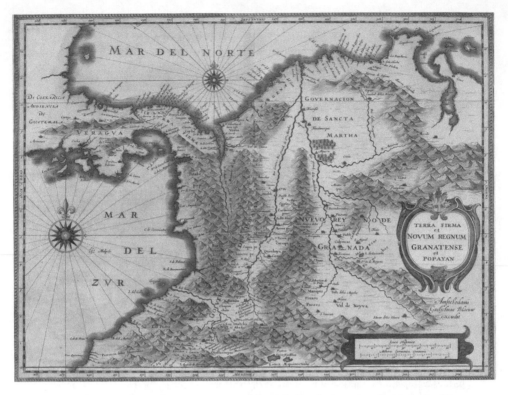

Figure 3.1. Seventeenth-century map of Spanish South America showing the New Kingdom of Granada and the Province of Popayan. "Terra Firma et Novum Regnum Granatense et Popayan," by Willem Janszoon Blaeu. Print, 1631. From the World Digital Library, Library of Congress, https://www.wdl.org/en/item/15674/.

Recopilación de Leyes de las Indias. Explicitly referencing the *Siete Partidas*, this code is a masterpiece of enlightened absolutism reflecting the underappreciated efforts of the regent Mariana of Austria to stabilize the Spanish Empire.

By 1580 the Spanish Empire's position as the first global superpower was undisputed, and the Age of Exploration receded in the face of the need to expand, defend, and consolidate Spain's control over the vast territories it claimed (figure 3.1). As Cartagena and Bogota guarded and ruled the New Kingdom of Granada, the colony's size, distance, and changing demographics required that flexible governance be built into the structure of imperial administration.[14] In light of this, metropolitan planners encouraged the symbiotic connection between administration, trade, and defense in Cartagena in particular. Indeed, the concentration of different types of officials, organized to support and limit each other, was a feature of Spanish imperium.[15] The traces left behind by this institutional layering show that enslaved Afroiberians engaged in all parts of the legal ecology. As a rule, it is probable that civil (as opposed to criminal) law was the most common basis for legal engagement by Africans and their descendants living in the region under the jurisdiction of Cartagena.[16]

The presence of a major imperial nexus like Cartagena had an effect on all the residents of the province. Secular and religious institutions were urban in their loci, concentrated in the largest cities and spreading their tendrils into smaller urban centers.[17] The closer that enslaved people lived to an urban node, the greater their chances of accessing imperial institutions.[18] Royal officers were spread thinly on the ground, forcing authorities to control immense territories with very limited manpower. It is estimated that in 1650, only about fifty thousand European-born Spaniards lived in the whole of the Spanish Indies.[19] Drawing on its medieval heritage, the crown addressed these structural limitations by focusing its limited resources on the towns that conquistadors organized in many of the strategic economic and military chokepoints of the empire.[20] Spanish authorities applied the template of Roman urban governance, concentrating diffuse, indigenous settlements through such policies as the *Reducciones de indios* (indigenous resettlement policy).[21] Concurrently the imperial response to the deepening indigenous demographic catastrophe violently pulled Africans to the Indies, where they spread throughout the Caribbean basin.[22] As valuable property, they tended to be concentrated in cities, towns, and the countryside directly around them, following the dispersion of the elites they were forced to serve. During the long seventeenth century, Afroiberians worked in every aspect of the economy as they became the primary settlers in Cartagena and its hinterlands.

LEARNING THE ROPES

As discussed in chapter 1, Africans in the Spanish Empire came from a wide variety of backgrounds. Although the time the enslaved subjects spent in the Indies did not solely determine their knowledge or ability (or lack thereof) to interact with the courts, most Africans acquired their practical knowledge of the workings of Spanish imperial justice after they were forcedly transported to the New World. Enslaved Africans arriving in the port of Cartagena were thrust into the ministrations of merchants, priests, and imperial officials.[23] Before anyone could disembark at the docks, they would be inspected by representatives of the governor and the *Asiento* (slaving concession), who were charged with verifying that the newly arrived were counted, taxed, and plague-free. Volume slave traders then took the people they had purchased to barracks that were prepared in the *solares* (yards) of their homes.[24] At this point, both the merchants, for whom slaves represented a substantial investment, and the Jesuits, who were charged with their Christianization, attended to the new arrivals.[25] The taxes paid on or by enslaved subjects were an important revenue stream for the crown, their work powered the local economy, and their souls represented a high-profile mission for the Jesuits; the arrival of a slave ship was therefore always a significant occasion.[26]

Court documents describing the arrival of slaves during this period note that merchants tended to them to ensure that the greatest number possible survived. This is unsurprising in Cartagena, where a healthy African off the boat could cost half as much as a small house or about a year's salary for an unskilled worker. An enslaved individual who appeared sick or hurt lost value because potential buyers were wary of their property dying after purchase, involving them in expensive and uncertain litigation to recover their investment.[27] After the enslaved Africans recovered somewhat from the arduous transatlantic crossing, merchants either transported them up the Magdalena to satisfy the demand for labor in the inland provinces or sold them into the local economy. For those sold locally, the moment of sale represented their first but likely not their last encounter with the notarial system, a mainstay of the legal ecology.

Pursuant to procedures largely unchanged since the medieval period, a notary recorded each transaction, and both seller and buyer were protected by laws specifically regulating the sale of Africans and by the terms of the contract of sale. As with many of the laws pertaining to the institution of slavery, they included a role for the enslaved subjects. While bozal Africans were usually sold unencumbered by legal restrictions on the owner, as the years passed, the slaves became active participants in the process of their own sale. Although the majority of enslaved people who came through Cartagena would be transported out of the province, for those who stayed the omnipresence of imperial institutions and the opportunities and costs of engaging them soon became apparent.[28]

For all three parties, the seller, the buyer, and the person being sold, the first sale was a risky transaction. When they all hailed from the local community, slaves and their potential new owners could somewhat gauge each other based on reputation. A first sale, however, took place without the prospective buyer's knowledge of the health or work habits of the person they were purchasing, while the recently arrived African would have very little knowledge of his new environment, adding even more opportunities for misunderstandings.[29]

Despite the formulaic disclaimers of responsibility contained in most sales contracts, the legal system provided protection for buyers in cases of fraud or a hidden tacha (defect). Sellers could be forced to refund all or part of the sale price to the buyer if the courts ruled the sale in bad faith.[30] As discussed further in this chapter, slaves served as witnesses in most cases involving disputes over the validity of sales or the cause of a slave's sickness or death. Because of the high evidentiary bar for the annulment of a first-sale contract, buyers usually took legal action only in cases in which the person in question died in the first few days after the sale, which naturally precluded them from being a witness in their own case.[31]

However, the Africans who managed to make it through the Middle Passage and then spent some time recuperating in the household of merchants usually survived the transfer to their new owners.[32] Upon entry into a household with slaves, arrivals would be surrounded by, and have the opportunity to learn from, people who had already lived in the colony for differing amounts of time and who possessed differing levels of socialization and understanding of the legal system. Near the top of their curricula would be learning their owners' vulnerabilities from cases like the one brought by Francisco Gutiérrez de Jereda, *notario eclesiástico* of Cartagena, against Josefa Melgarejo for the *redhibitoria* (restitution/refund for cause) of the sale of a slave woman who fell ill after purchase.[33] A local judge absolved Melgarejo of responsibility because too much time had passed since the date of sale to assume automatically that she had been sick when sold. However, de Jereda appealed and, based partially on slaves' first-hand testimony, the oidores of the Real Audiencia in Bogota modulated this ruling, ordering Melgarejo to return half of the sale price to de Jereda.[34]

Africans who joined households with few or no other enslaved workers were not necessarily disadvantaged, as they could interact with others in the social spaces created by work and religion. These opportunities could be especially abundant for those living in urban households with only one or two slaves, as they might be sent out to run errands or rented out to earn cash for their owners. Africans and their descendants performed the majority of domestic economic activity in the Province of Cartagena, so, unless their enslaver isolated them, they would generally come in contact with other enslaved workers throughout the day and, sometimes, the night.

Most slave labor revolved around the principal economic activities of the province: mining, commerce, agriculture, defense, and administration. The frontier nature of early settlements in the Province of Cartagena forced cities and towns to be largely self-sufficient.[35] Some goods could be brought from Europe or from other parts of the continent, but prohibitive transportation costs limited long-distance trade to largely high-value, low-weight items. Therefore, from the beginning, workshops in urban areas depended on unfree craftsmen to produce all the necessities of life. Enslaved Afroiberians participated in the economic activity of the province at every level, starting with the most menial jobs and progressing upwards as their skills, dedication, and opportunities allowed.[36]

Bozales might find themselves part of the same household as enslaved workers in the process of *coartación* (self-purchase). A recent arrival might be assigned to work with an enslaved woman who lived outside the household and paid her enslaver a rent on herself.[37] They might also encounter freedpeople who had negotiated their emancipation through long or signal service,[38] as well as freedpeople utilizing the courts to preserve their freedom,[39] or even freedpeople who had prospered to the point that they had acquired slaves of their own.[40] All of these actors frequently engaged with the legal ecology.[41] They provided frames of reference for newcomers attempting to understand and better their condition.[42]

Despite the cavalier attitude sometimes attributed to litigants in Spanish America, legal battles tended to be deadly serious business for enslaved subjects. Both sides risked loss, their reputation, and numerous costs when using the courts to resolve conflict. Additionally, enslaved litigants were usually risking grievous bodily harm or even their lives. Unsurprisingly, masters and slaves often sought to reach a negotiated settlement multiple times before calling in the lawyers.

Over time, enslaved Afroiberians and freedpeople would become enmeshed in a web of ongoing negotiations.[43] Gossip was a crucial means of educating new arrivals and young people on the risks they faced and ways of mitigating the same. For example, hearing about a conflict caused by a slave owner's breach of an undocumented agreement would tend to impress the utility of the notarial system upon those with access. Documenting agreements was a form of insurance. My survey of cases suggests that masters were generally amenable to the process, probably because clear terms maximized the chances that both sides would get what they expected. Moreover, a master's reputation for good faith with the members of their household represented a key part of their authority. Breaching written or spoken contracts could push the conflict into the courts, which often proved to be expensive, time-consuming, and disruptive to the order and productivity in a household. Familial enterprises that included enslaved workers and freedpeople sought to balance coercion and consensus building as a competitive advantage. Few cases illustrate this better than the legal storm unleashed by Francisco Aguirre Morado.[44]

PROTECTED WITNESS?

In 1661, Francisco Aguirre Morado sued *maestro de campo* (marshal) don Francisco Jiménez de Enciso, requesting his own liberation. This was a bold move. Don Francisco was a high sheriff of the Holy Office of the Inquisition, Provincial of the Santa Hermandad, and, as he never failed to point out in his many long-winded court declarations, Cartagena's longest-serving *alcalde ordinario* (municipal councilman).[45] He was firmly ensconced among the powerful oligarchy that felt themselves the rightful leaders of the towns and cities of the New Kingdom of Granada.

Francisco Morado, in contrast, was a creole slave. His mother was born in Angola and sold as a young woman in the slave market of Cartagena. The circumstances of Morado's birth enmeshed him in the province's politics and serve as an example of the balancing function of the courts. According to later testimony, he was the firstborn slave in the newly established household of Antonio Luis de Aguirre, royal treasurer of the town of Río de la Hacha. As was customary among pious provincial elites or those who aspired to be seen as such, Francisco's owner celebrated his birth by declaring him free and adopting him as a dependent of the family. It is also possible that he was the son of his owner, but the record is unclear.

Unfortunately, financial and political difficulties struck the household, with tragic consequences for its most vulnerable members. Antonio de Aguirre fell behind in his payments to the royal treasury, which ordered the seizure of his movable goods and property and their sale at auction to offset the shortfall in the accounts. The seized property included Francisco Morado, still a small child, and his mother, sold together to the powerful and wealthy don Francisco Jiménez de Enciso. During this time, Antonio de Aguirre died, sick and impoverished. In the confusion and chaos inherent in the dismantling of a household, the freedom granted to Francisco Morado remained only in memory. However, neither he nor his mother forgot the reality of his freedom or the unfortunate events that led to his bondage.

Twenty years later, Francisco Morado found himself again at the center of an intervention by the royal treasury. However, this time he was not a helpless child but the experienced supervisor of one of don Francisco's pearl fisheries. At issue were chronic back taxes owed on most gold mines and pearl fisheries. When fiscal agents arrived to take inventory and begin the process of seizing assets, don Francisco frantically sent word that Morado should obstruct their work. Unexpectedly, Francisco Morado refused and instead opened the books and turned over thirty thousand pesos in cash and property.

This was a substantial fortune and its loss could be a crippling blow to even the strongest family enterprise. Don Francisco immediately sued the tax collector, alleging he had overstepped his authority, and requested the return of his property. Meanwhile, to coerce Morado's testimony and in reprisal for his cooperation, don Francisco Jiménez had him put in chains and beaten. Don Francisco's rage reached the point of sending to Cartagena for the "Jesús María," a collar and chain specifically designed for torment.[46]

In his complaint, Morado describes how, after several days of cruel treatment, a corrupt alcalde in don Francisco's employ transported him, beaten and cowed, to testify. However, elbowing one of his captors in the nose, he broke away from them and barely escaped with his life. While hiding out, he heard from friends that don Francisco had ordered him captured or killed. At this point Morado could have left town and joined one of the groups of cimarrones perennially coalescing in the borderlands; but his life was in Cartagena and he chose to fight for it. Looking for allies, he sought out the royal officer auditing don Francisco and placed himself under his care. Knowing full well don Francisco's sway over local officials, the officer took Morado to the city of Santa Marta.

Once under protection of the governor of Santa Marta, Francisco Morado sued his owner, alleging that don Francisco had never legally possessed him and had kept him in his household against his will. Morado testified that don Francisco knew of his previous owner's grant of freedom and illegally kept him as a slave regardless. He also stated he had served don Francisco well, hoping he would vouchsafe his freedom. However, don Francisco had failed to free him, and the punishments meted out unjustly to Morado were the last straw. Describing himself as a faithful subject, Morado proclaimed that his loyalty to the king superseded any duty to don Francisco, obligating him to cooperate with the treasury officials. In his words, obedience to the king was his highest duty.

The voluminous records of the court case between don Francisco and Francisco Morado provide a clear insight into their erstwhile trusting relationship. Morado and other witnesses attested that on several occasions don Francisco had promised him freedom. His disappointment and resentment at don Francisco repeatedly putting off his liberation probably contributed to Morado's sudden rush to cooperate with royal auditors. Regardless, as Morado explained to the court, he had been a hardworking and responsible foreman for years, whose only crime was cooperating with the authorities. In this light, don Francisco's punishments and attacks became a terrible betrayal. He requested the court set him free and order don Francisco pay him the wages Morado should have received for the years of work he had performed while in illegal bondage.

The legal ecology strained to diffuse the conflict unleashed by the dysfunctional relationship between two proud and hurt men who had been close collaborators. The case brought against don Francisco deeply offended him, calling into question his honor and strength. Accordingly, he responded to Morado's claims by countersuing, presenting rather complete documentation proving his ownership; then requested that, given the grave harm he had suffered because of Morado's disloyalty and disobedience, the court order his execution. As he put it, "Francisco Morado . . . betrayed my trust as his master and he deserves the death penalty for the so atrocious crimes, he should be put to death and should be executed publicly as an example to the other slaves including those that I have, and the slaves of the vecinos."[47] By the time of its conclusion, the case had offended much more than his sensibilities.

Including two appeals, arriving at a final resolution took most of the 1680s and accumulated over four hundred pesos in court fees. One can reasonably estimate the total legal fees to have been much greater. This great expense of money, time, and people resulted in, at best, a pyrrhic victory for don Francisco. In the final appeal, the Real Audiencia de Santafé found both parties culpable. They affirmed Morado's enslaved condition, citing voluminous evidence and the fact that he had waited so long before pressing his claim. However, they also firmly denied his owner's request for execution. The court ordered that Morado receive fifty lashes for his *desacato* (willful disobedience). Simultaneously, the oidores instructed don Francisco to sell Morado to an owner, approved by Morado and royal officials, outside of the province. For Morado's security, the court established that if any harm came to Morado, don Francisco would be liable in his person and property for four hundred ducats.

Morado's ability to moderate his master's power was rooted in the DNA of the empire. Royal authorities did not always favor enslavers, even in cases involving wealthy and powerful subjects. Francisco Morado, familiar with the legal ecology, effectively fought one of the richest and most well-connected men of the province to a standstill. Furthermore, since Morado had been confirmed as his property, don Francisco was required to pay all the expenses of the case against him. Nonetheless, Morado did not achieve his freedom and suffered fifty lashes. He was alive and his rebellion had extracted a high price from don Francisco. Unfortunately, he was probably going to have to start from close to zero with a new owner.

Taming the fractious nobility's power and establishing the supremacy of royal over private justice propelled imperial Spain out of the medieval period. Consequently, curtailing the power of local elites remained one of the crown's enduring preoccupations. Partially in service to this, judicial officials consistently admitted and adjudicated lawsuits presented by enslaved subjects against their masters and other social superiors. Experienced royal officials were past masters in the art of encouraging the disaffected parties of a lawsuit to collaborate in finding a mutually acceptable solution. Knowledge gave the "enemies and familiars" of powerful and wealthy families leverage. The asymmetrical relationship between an enslaved person and a master prevented even the most trusted of collaborators like Francisco Morado from attacking the master class at will. Nevertheless, for the trusted and disaffected, opportunities for some form of payback were seldom far away.

STANDING WITNESS

In accordance with Iberian law, slaves possessed legal personhood. Mutually reinforcing Roman, medieval, and Catholic law established their juridical personality, allowing them (theoretically) to participate in legal actions on all levels. The ramifications of this legal principle cascaded throughout the Iberian Atlantic. Enslaved Afroiberians and freedpeople could initiate suits in defense of their rights and could also testify on their own behalf or as part of other legal processes. Scholars have somewhat neglected the role of enslaved witnesses in the Spanish judicial system, despite their ubiquity in the records.[48] Significantly, they could testify even in cases in which the legal status of the plaintiff was the matter in dispute.

As many scholars have noted, Spanish America was a litigious place.[49] Enslaved people were valuable property and, in many cases, worked closely with their owners. Even if obliquely, enslaved subjects drew power from their ability to testify in court. They could be given in a will, donated to the church, mortgaged, rented, or sold outright. Every aspect of each transaction could be contested in the courts, and often was. When the judges addressed questions of ownership, the testimony of the enslaved people usually played a key role in the adjudication of the case.[50]

Having a judge involved made disputes in which enslaved Afroiberians participated more volatile for their masters. Theoretically at least, a person being held as a slave could challenge their bondage in court. Unlike a contested house or livestock, the people in question could participate in their own cases. Of course, laws do not enforce themselves, and it is significant that assimilated, urban slaves are vastly overrepresented in the surviving records. Nonetheless, for enslaved people, serving as witnesses was probably the most common form, and one of the most important, of their engagement with the courts. Furthermore, Africans and their descendants are commonly found as witnesses in cases involving disputes over the validity of a sale or the cause of death or sickness of other enslaved people. Because experienced captives generally had the responsibility of caring for and supervising newly acquired bondspeople, they often possessed information that allowed them to testify to both the initial condition and subsequent treatment of recent arrivals.

The growing demographic preponderance of Africans and their descendants in the Province of Cartagena throughout the long seventeenth century meant that there were few cases that did not include testimony from at least one unfree witness. Complicating this tangled social fabric are the opaque, competing social networks Africans and their descendants built. We cannot assume that any person, regardless of their legal condition or "race," was acting to benefit their peers as we might perceive them. The following case developed in the aftermath of the death of a respected community leader, giving us some sense of the social network she built and the weight judges gave to the testimony of different classes of witnesses.

THE DEATH OF ISABEL BRAN

In May 1653, Doctor of Theology Matías Suarez de Melo, canon of the cathedral of Cartagena, appeared before a royal notary and recorded his purchase of Isabel Bran. The sellers were Juana Gonzáles and her son-in-law Antonio de Villalobos. Only two weeks after the transfer to Suarez de Melo, Isabel Bran fell gravely ill. As her condition worsened, her new owner brought in a variety of medical personnel, but her health continued to deteriorate. On May 21, she perished, and her friends and family buried her in the local cemetery. However, Isabel Bran was valuable property, and her death did not end her story.

For two months after her death, Suarez de Melo tried to negotiate with the sellers to recover part of his investment. However, González and Villalobos refused to settle, insisting that they had no blame in her death.[51] This was a gamble on their part, as Isabel's death occurred soon after her sale and the law provided avenues for redress. The costs of litigation could be high for Suarez de Melo, and engaging the legal ecology always involved risk. Simple litigiousness for the sake of litigiousness could result in the dismissal of the case and the guilty party having to pay all the legal costs for both sides.[52] However, the chance of recovering or losing the substantial sum of 385 pesos pushed both sides toward litigation.

Very much like modern property law, Spanish law obligated a seller who knew that the enslaved person being sold had some major tacha of body or character to disclose it to the buyer. If a serious tacha was not disclosed in writing in the contract of sale, then the buyer could request a refund of the purchase price through a redhibitoria lawsuit. The law and custom restricted what could be claimed as a tacha. Additionally, the rudimentary state of medical diagnostics guaranteed uncertainty in disputes over the exact origin and type of illnesses that caused the death of a slave.

Like many (many) others, the case initiated by Suarez de Melo hinged on three interrelated questions: What type of sickness caused the death of Isabel Bran? When did she contract this sickness? Finally, did physical mistreatment contribute to her sickness and death? In his initial statement, Suarez de Melo presented a strong narrative that answered all three questions. As he told it, Isabel Bran approached him in early 1653 requesting that he purchase her. Her owners planned to sell her, but her husband belonged to the Cartagena cathedral.

Therefore, so she could remain near her family, she lobbied Suarez de Melo to purchase her as his personal slave.[53] After hearing Isabel's pitch and checking her character and work references from other members of the community, Suarez de Melo agreed to purchase her and invited her to stay with him for several days. Law and custom encouraged a trial period wherein a prospective member of a household could come to live in the house of their new owner. During this week, Isabel comported herself as a model slave, and by all accounts was happy with the treatment she received in the de Melo household. All parties being satisfied, the notary recorded the sale and the parties exchanged the considerable sum of 385 pieces of eight.[54]

Despite all the care put into making this transaction seamless, problems arose. About two weeks after the finalization of the sale, Isabel began to feel sick and complain of pain. Initially, she treated her illness through potions and *totumas* (compresses) acquired from various members of the community that had side trades as healers.[55] As mentioned, her condition continued to worsen, and Suarez de Melo intervened. Over the course of her illness, he invited four different doctors to his house in attempts to cure her. Sadly, the disease proved stronger than any of the remedies prescribed and, by the time of Isabel's death, her room had acquired such a stench that it could no longer be used for any purpose.[56]

After describing how he came to possess Isabel and how she died, Suarez de Melo presented information that he acquired after her death, ostensibly proving the sellers defrauded him. In his statement, he portrayed the sellers as deliberately dishonest and conniving.[57] He claimed to have discovered that González and Villalobos physically abused and constantly overworked Bran, not giving her enough food, medical attention, or even decent clothes. Furthermore, they had previously tried to sell her to another *castellano* (Castilian) but the prospective buyer cancelled the transaction upon receiving a negative evaluation from a doctor who examined Isabel.[58]

In Suarez de Melo's version of events, after the first sale fell through, Isabel set about finding another buyer. Through her husband Domingo Carabalí, who belonged to the cathedral, Isabel learned that Suarez de Melo was looking for a female

slave to complement his household. Approaching him, she deliberately hid her illness and the bad treatment to which she had been subjected. Desperate to escape
her terrible masters, not only did she lie when asked about her life, she also convinced her community to lie to Suarez de Melo when he checked her references.

Considering the impact changing owners could have on their quality of life, Africans and their descendants were continually aware of their possible commercial-
ization. While the strategy that Suarez de Melo attributed to Isabel constituted an
extreme case of coordinated trickery, much smaller manipulations could have a big
effect on sales. Throughout the records we find regular, unremarked-on references
to the methods by which the community and individuals managed the information
available to prospective sellers and buyers to influence their decisions.

Suarez de Melo depended on this communal knowledge to show that Isabel's
owners sold her with a serious hidden tacha. He alleged that they not only knew
about her condition but that its root in their maltreatment made them fully liable.
The theme of unchristian and cruel ownership is central to this case and many others. This case deployed it on three levels. First, Suarez de Melo contended that Isabel's maltreatment at the hands of her previous owners contributed to her sickness,
making them indirectly responsible for her death. Second, the fear of continued
mistreatment at their hands forced Isabel to lie about her condition, and it convinced her community to go along with it. Third, and probably most consequential,
treating your slave cruelly and carelessly marked you as a bad master, and bad masters faced the presumption of liability in cases in which they sold someone and the
new owner found a major tacha.

Unsurprisingly, Juana González and Antonio de Villalobos presented a very different picture of the life of Isabel Bran and their relationship with her. They stressed
their status as good Christians, faithful subjects of the king, and upstanding members of their community. Building up from the bedrock of those qualities, they presented themselves as inherently good masters. Additionally, they spoke of caring
for Isabel as a person while praising her work ethic and business initiative. In their
version of events, when they decided they needed to sell Isabel, they informed her,
asking her to find an owner with whom she would like to live; Isabel then arranged
her own sale to Suarez de Melo to be closer to her husband. They asserted that a
sudden attack of disease, an act of God for which they had no responsibility, caused
her death. They also stated that their reputation in the community would substantiate their declarations.[59]

In support of their respective declarations, each party in the lawsuit presented
a group of witnesses. A close examination of the composition of these groups allows us to parse the weight that Spanish officials gave to the testimony of different
types of people. Isabel's case provides a particularly useful case study, as it involves
a common cause for litigation and a broad slate of witnesses.

Witnesses for Canon Matías Suarez de Melo:

Gabriel de Esquivel, doctor

Juan Suárez, treasurer (cousin of plaintiff)

Ambrosio Herrera, *vecino*

Jacinto de León, *vecino*

Luis Melgarejo, previous prospective buyer

Domingo Carabalí, husband (enslaved)

Isabel Bran, aunt (enslaved)

Francisca Bran, friend (enslaved)

María Angola, friend (enslaved)

Juana Criolla, friend (enslaved)

Josefa Mulata, friend (enslaved)

Witnesses for Juana Gonzáles and Antonio de Villalobos:

Fray Bartolomé de San Agustine, *religioso descalzo*

Doctor Francisca de Salazar, *comadre de parir* (midwife) *y vecina*

Francisco Ortiz, city doctor

María Gómez Palomino, employer of Isabel Bran

Luis de Salazar, *vecino*

Pedro de Aguilar, *vecino*

Isabel Núñez, *vecina*

Ana Marín Morena, freedwoman

Three noteworthy contrasts emerge from a comparison of the witness lists. First, three doctors, including the city's official doctor, supported the testimony of Juana Gonzáles, while Suarez de Melo had the support of only one doctor. The preponderance of medical testimony should have provided a major advantage to Juana Gonzáles since the core of the litigation pertained to Isabel's health prior to her sale. Second, enslaved people made up the majority of Suarez de Melo's witnesses, while no enslaved people stood as witnesses for Juana Gonzáles. In the standard understanding of early-modern society, the low social status of Suarez de Melo's witnesses would seem to disadvantage him. Third, the enslaved witnesses Suarez de Melo presented knew Isabel well, as they were either family members or life-long friends; in contrast, the witnesses Juana Gonzáles presented mostly knew *of* Isabel, as they were predominantly doctors or people of standing in the community who could testify to her reputation.

Transposing the testimony of the various witnesses gives us a broadly accurate picture of Isabel's life. Aside from the doctors, all the witnesses agreed on several relevant points, the first and most important of which was that Juana Gonzáles was not a bad mistress. Isabel and Juana had a good working relationship for years, and Juana allowed Isabel to hire herself out to work for different people as a way to earn extra money. Secondly, all the witnesses except the doctors agreed that Isabel had complained and sought treatment for a variety of illnesses during the final years of her life.

On August 17, 1654, after considering almost two hundred pages of testimony, José de Arbicu, an alcalde of Cartagena, gave his ruling. Each part of his decision had a strong monetary consequence. He found that the weight of the testimony proved that at the time of her sale, Isabel Bran had been seriously ill. Therefore, Juana Gonzáles should return the 385 pesos Suarez de Melo paid for her. However, the judge found the charge of her being a bad mistress without merit, finding that Juana Gonzáles intended no fraud. Because of this part of the ruling, the judge ordered each side to pay their own legal costs and split the court fees, instead of the total cost falling solely upon Gonzáles.[60]

Considering the large amount of money at stake, neither side accepted the ruling. The case dragged on for another two years, eventually reaching the Real Audiencia in Bogota. On February 11, 1656, a definitive judgment was handed down. The oidores reaffirmed the conclusions of the original judgment but changed the actual monetary award. Citing Juana Gonzáles's lack of intent to commit fraud and Suarez de Melo's failure to conduct a thorough check of Isabel's health, they reduced the original award of 385 pesos to 150 pesos. An examination of other cases shows that this outcome was fairly standard. The oidores of the Audiencia usually leaned toward providing nuanced responses to cases in which they found no clear criminal intent, opting instead to spread around the financial pain.

Analyzing the trajectory and outcome of this case and the many others like it complicates several narratives commonly found in the historiography of the early modern Spanish Empire. First, according to the standard interpretation, the courts gave greater weight to witnesses of higher social standing. However, as this and other cases show, the determinative testimony as to whether or not Isabel had a long-standing sickness was provided by her enslaved family and friends. Juana Gonzáles's use of three doctors and four high-class members of society as her witnesses did not sway the judges. Neither medical experience nor social class trumped the testimony of those who knew Isabel best. Royal judges were most susceptible to reinforcing the advantages of class and race when these were marshaled to support narratives that nudged all parties in a lawsuit toward broadly agreed prosocial behaviors.

Another salient point illustrated by this case is that the testimony of enslaved witnesses seldom matched exactly those of the principals in the case. Suarez de Melo likely would have preferred for his witnesses to support his declarations in their entirety, but he was unable to persuade or pressure them into compliance, in spite of their position as slaves and his as a high-ranking member of society. While generally supportive of the initial declaration presented by Suarez de Melo, especially in regard to Isabel's long-standing illness, the enslaved witnesses differed considerably with him on several key details. While he worked hard to portray Juana Gonzáles as a bad mistress, all the enslaved witnesses he presented to the court contradicted this declaration, testifying instead that Isabel and her mistress had a good working relationship. They also repudiated any notion that they participated in covering up Isabel's sickness. This part of their testimony was particularly significant as the case was appealed through the courts. The Real Audiencia decided to reduce the monetary award largely based upon the determination that Juana González was neither a bad mistress nor intent on any fraud.

Regardless of the particulars of Suarez de Melo's testimony, it lets us see a legal ecology in which the Africans and their descendants had a measure of control over who purchased them and at what price. His presentation to the court illustrates what was considered plausible in the early-modern Spanish Empire. In his narrative we can see Isabel Bran leveraging her social capital to control her destiny by coordinating with her community to provide or withhold critical information.[61]

In addition to their concern for their own fate, enslaved Africans and their descendants were the principal economic actors of the province; consequently, they were the main witnesses in many different types of cases. In a litigious society in which slaves were valuable property, matters regarding their ownership, the validity of sales, their treatment, their identities, and other disputes pertaining to their work and personhood were constantly brought before the courts. Who better to testify about many of these aspects than the very property in litigation?

MANUELA COMES HOME

The case between Paula Gómez, a vecina of Honda, and Juan de Cáceres Hidalgo, a vecino of Cartagena, provides another example of enslaved people controlling information and serving as determinant witnesses in legal disputes.[62] Gómez sued Cáceres over the ownership of a woman named Manuela, claiming that her grandmother, María Gómez, had given Manuela to her in an irrevocable donation before her death. She explained that, while she was still a minor, creditors of her grandmother's estate had seized and sold Manuela to pay for delinquent debts incurred in the wedding of one of María Gómez's daughters.

Neither party alleged that the transaction by which Juan de Cáceres had acquired Manuela was illegal. The dispute instead became centered on whether the Manuela in the possession of Juan de Cáceres Hidalgo was the same person given to Paula Gómez by her grandmother years before.[63] If the court determined that they were indeed one and the same, possession should revert back to Paula since her grandmother deeded Manuela to her before incurring any of the debts at issue, making her creditors' seizure of Manuela illegal and invalidating all the intervening transactions.[64]

Arguing his purchase of Manuela had been completely legal, Juan de Cáceres

Hidalgo fought mightily to preserve his rights over her. Manuela was capable, hard-working, intelligent, and both parties' statements described her as a loyal and valu-able slave. At the time the creditors seized and sold her, Manuela worked in the gold mines of San Lucas. Several witnesses who worked with or knew her testified that she was one of the better-paid slaves in the mines. Typically, enslaved work-ers in the mines received anywhere from one half to one-and-a-half gold pesos a week on top of their maintenance costs and the mine owner's cut, depending on their productivity. Manuela was among those receiving one-and-a-half gold pesos a week, due to her skill and dependability.[65]

A network of enslaved people, serving as witnesses and informants for Paula Gómez and Manuela, frustrated de Cáceres Hidalgo's efforts to maintain owner-ship at every turn. When Gómez initiated the case, Manuela was passing through the city of Cartagena and managed to get word of her location to her previous owner. The available documentation leaves unclear exactly how Manuela transmit-ted this information. However, considering the prominent role played by Manuela's network of enslaved friends and acquaintances in the subsequent case, we can rea-sonably assume that she utilized this network to communicate information to her previous owner.

After Paula Gómez discovered Manuela's whereabouts, she petitioned the lo-cal authorities to detain Manuela and requested they return the slave to her. In response to this, Juan de Cáceres first argued that his Manuela was not the one Gómez's grandmother had given to her. This argument was stymied when several enslaved witnesses testified to the contrary. The most important witness, a slave named Isabel who had belonged to the provincial governor at the time of the do-nation, testified that she knew her when Manuela lived in María Gómez's house. She also testified that she had witnessed the donation.[66] After Isabel, four more en-slaved people and assorted residents corroborated that María Gómez owned Man-uela and gave her to her granddaughter in perpetual donation before her death. Once again, just as with the death of Isabel Bran, enslaved witnesses provided the key testimony that made Paula Gómez's lawsuit possible.

The strength of the evidence left Juan de Cáceres with no recourse but to re-quest that the judge name the merchants who originally seized and sold Manuela as codefendants in the case so that they would share the financial loss of returning Manuela.[67] Unfortunately for him, he was unable to get any traction with the local authorities, who ordered de Cáceres to return Manuela to Paula Gómez.[68] Facing the loss of his investment in Manuela, Juan de Cáceres appealed the initial ruling to the Real Audiencia de Santafé. In his appeal, he testified that he had possessed Manuela peacefully for several years and described himself as a good master, having never been accused of mistreating his slaves.[69] Nonetheless, the Audiencia judges found the weight of the evidence against him overwhelming and ratified the lower court's order that he return Manuela to Paula Gómez.[70]

MANUMISSION: *COARTACIÓN* AND *LIBERACIÓN GRACIOSA*

The ethos of the Spanish Empire generally encouraged masters to manumit model slaves, and the institutions of the crown worked to support and protect manumission. The importation of captive Africans to the Caribbean basin exploded during the Union of Crowns, so much so that African-born people became a substantial part of the population. Starting at the bottom of the social ladder, Africans arrived in an environment where, with effort and luck, they might provide themselves or their children with means of advancement. During assimilation into Iberoamerican society, Africans learned Spanish and the local pidgin, created social networks with their work and church-mates, and became aware of different pathways to manumission.

However, the path to freedom was seldom easy or uncontested. Given their social and economic value, unscrupulous slave owners and their heirs found many ways to extract more value from enslaved people.[71] As a counterbalance, Africans and their descendants leveraged social norms, the church, and the legal system to protect their life, acquire freedom, and defend their property. Facilitating this, the Catholic Church and Spanish Crown generally encouraged the maintenance of mechanisms that promoted assimilation and manumission.[72] Crucially, and unlike other slave systems, Iberian law provided a clear mechanism for self-purchase.[73]

Coartación (legal self-purchase), the most effective and powerful tool enslaved Afroiberians possessed to acquire their freedom, arose out of the principle that enslavement was contrary to human nature and happiness.[74] Therefore, the state should, where possible, support freedom. Coartación allowed a slave to agree on a purchase price, depositing a minimum of one-fourth of this amount with their owner, subsequently making payments on the balance until achieving self-purchase. Once the enslaved person deposited the initial payment, if the owner decided to sell, the law maintained that the former keep control of the part of her or his person already paid for. Coartación differed from *liberación graciosa* (manumission by grace) because it did not depend on the owner's goodwill. If an enslaved person offered a down payment, the law obligated his or her owner to accept it.

In cases in which a price could not be agreed upon, an alternative path was available. Enslaved people could ask officials in their locality, at any point during their captivity, to evaluate and determine the fair value of their person. Once officials determined the fair price, the slave could give a down payment to the owner, commencing the process of coartación, and ensuring it would continue even if said owner sold him or her. The court determined a price, which could not increase as long as enslaved people made regular payments. Eventually the enslaved person would finish paying for her or himself and would be free by right of law.

To ensure the security of the payments made by the enslaved person, the parties could have a royal notary record the transactions. The official protection of the

arrangement reduced the ability of an owner to cheat the enslaved person in informally negotiated agreements. Fuzzy agreements could be subject to litigation
when the untimely death of an owner or a moment of financial stress opened the
door to assets being seized and liquidated. The scarcity of cases in which owners
tried to renege on contracts of coartación provides some evidence of the effectiveness of this pathway to freedom. Although imperial authorities did not specifically
codify coartación in law until the nineteenth century, it was a common practice in
the medieval period, and as such, the courts throughout the Spanish Empire upheld
it.[75] For example, in the case discussed at the start of the chapter, Francisco Aguirre
Morado asked for and received the services of a "lawyer for the poor" to aid his efforts to force his emancipation despite the opposition of his elite owner.[76]

In the early modern Spanish Empire, enslaved people served not only as pro-
ducers of revenue but also markers of honor.[77] Ownership of human beings is rife
with meaning, meaning from which some slaves could extract the social energy
needed to acquire their freedom.[78] The economic value of enslaved people meant
that ownership, more so the display of ostentatious possession, signaled status and
power. Throughout the Indies, social custom dictated that wealthy residents have,
almost out of necessity, an entourage of enslaved people following them around
town. Owning slaves was such a coveted marker of honor that many indigenous
leaders petitioned the crown for the grant of a coat of arms and the right to have
enslaved Africans in their retinue.[79]

Despite, or maybe because of, the multivalent value of enslaved people, most
elites in the Spanish Empire during the Hapsburg dynasty, and even after, considered it honorable and righteous to free one's slaves. Notarial records, Inquisition
records, and contemporary histories show that owners regularly granted liberación
graciosa to the enslaved people in their possession during weddings, births, military victories, religious festivals, and, most commonly, upon death.[80] The value
of displaying magnanimous ownership was multifaceted. Owners used their relationship with enslaved people to display honor, loyalty, and piety. By freeing a slave
during key social and religious events, owners displayed their devotion and piety
to the community. This was also meant to show the righteousness of Catholic masters over any other kind, displaying and reinforcing their good relationships with
the enslaved people they owned. Within a slave owner's household, the judicious
use of liberación graciosa created a powerful incentive for good behavior among
her or his slaves. The presence of this positive incentive was of paramount importance considering the intimacy of many masters' connections with Africans and
their descendants.

COMING TO TERMS

A slave who could not earn enough to make the regular payments required by
coartación and who did not receive liberación graciosa could still hope to attain

freedom through negotiation with their owner.[81] Africans and their descendants were the province's key economic engine, working at almost all levels in every business. The depth of their engagement in the economy provided them with opportunities to create extra value for their masters. As an incentive, masters sometimes offered manumission, usually during certain feasts or upon the master's death, in exchange for signal service.[82]

In some cases, masters and enslaved people recorded their agreements using a royal notary.[83] However, most such deals remained verbal and, therefore, dependent on the honor of both parties. Despite the undocumented nature of these agreements, the courts provided some recourse to enslaved subjects in their enforcement.[84] Slaves could request that local judicial or religious officials mediate in case of a dispute.[85] If that failed, they could initiate a legal case against their masters. A master's breach of faith also had social consequences. As we have seen, enslaved people served as witnesses in many cases and could, either personally or through their network, damage a faithless owner's interests. Additionally, acting dishonorably toward an enslaved person injured an owner's reputation and reduced their credibility.

Humanity being what it is, not all deals negotiated in exchange for freedom involved strictly legal actions. It is a negotiation of dubious legality that led one enslaved man named Lorenzo, on the night of *Jueves Santo* 1572, to stab *capitán* Pedro Pérez in the face just outside of the town of Tolú in the Province of Cartagena.[86] The incident was part of a long-running feud between Francisco Marmolejo, Lorenzo's owner, and Pérez. Marmolejo initiated a revenge plot after the *capitán* accused him of illegal dealings, inducing Lorenzo to commit the crime in exchange for a promise of safety and his freedom.

The details of the crime are delicious in their deviousness. Marmolejo's associates provided Lorenzo, the designated hit man, with a complete disguise, allowing him to infiltrate the religious procession of the *Disciplinantes* (religious fraternity) in which *capitán* Pedro Pérez was marching. They dressed him in a robe, a hood, canvas leggings, sandals, and gloves to avoid recognition. Lorenzo then hid under a small boat on the beach near the Disciplinantes' path, waiting for his chance. To facilitate the attack, one of Marmolejo's accomplices sent a boy to douse all the fires lighting the marchers' way.

The attack against *capitán* Pérez went off without a hitch, Lorenzo joined the procession long enough to strike, and, in the confusion, waiting conspirators spirited Lorenzo out of the city. The deal between Lorenzo and Marmolejo stipulated that upon completion of the crime, Marmolejo would *enhorrar* (free) Lorenzo, and set him up to live somewhere far away. However, before the strike, Lorenzo, showing a distinct lack of discretion, bragged to several of his friends about his impending plans, and more than one bystander overheard his statements.[87]

After escaping from Tolú, Lorenzo next surfaced in the town of Veragua, where he continued to practice his lack of discretion. Constant information leaks placed all the conspirators under the onus of justice. Strangers, later witnesses, again overheard him talking about the crime, this time complaining publicly that, while he fulfilled his bond with Marmolejo, his old owner had not done the same.[88] The mastermind of a public vendetta aspires to be suspected and feared, not hauled to court in chains. Lorenzo's dissatisfaction with his treatment, combined with his general inability to keep things to himself, landed Marmolejo in this situation.

Unfortunately, the conclusion of the case has been lost. However, the strength of the evidence presented by *capitán* Pedro Pérez was overwhelming and did not bode well for Marmolejo's chances of escaping punishment. And regardless of the final outcome, Marmolejo's imprisonment as he awaited judgment and the financial burden of defending against an accusation of this severity already constituted a serious chastisement.

The standard historiographical interpretation of slave owners' use of enslaved people to commit crimes stems from the theory that they existed as pawns in the hands of their masters. Scholars commonly argue that the power differential inherent to their condition put enslaved people at terminal disadvantage in negotiating and enforcing deals.[89] A more nuanced evaluation of the early Spanish Empire's legal environment provides a useful corrective. The courts used what was *sabido y notorio* (well known by all) in the community when making legal determinations. The ability of enslaved Afroiberians to testify, spread rumors, or gossip gave them substantial leverage in negotiating and enforcing deals. When deciding how to treat their property, wise masters would keep in mind that, in the eyes of royal justice, they were dealing with people. Making an enslaved person a partner in crime and not keeping one's word were risky propositions.

CONCLUSION

As the indigenous population continued to collapse, Africans and their descendants, arrivals and survivors, participated in all aspects of economic and social life in Spanish America.[90] Growing ubiquity allowed some slaves and freedpeople to access the avenues of legal engagement rooted in the empire's medieval background. Participation in the legal ecology solidified their access to the same and built an unequal but interdependent relationship with imperial institutions. Growing legal entanglement, in turn, provided slaves and their communities with some means of redressing the chronic power imbalance characteristic of their lives. Throughout, owners, who controlled much of local government, pushed back against any limitations on their power. The complexity of this interplay has not been sufficiently appreciated in the historiography of Spanish slavery.[91]

Early modern Spanish society possessed a coherent narrative that pervaded the legal and moral theory of slave owning. As both source and guide, the law clearly defined and valued righteous masterhood. The law established that a slave owner should only punish his slave for minor offenses, deferring otherwise to royal officials. The law also required a master to provide his slaves with sufficient food, shelter, clothing, and rest and to support their Christian education.[92]

Of course, Christian goodwill and legal strictures did not guarantee righteous treatment. Nonetheless, in almost every case examined, slave owners endeavored to portray themselves as good, kind, Christian masters. Within the towns and cities of the early Spanish Empire, information was widely and notoriously shared.[93] To a degree, the courts and the community held owners accountable for their reputations. Reputation in the small, close-knit communities of the New Kingdom of Granada represented a key avenue for social and business capital. Almost all the legal cases in this period reference the phrase "sabido y notorio." Local knowledge strengthened and legitimized the law.

Slave owners often and vociferously proclaimed themselves model owners—a standard to which society could then hold them.[94] If it were sabido y notorio that a slave owner behaved badly, he or she could incur social, legal, and monetary costs. Slaves and freedpeople with the necessary cultural capital and location took advantage of this. Legal action by enslaved people against their owners could result in fines, forced sale, or even outright confiscation. Additionally, judges at every level, when adjudicating cases of disputed ownership, considered the treatment of enslaved people in their judgments. In some cases, enslaved people suffering abuse temporarily absconded as a negotiation tactic. They would stay away until their owners offered some remedy. In these cases, royal officials often mediated between the parties.[95] Furthermore, a reputedly bad master found it harder to prosecute cases in the courts against the enslaved people he owned.[96]

The legal and social environment imposed a broad range of costs on "bad" masters beyond those directly imposed by imperial officials. A good reputation aided in the monetization of one's slaves. Conversely, notoriously bad behavior reduced an owner's ability to sell any slave. Socialized and/or skilled people actively fought their sale to masters with bad reputations. Furthermore, proprietors with a reputation for abuse exposed themselves to greater risk of losing a redhibitoria lawsuit if, as discussed earlier in this chapter, buyers discovered a major tacha after a slave sale.

Finally, slaves' testimonies often decisively influenced the outcome of commercial cases. A reputation for cruelty or unrighteous masterhood discredited any slave owner. A bad reputation complicated procuring favorable witnesses from an interconnected and self-aware community. None of these advantages offered enslaved people complete protection against abuse, as the crown and church directly sanctioned their exploitation. Nonetheless, the legal environment promoted and rewarded "good" relations between master and enslaved people. The form and substance of the legal ecology tended to ameliorate, most often generationally, the exploitation inherent in slavery.

4

ROYAL JUSTICE

Justice is the constant and perpetual wish to render everyone his due.
—*The Institutes of Justinian 535 CE, Book I. of Persons*

The popularization of royal justice typifies the transition from medieval to early modern governance. During the long seventeenth century, this process extended to Cartagena de Indias, where, despite the difficulties inherent in administering an Atlantic empire, enslaved people felt the presence of the king's law on the other side of the world. The documents examined for this book give us some sense of the complexity in the judiciary's treatment of unfree subjects accused of crimes during the golden age of the Spanish Empire. Throughout this chapter we follow slaves and freedpeople as they navigate the criminal justice system, tracing the praxis of Spanish royal justice. The relevance of state justice to the institution of slavery varied across the European outposts in the Caribbean basin. Access to the courts had a clear, but hard to define, connection to the relative moral self-conceptions of the competing empires.

Empires are made up of people, and people's understanding of the application of justice and good governance is no more linear in its development than any other human construct.[1] For example, when the French pushed the Spanish out of the part of Hispaniola that became Saint Domingue, French law and its enforcement initially resembled Spanish law in Cartagena. However, over the course of the long seventeenth century the infrastructure of enforcement in Saint Domingue was disassembled, as plantation slavery intensified the penetration of racial ideas.[2] The change in social mores and legal practices between Saint Domingue and Cartagena led to increasingly divergent legal ecologies. Even more comprehensively racialized exclusion developed in the English colonies of Jamaica and Virginia, as local elites controlling colonial legislatures moved to actively deny their black and enslaved residents any access to channels of royal justice.[3]

Meanwhile the size, complexity, economy, and population of Spanish America anchored the codified procedures and long-established customs guiding the acts of judicial authorities.[4] Because of the widespread understanding that Spanish law recognized enslaved Afroiberians as subjects of the king possessing legal personhood, officials were less likely to handle the cases of enslaved criminals in an ad hoc or summary manner. For the enslaved population, checks and balances aimed at enforcing proper procedure in the application of the law served as a buffer against human passions and the vagaries of circumstance.[5]

Iberian legal tradition accepted the trade-offs between swiftness and justice.[6] As we have seen, convicting anyone of a crime in the New Kingdom of Granada was not an easy procedure. The legal and administrative system depended on owners, officials, the unfree, and other subjects cooperating in a complex, flexible balancing act to foster stability in a volatile and threatened region of the empire.[7] This interplay produced a plethora of diverse outcomes from interactions between the courts and enslaved people. Though there were no guarantees of equity throughout the system, access to the legal ecology empowered slaves to exert agency on adjudications.[8]

THE PASSION OF DOMINGO ANGOLA

In Mompós on the morning of February 15, 1644, Lieutenant Governor and Captain General Sergeant Major Antonio del Castillo received news of an unusual fight.[9] An enslaved man named Domingo Angola had attacked Lorenzo Domínguez Camargo, the *alcalde mayor* of the Santa Hermandad (head of the rural constabulary). The night before, Domingo, an African-born but assimilated and popular young man, had been fighting with an enslaved woman who belonged to the alcalde mayor. When Lorenzo intervened, Domingo attacked him. Simultaneously, several bystanders intervened and disarmed Domingo, who ran away. Seeking to redeem his honor, Domingo went home, rearmed himself with his master's dagger and sword, and then went back looking for Lorenzo. Fortunately for him, he ran into the city guard who subdued him and carried him off to jail.

This seemed to be an open and shut case. Domingo Angola had been in illegal possession of two different sets of weapons. Despite being disarmed once, he compounded his guilt by returning to his master's home to rearm. Sword in hand, he attempted to attack a high-ranking official of the royal constabulary in front of multiple witnesses, twice. We would be forgiven for assuming that an African slave who violently challenged both the social order and the authority of the state would be swiftly and brutally punished.[10] However, in Domingo's case, arriving at a final sentence took over a year, during which individual and institutional actors mediated the final verdict to Domingo's benefit, an altogether unusual outcome among Atlantic empires.[11] In the finest Castilian tradition, Lieutenant Governor Castillo reacted to Domingo Angola's outburst by filing paperwork. Instead of relying solely on the testimony of the victims, Castillo searched for other witnesses to the incident. He found three individuals willing to give statements to the city's royal scribe. They all concurred that Domingo Angola had engaged in an altercation with a woman who had spurned his advances; when her owner, Lorenzo Domínguez, intervened to protect her, Domingo Angola attacked him. Having established a foundation of evidence against Domingo as well as a motive for the crime, Castillo appointed the fiscal Diego Laurencio to proceed with the case.

Laurencio first took a longer statement from Lorenzo Domínguez and then compiled and considered the evidence. He recommended that Domingo Angola be charged with illegally carrying weapons, attempting harm on a vecino, and desacato of the lawful authorities. The lack of an attempted murder charge is noteworthy because in the *Siete Partidas*, the punishment prescribed for a slave who attacked a royal official was death. Once the charges were formalized, the court notified Domingo Angola and his owner Juan Díaz of the case and appointed an advocate to represent the accused. With his advocate present and a royal scribe recording the proceedings, Domingo threw himself at the mercy of the court.

Aware of the exemplary punishments that the spectacle he had put on invited, Domingo carefully navigated his confession. He tried to exculpate himself by claiming that his actions were an unthinking response to an intolerable provocation from the woman he was courting, aggravated by the fact that he was on *chicha* (homemade liquor) at the time.[12] Seeking to support him, Juan Díaz certified that Domingo was "a slave respectful of those who provide justice and of my orders, who does not go about armed without my permission."[13] Domingo and his owner also presented several local residents as character witnesses; they attested to Domingo Angola's good behavior and demeanor.[14] The witnesses in this case reflect the imagined communities forming and re-forming in the cauldron of Cartagena. The strength and depth of Domingo Angola's social networks provided him with essential support when he engaged with the legal ecology. Overall Domingo presented himself as a responsible, law-abiding Christian slave with a spotless record who regretted his mistake and deserved a second chance.

In meting out punishments, Spanish legal tradition and procedures encouraged judicial officials to take into account the character, local reputation, criminal history, and other extenuating circumstances of defendants. This relatively holistic perspective gave enslaved Afroiberians and their allies incentives and platforms upon which to profess their belonging in the Christian community, their loyalty to the crown, and their trust in royal justice. Assessing the treatment of enslaved people solely in the context of victimization obscures the utility that they derived from the Spanish legal ecology. If an enslaved defendant were to be given short shrift by local officials, it would probably happen in a case of the type discussed here. Instead, local officials in Mompós generally followed procedure in applying the law to Domingo.

Royal officials could be admirably efficient, and, as occurred in most criminal cases, in Domingo's they carried out all steps prescribed by law in less than two weeks after the initial crime. Given the evidence, only the severity of the punishment remained uncertain. At the end of February 1644, Lieutenant Governor Castillo sentenced Domingo Angola to one hundred lashes in the town plaza and one year of exile from the town. He also ordered Domingo's owner, Juan Díaz, to pay the costs incurred in the case, according to the official scale.[15] Within the context of similar cases and the standard penalties recommended by legal codes, this was a mild sentence.

Domingo Angola twice confessed upfront to possessing weapons illegally. Leaving aside the assaults he carried out with said weapons, the relevant section of Cartagena's ordinances reads, "It is ordered that no black person may carry firearms or knifes or machetes or *macanas* (Taino wooden swords) or any other offensive weapon, upon pain that on the first offense they be taken to the public whipping post and receive one hundred lashes, and that they be left there tied up all day naked, until sunset. They shall not be able to carry weapons even when accompanying their master. And if they are caught with weapons a second time, they shall have their genitals bound at the discretion of the judge according to the quality of the crime, because depending on their shamelessness and the crimes they commit with said weapons, so must be the rigorousness of their punishments."[16] Thus, the full punishment Domingo received and more could have been applied for merely carrying weapons, arguably the least significant part of his crime.

Nevertheless, from the perspective of Domingo Angola and Juan Díaz, this comparatively light sentence still entailed severe economic and social costs. On top of Domingo's pain and the chance of death from an infection resulting from the wounds of the lashes, the year of exile disrupted carefully constructed, mutually beneficial arrangements. As a small, local artisan, the relationship of trust and the training Juan Díaz had established with Domingo Angola was a key part of what made his workshop profitable. Domingo, in turn, had showed himself to be so valuable a worker that he had negotiated an arrangement wherein after he finished his quota for the day, Juan permitted him to go out on his own and find work around town, keeping what he earned.

Banishment was a versatile punishment, and Lieutenant Governor Castillo recognized that sending Domingo Angola away from Mompós and the life he had made for himself would leave him alive but strip him of much of the social worth that enhanced his life. Banishment also punished Juan Díaz by forcing him to sell Domingo Angola away from town under conditions that almost certainly diminished his value. Neither Domingo Angola nor Juan Díaz had the cash reserves that would allow Juan to replace his only worker and pay the full costs of the legal battle without selling Domingo. Fortunately for them, the Spanish legal system provided for multiple levels of appeal. By restating his case in front of a different judge, they could plead for review and hope for a more favorable judgment or at least buy some time.

Therefore, after receiving notice of the sentence, Juan Díaz appealed it to the Real Audiencia de Santafé. The oidores in Bogota reviewed the case and handed down a modified sentence in early 1645. They revoked the sentence of lashes and exile, probably because by that time Domingo Angola had already spent close to a year in jail and partly in recognition of his previous good conduct. Nonetheless, Juan Díaz was still ordered to pay the legal costs and fined an additional fifty pieces of eight. It is likely, as in other cases, that Domingo was encouraged to contribute toward the payment of the fine and the legal fees incurred in his defense.[17] The oidores also reiterated the lower court's ruling forbidding Domingo from carrying weapons under any circumstances.[18]

The oidores' response to the appeal suggests consideration of Domingo's character, the original case, and what had transpired since. They still condemned his criminal behavior but lightened and changed the penalty from lashes and banishment to time served and a fine. In a sense, the switch from a potentially deadly physical punishment to a fine can be understood as recognition of Domingo Angola's integration into imperial society and his value to the same. We can reasonably assume that Juan passed this fine on to Domingo, who almost certainly preferred paying fifty pesos to receiving one hundred lashes in the plaza. While fifty pesos is a significant amount of money, a hardworking and skilled slave such as Domingo might be able to gather that amount in about a year. On the whole, this sentence exemplifies the moderating role of the Real Audiencia in local criminal cases. While not binding, precedents had a cumulative effect on the treatment of Africans and their descendants.

TROUBLESOME PROPERTY

As moral actors with legal personhood and codified rights and responsibilities, enslaved defendants were held responsible for their actions but received the protection of legal procedure when they faced criminal accusations. The case of Domingo Angola and Juan Díaz echoes structures, themes, and challenges common to most unfree people engaged in criminal cases in Cartagena. In the next sections, we will further explore the relationship between the legal ecology and enslaved Afroiberians in their roles as defendants, plaintiffs, accusers, and accused, and in their important but underappreciated role as witnesses.

To understand how Afroiberians fulfilled these roles we have to be sensitive to the laws and policies that regulated how Africans became part of Iberoamerica, as well as the circumstances of the early Spanish Empire, starting with how they shaped the role of slave owners in the legal ecology. An enslaved population was a lucrative liability to the state. On the one hand, slaves powered the local economy; on the other, if not managed carefully they could become a dangerously disaffected group. Spanish laws regarding owners' share of this liability derived from Roman law, which defined enslaved people as members of the household of their owners, the paterfamilias. Building on the Renaissance of the twelfth century, Alfonso X's transmutation of Justinian's Code into the *Siete Partidas* established Christianized Roman law as the basis of Spanish jurisprudence. In promoting responsible slave owning, adherence to Christian masterhood was the measure in evaluating the fitness of an owner and his or her culpability in any crime committed by a member of their household.[19]

Domingo Angola could not call on a powerful or rich owner to defend him, but an elite man would call on personal honor to argue for his guiltlessness or that of his retainers. Against the king's justice, Spanish men and women of high status deployed a complementary social and legal narrative that was built around validating the status and honor of the highborn. Of course, the narrative that accorded privilege to the honor and status of slave owners could be undermined if contradicted by their reputation in the community. Under this system, it was dishonorable for elite men or women to be in the position of defendants in a case initiated by a slave.[20] Thus we see slave owners like Juan Díaz standing beside their slaves when they tangled with royal justice.

The closeness with which they were legally tied to their master's household distinguished attitudes toward enslaved people in the Spanish Indies from attitudes found in contemporaneous imperial societies.[21] In general, some of the differences in the roles of owners in the legal ecology are reflected in the contrast between Spanish handling of enslaved subjects in criminal cases and English colonial practice. Slavery became significant in Anglo-America during a time when the metropolis was in the midst of a civil war, the deadliest conflict for the English before World War I, preventing Britain from imposing a legal framework to regulate slavery in its colonies. Unsurprisingly, unencumbered provincial slave-owning elites framed the imperial state's legitimate interventions as protectors of property, promoting the repression of enslaved people as a common responsibility of all "respectable" residents. These societal goals were expressed through the slave codes created by the colonial legislatures in the British Americas, which all increasingly focused on control and exploitation. To encourage masters to turn in and support punishment of enslaved people who had committed crimes, British colonial authorities compensated owners when people they owned were sentenced to judicially mandated maimings or execution.[22]

In the Spanish Empire, owners paid for the mistakes of the enslaved people in their household and received no compensation in return. Sometimes, as in the cases examined here, owners paid for the defense of their slaves and advocated on their behalf, even when the "victim" of the misconduct was the owner himself. Overall, the legal ecology tended toward continuity and self-preservation, sometimes in opposition to the patriarchy or social elites; thus, imperial interests modulated the consequences of Domingo Angola's attack on chief constable Lorenzo Domínguez. In a different kind of legal tradition, one that valued and defended honor or personal property above effective governance, the disparities of wealth and power could have resulted in the ad hoc handling of the case and/or a more onerous sentence.

ROYAL SURVEILLANCE

Enslaved Afroiberians lived in an environment rich in supervision. Information was a crucial input of royal power. As Philip II, the prudent king, wrote to his to provincial officials, "we need to know everything that occurs."[23] This was reinforced in

Cartagena during the long seventeenth century as the focus of the region centered on defense, administration, and trade. This emphasis resulted in a concentration of soldiers and officers, as well as an abundance of imperial officials in the cities and towns of the province. The financially challenged Spanish Crown also created redundant and/or superfluous offices to sell them to local elites, thereby inflating the number of municipal officials.[24] As a consequence, many vecinos who had very little responsibility within the government of the province held official titles and had authority to arrest and present an accusation against anyone whom they witnessed committing a crime.

Most criminal cases were adjudicated along generally aligned principles using a common legal corpus by the senior alcaldes of the cabildo, provincial governors and their lieutenants, and the senior constables of the Santa Hermandad. When crime occurred in a city or town, an alcalde or a representative of the governor handled the case. If the crime was committed in the countryside, or by a runaway slave, the Santa Hermandad held jurisdiction. These were the royal officials *de primera instancia* (lower courts); they had the first call to investigate, judge, and sentence most crimes in their jurisdiction.

As in any complex system, mistakes and procedural breakdowns occurred. The heterogeneity in the quality of royal officials combined with overlapping jurisdictions to create plenty of opportunities for errors of commission and omission. As the highest courts in the Indies, below only the Council of the Indies and the king, the reales audiencias were responsible for protecting the integrity of the law and procedures by reviewing, validating, or modulating decisions made by local officials. As they did for Domingo Angola, they could adjust sentences to better fit the circumstances of the crime. Without the oidores of the Real Audiencia figuratively looking over their shoulders, local officials would have tended to further shirk from their duties to a class of defendants who were structurally disadvantaged in their ability to seek redress.

The operating logic of the Real Audiencia provided incentives for its oidores to police the officials under their jurisdiction. The position and prestige of the institution and its judges depended on the public's perception of their verdicts as just, moderate, and consensual. Popular legitimacy required that courts provide a dependable and useful service to their constituents so as to attract a steady supply of cases, the lifeblood of any legal ecology. At its most basic, courts in the early modern world were almost entirely financially dependent upon the various fees and fines paid by litigants, and the audiencias were no exception.

Unlike courts in the English Caribbean, courts in the Spanish Empire promoted the monarch's image as the protector of all, not the defender of property rights above all. Judicial policy generally valued respect for the law and social stability over blind enforcement of social repression and discipline. Slavery, while important, was by no means the court's primary concern. Because their authority, positions, and incomes rested on the social respect for and credibility of the law, the oidores of the audiencias generally prioritized maintaining control over local officials over economic efficiency.

The density of supervision over all social classes in the region under Cartagena's jurisdiction was unusual but did not differ in type and purpose from what existed in the rest of the empire. Overall, for enslaved Afroiberians most private and imperial supervision explicitly focused on control and discipline to extract the greatest possible value even from the "fractionally free." However, both the crown and enslaved people had other priorities than enriching slave owners and these sometimes complemented each other. Strategic cooperation between a marginalized (but intimately connected to the elite) minority and a distant metropolis is particularly evident among enslaved witnesses in criminal cases.

ACCESS AND PUNISH

The story that can be discerned from the primary sources and the gaps therein is shaped by where Africans and their descendants lived and how well they had familiarized themselves with Spanish language, law, and culture. At a minimum location and socialization largely determined the type and intensity of documented supervision. The institutionally rich environment of Cartagena, bounded, as always, by the limitations of early modern governance, framed but did not determine slaves' encounters with royal and local authorities. Domingo Angola's responsible behavior earned him the trust that allowed him to build the social network that rallied around him during the trial. Without the trust Domingo's owner had in him, Domingo would never have had his access to weapons; without his social network, he wouldn't have come into conflict with his lover's owner in the first place.

During the long seventeenth century, as enslaved Africans and their descendants achieved demographic preponderance, they worked closely with government officials, merchants, and the artisans of the cities and towns of the Spanish Empire, from the highest to the lowest. As a royal cédula responding to a viceroy's request states, "in that land there is a great lack of Spanish people to serve as companions, due to which you have included in your retinue some black slaves, and it was asked of me that I give you license so that you may arm them, so that they might serve as guards and defend your person, and so that you might execute our justice . . . having been reviewed by our Council of Indies it was agreed . . . and I authorize it." The cédula went on to instruct the viceroy that this exception to the prohibitions of enslaved people carrying weapons only counted when they were with him, but this was obviously a fuzzy line.[25]

The use of Afroiberians as bodyguards at the highest levels of imperial administration gives us an idea of the range of their work. Enslaved Africans and their descendants were not only treated as trusted employees but occasionally and usually informally moved into the role of their owners' partner. While the partnership was seldom equal, there were incentives for mutual cooperation. One of the most important of these was the halo effect of responsible high-skill work. Socialization and location intersected with occupation to shape how the unfree pursued their interests through the courts. Whether enslaved or free, Afroiberians' social and economic capital was expressed and reinforced through their heft in court proceedings, including criminal prosecutions.

Enslaved Afroiberians most often came before the judiciary as defendants in cases of robbery, fighting, disturbing the peace, desacato, possession of weapons, and attempted flight. Whereas some of these acts were defined as crimes only if committed by enslaved people (e.g., some of the prohibitions on carrying weapons and travel), free individuals could be charged for robbery, fighting, illegal possession of weapons, disturbing the peace, and desacato. In cases which could have been committed by either enslaved or free people, it was commonplace for the former to suffer greater physical penalties as punishment.

Scholars have sometimes assumed slaves' race explains this disparity.[26] However, court documents do not substantiate such a claim. The different institutions of the Spanish Empire did not simply preserve and reinforce racial privilege or oppress enslaved people. As the example of the Inquisition has shown, the institutions of the crown tended to target the richer and more powerful members of society because of their reliance on the fines they levied to fund their budget and salaries. Prosecutions of that sort would focus on the paterfamilias, as such a target would more likely have the resources to pay for the costs of whatever transgressions occurred. Furthermore, all royal institutions had the implicit function of offering solace to those weaker subjects of the crown who were vulnerable to abuse by unjust elites.

An important but neglected area of the historiography addressed in this chapter is the role of enslaved Afroiberians as plaintiffs. Because Spanish law coded slaves as subjects of the king, they received the protection of royal justice. In the clearest expression of this, Spanish law classified the killing of an enslaved person as murder, punishable by death. Owners' right to physically punish the enslaved people in their households complicated this legal principle.[27] These contradictions within the legal system created grey areas for local officials, who generally exercised great care in handling cases involving criminal abuse by masters.[28] Given their more distant and elevated judicial position, it would usually fall to the judges of the audiencias to take exemplary action against people who abused or killed enslaved subjects.[29]

The law provided a variety of penalties for crimes against enslaved people, discriminating according to gender, social, and economic status. Those convicted of attacking or murdering slaves were often given the option to substitute a fine for other penalties. The type of punishment varied depending on the social position, financial situation, and preferences of the accused. Possible penalties included physical punishment, imprisonment, public shaming, hard labor, monetary fines, and exile. Judges adjusted the punishment mix in an effort to distribute the consequences along an arc that utilized physical, economic, and social levers. Since enslaved people seldom possessed the financial means to pay fines, exile and physical punishment were the most common consequences. The lives and writings of contemporary commentators such as Alonso de Sandoval show how a slave's physical body largely determined their position in society. Even those who dedicated themselves to the health and salvation of slaves' eternal souls were aware of the physicality of enslavement.[30] Thus, physical punishment reinforced the structures of social control without which slavery could not exist. Exile cost the owner money and time, while also breaking up the social network that a troublesome captive might have built. Banishment for any length of time drained economic and social capital.

Most cases show local officials and audiencia judges applying generally consistent sentences over time. To Domingo Angola's at least partial relief, punishments were usually not as harsh as those recommended in the legal codes and ordinances. In the understanding of Cartagena society, sentences given to slaves and other nonelites did not differ substantially in their severity. Owners and local officials administered penalties for misbehaviors along a widely agreed-upon scale. Only major crimes merited the harsher penalties formally administered by the state, such as monetary damages levied against the owners and public corporal punishments for enslaved litigants. The next tranche of cases examined here hinges on procedure. What risks and opportunities opened up when local officials did not follow established guidelines in applying the law or applied the law correctly but harshly?

Critical to understanding the durability of the Spanish Empire, these cases explore a virtuous cycle whereby the actions of local officials, moderated and reinforced by regional supervision, strengthened and legitimized the law. Everywhere within the cases from Cartagena there exists power and the trade-offs between resistance and accommodation. Part of the inner logic of Spanish governance was that it created stakeholders and enforcers out of the very subjects it oversaw. Faced with a chronic shortage of European settlers and enforcement personnel, Spanish institutions necessarily harnessed centripetal social forces and economic self-interest. The perceived legitimacy of the legal ecology channeled and diffused resistance to the exploitation inherent in slavery.

DISCIPLINING CUADRADO

In December 1643 Juan Angola, Francisco Criollo, and Antonio Angola were captured along the edge of a hacienda in the Montes de María region of the Province of Cartagena.[31] As they passed by, they were hailed and, when they reacted suspiciously, detained by workers of the hacienda. Questioned by an overseer, they explained that eight months ago they had escaped from the hacienda of *capitán* Francisco de Trejo Atienza, lieutenant of the provincial governor and *capitán de guerra* (war captain) of the city of Santiago de Tolú.[32]

As required by laws regarding cimarrones, the overseers transferred the three young men to the custody of the Santa Hermandad. Constables brought them to Cartagena and delivered them into the tender mercies of *capitán* Alonso Cuadrado Cid, *alcalde provincial* (provincial head) of the Santa Hermandad.[33] From what can be gleaned from the case, *capitán* Cuadrado was a young, brash official, rising in the ranks, quick and severe in his efforts to enforce law and order as he saw it.

Meanwhile in the municipal jail, the prisoners awaited their official deposition. On January 4, 1644, royal officials interviewed them one by one. With scribe Lorenzo de Soto recording, each prisoner promptly confessed to running away approximately eight months ago. None of the accused denied that they were cimarrones; nor did they challenge their status as slaves. All three independently presented similar narratives of their activities and motivations. Even though all three had the same experiences as cimarrones, the framing and synchronicity of their stories suggests that they were all following a commonly agreed upon script, as opposed to coincidentally voicing precisely the same story in separate depositions.

All three swore loyalty to the crown and obedience to their owner and blamed their escape on intolerable abuses at the hands of mayordomo Mateo López in their master's absence. The prisoners leveled a long and detailed list of accusations against the mayordomo, describing how he had beaten them, insulted them, taken fish they had caught in their off hours, and prevented them from attending church on Sundays. Antonio Angola even alleged that in a fit of rage Mateo López had hanged a man by the testicles to punish him.[34] The particular emphasis that the prisoners put on this last detail is important because the *Siete Partidas* explicitly prohibits the genital mutilation of slaves (in accordance with what is established in Justinian's *Corpus Juris Civilis* upon which the *Siete Partidas* is based).

As they told it, fearful of unbearable future punishments, Juan, Francisco, and Antonio had decided to flee. They initially planned to leave for a short time until their owner came back to the hacienda. Once he returned, they hoped to take their complaints directly to him and ask for the removal of the abusive overseer—a practice known as "petit marronage." However, despite their protestations of virtue, they had no good explanation for why they had absconded for eight months, much longer than acceptable within the negotiated world of owner, slave, and overseer politics.[35]

Juan Angola, Francisco Criollo, and Antonio Angola appeared to be in good health and not undernourished, leading royal officials to suspect that they had found shelter in a *quilombo* (runaway slave community). This prompted careful questioning. Officers of the Santa Hermandad interrogated each slave regarding their coordination with or awareness of other runaway slaves, and if they had stolen or performed any other illegal acts while absconding. All three, separately, vehemently denied they had "*noticias de eso* (knowledge of anything like that)."[36] The three men presented a well-rehearsed repertoire of the acceptable excuses for running away and what runaways should and should not say if they were caught.[37]

Their coordinated answers are even more exceptional because only one of them,

Francisco Criollo, had been born in the Indies. Juan Angola and Antonio Angola had only recently arrived from Africa. Most likely, Francisco had prepared his more bozal companions for the rigors of the courts and coached them to coordinate their statements. The use by enslaved Afroiberians of narratives that fit into the understanding of Spanish officials further cemented a lexicon that expressed reality in a way that meshed with Spanish law. Notwithstanding their stories of abuse and their denial of any undue contact with cimarrones, on January 8, 1644, after only four days of interrogation, testimony, and deliberation, Cuadrado passed judgment. He commanded the runaways each receive two hundred lashes through the streets of Cartagena and spend a year laboring in the royal factories and galleys. He also fined their owner twenty pieces of eight per slave to cover the costs of catching and transporting the prisoners.[38]

Though this sentence was harsh it was not extreme, given that Francisco, Juan, and Antonio were confessed cimarrones who had spent eight months out of their master's custody. Yet, we still find a record of this case in the archives of the Audiencia of Bogota. Why was this sentence appealed? The punishment matches those given to other slaves for similar crimes.

Procedural mistakes in arriving at the sentence provided the necessary justification for appeal. For the prosecution of crimes, procedure mandated that a slave charged with *marronage* should be held while his owner was notified and responded to the charges. If the slave was found guilty then he would be punished, and his owner billed for some of the costs incurred in capturing and transporting his slave. Spanish legal tradition also provided anyone on trial, including a slave, the right to an advocate. To reinforce this requirement, a complementary provision of Spanish law established that anyone under twenty-five years of age was considered a minor and, as such, could not be tried criminally without notifying their paterfamilias and appointing an advocate in their favor. In this particular case, two of the slaves were under twenty-five years of age.[39]

Capitán Cuadrado, therefore, made three procedural mistakes that provided justification for an appeal. First, he did not notify the slave's owner that his slaves had been caught. Second, he did not assign a *procurador de oficio* (advocate) to represent the captured slaves when they were interrogated. Finally, and most problematic of all, he did not notify their owner before initiating the procedures that resulted in their judgment and sentence.

When the owner, *capitán* Francisco de Trejo Atienza, first heard of the fate of his slaves, they had already been sentenced to two hundred lashes in the streets of Cartagena and a year of convict labor in the royal factory. To top it off, he also discovered that he owed sixty gold pesos to the coffers of the Santa Hermandad. An elite and prosperous member of society, Trejo Atienza was familiar with proper procedure for the capture of runaways and knew that Cuadrado had violated his slaves' as well as his own legal rights. He moved to seek redress in the Audiencia in Bogota.

Trejo Atienza moved swiftly. Immediately after receiving notification of his slaves' sentence and current status, he appointed a local advocate, Pedro Sánchez, to represent him and investigate. After paying the fine of sixty pesos necessary to proceed with the case, Sánchez tried to get access to copies of all the legal documents that made up the case file to review and prepare his appeal. Careless officials, afraid of being caught in their mistakes, commonly tried to prevent the reopening of their case records to stymie any investigation into their mistakes. Accordingly, Sánchez's requests for documentation created a three-month long, three-way tug-of-war between the lawyer Sánchez, a long-suffering royal notary named Velásquez, and *capitán* Cuadrado.

Once *capitán* Cuadrado realized this case faced an appeal and review by the Real Audiencia de Santafé, he pulled all the records from the archives to organize them more to his favor. He also added to the file a local ordinance dating from 1570 that dealt harshly with runaway slaves to show that he had shown greater mercy to the slaves than what was prescribed by the law. He failed to note that neither the king nor the Council of Indies had ever approved that same local ordinance. At the same time, Sánchez, the slaves' advocate, continued to badger Velásquez to give him the case files. Velásquez responded to Sánchez with exasperation, informing him this was not possible since *capitán* Cuadrado had taken the records so that legal advisors associated with the Santa Hermandad could review them.[40] Eventually, Sánchez had to write to the Audiencia to register two formal *requerimientos* (orders) demanding the documents. Finally, in November 1644, under threat from the oidores of the Audiencia in Santafé de Bogota, *capitán* Cuadrado returned the files to Velásquez so he could copy them and give a set to Sánchez.

Based on the material, Sánchez prepared an appeal to the Real Audiencia de Santafé de Bogota not on the actual sentence but on Cuadrado's procedural errors. Appealing on procedural grounds obviated the strongest part of the defense presented by *capitán* Cuadrado, whose declarations emphasized the fact that the three captured slaves were confessed cimarrones, and that their sentence was lenient when compared to established law (figure 4.1).[41]

Because this case involved a review of the official conduct of an alcalde provincial of the Santa Hermandad, a group of three different oidores (instead of the usual one) examined Cuadrado's process. Sánchez presented the appeal in a public hearing in Bogota in April 1645, and in May of the same year the Audiencia judges began reviewing the case, considering the capture, initial interrogation, witness statements, and the mass of declarations and counter declarations the file contained.[42] On February 7, 1646, they handed down a stinging rebuke, nullifying the entire sentence pronounced against Trejo Atienza's slaves and ordering that the Santa Hermandad return the fine of sixty gold pesos. They also released Juan, Francisco, and Antonio from jail into Trejo Atienza's custody.

As seen in the other cases discussed in this book, the Real Audiencia regularly

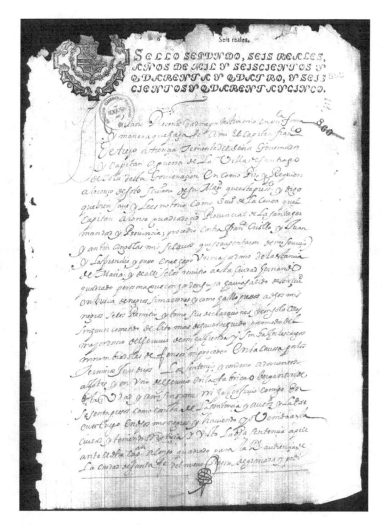

Figure 4.1. Page of imperial stamped paper containing part of the defense of three enslaved men, Francisco Criollo, Juan, and Antonio Angola, by their owner, Captain Francisco Trejo Atienza, 1645. From Fondo: Colonia. Grupo: Negros y esclavos de Bolívar, Legajo 9, Documento 13, Folios 898r, Archivo General de la Nación, Bogota.

modified and adjusted the sentences given by lower officials. However, in this case, they clearly set out to make an example of *capitán* Cuadrado. Not only did they annul the sentence he had given but they also declared it an *atentado* (gross violation) of royal law, ordering him to pay a fine of fifty *patacones* (silver coins) from his own funds. They also admonished him to observe legal procedure more strictly in the future, declaring that, to ensure this, an *asesor letrado* (expert jurist) would supervise all of his sentences and that he had to send a report to the Audiencia in Bogota for each case he handled.

Capitán Cuadrado tried to delay and otherwise thwart the appeal against him. A less wealthy, influential, and informed slave owner faced with these obstacles might have simply given up. However, Trejo Atienza had wealth, power, and an imperial position. He possessed both the means and the knowledge to frustrate Cuadrado's attempts to block his appeal. Still, while the high costs of owning slaves during this period required substantial wealth, it did not mean that only slaves of the rich could count on the protection of the courts. The archives offer many cases in which poorer, less prestigious slave owners successfully used the courts to gain redress against those who could be considered their social and economic superiors.[43]

Trejo Atienza's appeal resulted in the exemplary disciplining of a local official who deviated from proper procedure. Not only was he disciplined, capitán Cuadrado also had to endure extra supervision going forward. Future defendants would benefit from this precedent, enjoying increased protection from Cuadrado's missteps. Wealthy subjects like Trejo Atienza jealously guarded their rights within the system, policing it to their advantage and to the benefit of all users.[44]

SWORDS UNCOVERED

On the night of November 17, 1622, residents living near Cartagena's Playa de la Ciénega awoke to shouts, curses, and the clamor of *espadas desnudas* (bare swords). Local resident *alférez* Rodrigo de Zárate, a lieutenant in the Spanish army, went to investigate. Outside he saw two young men, García Mulato and Juan Criollo, swords in hand, running up the street cursing up a storm; to add insult to injury, Juan was completely naked. Rodrigo de Zárate confronted the young men, yelling, "You cannot be here! You will be sent to work in the galleys for acting so scandalously and carrying weapons!" Juan and García reacted with a stream of insults and curses. Brandishing his sword, Juan challenged him: "You and how many others will take us to the galleys?" and chased Zárate back into his house.[45]

The next day, Zárate went to Benito Maldonado Millán, alcalde ordinario of Cartagena, and in high dudgeon denounced the young men. Maldonado questioned Zárate and was convinced to open a formal case. He took testimony from the free *morena* María Sánchez who lived down the street and from Zárate's creole enslaved woman Dominga. Both women testified that on the night of November 17 they saw a group of blacks fighting, two of whom threatened Zárate before running off. They had been frightened and subsequently accused Juan Criollo and García Mulato of being *pendencieros* (troublemakers).[46]

On November 26, royal notary Francisco Pachecho accompanied members of the city guard in searching "through all the streets and street corners, and it being very late at night, the wanted *negro* was found, and he was walking with a mulato that ran away, and the negro was captured and he had in his possession a cape and a sword."[47] Maldonado Millán assigned Juan Criollo an advocate named Pedro de Quintanilla and notified his owner of the legal proceedings.[48] Juan Criollo belonged to Juan de Salinas, who ran a *pulperia* (small retail store that usually sold alcohol) located in the front part of his home.

In late December 1622, Quintanilla interviewed Criollo and presented a memorial to the alcalde Benito Maldonado Millán, asking that his client be absolved and freed. The petition explained that, at the time of the crime, Juan was at the home of his master. Quintanilla also stated that, while many witnesses saw a fight during the night of November 17, they did not witness Juan Criollo's participation. According to Quintanilla, Juan de Salinas habitually forgot his sword and *broqueles* (small shield) in various parts of the city while out drinking and that night had sent Juan Criollo out to retrieve them. He argued that if Juan Criollo had in fact carried weapons on the night of the fight, it was because he was recovering his master's weapons and did not prove that Criollo had taken part in any kind of *pendencia* (public disturbance). Quintanilla also argued for the dismissal of the charges relating to the supposed insults and *palabras desvergonzadas* (shameless words), because Zárate's accusation did not specify Juan Criollo's actual words.

In response to Millán's emphasis on pendencia, defense attorney Quintanilla focused on mitigating the crime by bringing forward character witnesses. One slave, two residents, and another vecino of Cartagena testified in favor of Juan Criollo. Their collective testimony confirmed what had been stated already by one of Juan's workmates: Criollo was described as a "humble and obedient black, a good worker and not troublesome."[49] Witnesses also testified that during the night in question they had each seen Juan either at home or looking for his master to give him his weapons. However, several of the witnesses also stated for the record that they had warned Criollo that carrying weapons in public was going to get him thrown in prison or sent to the galleys. These statements complicated matters for the defense.

Echoing previous cases, the defense focused on creating doubts about the night in question while portraying Juan Criollo as an obedient, hard-working subject. Unfortunately, it was not enough; the evidence against him was too strong. Even defense witnesses had confirmed some of the accusations. On December 7, alcalde Maldonado Millán sentenced Juan to be paraded naked through the streets on the back of a mule, with his wrists and feet bound and a rope around his neck, after which he would receive two hundred lashes in the main plaza. He also sentenced him to exile from the city for six years. While a harsh sentence, it was well within the bounds of the law considering the seriousness of Juan's crime.[50]

Understandably, neither of the two Juans accepted the humiliation, lashings, and six-year banishment from the city. While the lashing and humiliation were problematic considering the affection Salinas professed for his slave and their close working relationship, exile was the more alarming punishment. To obey the sentence, he would likely have to sell Juan, thereby losing a trained business partner.

Moreover, considering the punishment Juan Criollo would receive and the damage to his reputation, Juan de Salinas could expect a substantial loss when selling him.

Accordingly, Salinas and Criollo told Pedro de Quintanilla to appeal the sentence to the highest authority in the city, Lieutenant Governor of Cartagena Fernando de Sarria. However, de Sarria was even less sympathetic to their case. On December 15, he reaffirmed the full sentence and added further punishments for good measure. The revised sentence decreed that, before Juan's exile from the city, he should spend eight years with a chain around his leg serving the crown: four years in the workshops of the convent of Our Lady of Mercy followed by four more years in the galleys. Furthermore, in a nod to Criollo's business reputation he specified Juan receive no salary for his work.[51]

This was bad for Juan de Salinas, as the sentence meant the practical confiscation of his slave. For the next eight years Juan Criollo would work for free for the church and the military. To continue to operate his business, Salinas would have to purchase another slave. A young and healthy bozal, newly arrived from Africa, required an investment of around 350 pesos. However, Juan Criollo was a well-trained socialized slave, and as such could command at least 500 pesos, the cost of a small house on the outskirts of town,[52] in the markets of Cartagena and much more inland.[53]

For Criollo, the sentence was catastrophic. Skilled and trusted, he had negotiated a favorable deal with his owner, developed a network of patrons he worked for, and built a strong social network in the community. Leaving aside the humiliation and brutality of two hundred lashes, forced labor and exile would rip him out of his social and economic networks.

Clutching at straws, they were left with a final hope—the Real Audiencia de Santafé de Bogota. The tribunal received the case in February 1623 and indicated the oidores would have a judgment ready in four months. During this period, the local authorities, having already twice confirmed the sentence's validity, paraded and whipped Juan Criollo. He may have felt some relief from the pain of this beating when he received news that the Real Audiencia had reduced his sentence. On May 11, 1623, the oidores reconfirmed the lashes he had already received but invalidated the rest of his sentence.

The Real Audiencia, far removed from the local passions and circumstances surrounding Juan's transgressions, sought to maintain public order but knew that excessive harshness could be counterproductive to the wider objectives of imperial development. Here once again, the Audiencia performed one of its roles—that of moderator. By ensuring that excess on both sides was checked, the royal judges maintained a balance that encouraged and legitimized participation in and obedience to the legal system.

OWNERS IN THE DOCK

Enslaved Afroiberians could be victims but also perpetrators of criminal offences.

The conflict between Isabel Criolla and Eufrasia Camargo, examined in detail subsequently, provides a window into how the Spanish legal ecology dealt with infamously cruel and abusive owners. Unlike most of the surviving cases found in the archives involving abuse, the secular authorities opened this case as a direct response to complaints from enslaved workers regarding their abusive owner.[54] This case does not arise out of a conflict between two different slave owners,[55] nor does it represent the efforts of enslaved people to engage the protections of the church, such as defending their right to marriage.[56]

On April 4, 1639, Gregorio Álvarez de Cepeda, the recently elected alcalde of the Santa Hermandad for the city of Mompós, set out into the borderlands of the Province of Cartagena hunting palenques. His mission was to destroy the palenques, return the cimarrones to their owners, and dissuade others from running away from their masters.[57] Gregorio and his men attacked two different settlements, captured over twenty-five people, and transported them back to Mompós for processing. Perennially worried about "increasing" runaways, members of the Mompós cabildo and Santa Hermandad interrogated the prisoners to determine the causes of the escapes and find possible solutions.[58]

The resulting declarations generally drew on a spectrum of accepted flight narratives. The captured cimarrones talked about being sold to unrighteous masters, conflicts with overseers, mistreatment by owners, or the desire to remain with partners, friends, or family members. Generally, these were problems that fell below the threshold that would have permitted enslaved people to make an effective complaint at a secular or religious institution. The homogeneity of the slaves' testimony speaks both to the commonality of experiences and the presence of a shared language of justice and mercy that gave weight to resisting unfair dominion. Most of the captives suffered physical punishments on a scale that accounted for the cause and duration of their escape.[59] In addition, their owners were required to pay fines. Local officials also issued a warning to the community that future episodes of *cimarrónaje* would be punished more severely.

However, during the interrogations, four slaves justified their cimarrónaje by alleging extreme abuse. The violence they purportedly suffered was beyond the pale and the authorities moved to investigate their declarations. The investigation focused on Eufrasia Camargo, the wife of Alonso Alvarez Ortíz. Eufrasia and Alonso were rich and powerful Mompós vecinos. Eufrasia owned many slaves in her own name, most of whom labored in the production and sale of cloth for the regional economy. Alonso was a wealthy merchant and a *regidor* (councilman), a member of the municipal council of Mompós. As a prominent Mompós family, together they owned several houses and over twenty slaves.

Accusations of minor cruelty at the hands of overseers and masters were common throughout the Spanish Empire and were usually dealt with by local officials in an informal manner.[60] The testimony of Eufrasia's enslaved workers, however, detailed egregious abuse, mistreatment so terrible it forced them to run away to save their lives. Claiming four people had died from Eufrasia's mistreatment, they illustrated their stories by showing the royal officials wounds and scars they said stemmed from recent torture. Confronted by the compelling verbal and physical evidence, the head of the rural constabulary collected testimonies from residents of Mompós to verify the allegations and remitted the case to the provincial governor, recommending further enquiry. After reading the testimonies of enslaved people and upon the advisement of local officials, the provincial governor, maestro de campo Melchor de Aguilera, ordered a full investigation of Eufrasia's treatment of the enslaved people in her household.[61]

The governor commissioned a local treasury official to inquire around Mompós about Eufrasia and her treatment of enslaved workers. The testimonies he collected further confirmed the allegations: the people of the town described Eufrasia as an inhuman and especially cruel master who regularly beat her slaves, forced them to eat their own excrement, and chained them at night. Two stories stand out. Francisco Ortíz, a long-standing local member of the clergy, testified he had tried to buy Isabel Criolla from Eufrasia to protect her from the bad treatment of her mistress. According to Ortíz, Eufrasia had refused to sell her slave and continued to abuse her. Multiple witnesses confirmed this accusation. A second, often-repeated anecdote described how, after Isabel Criolla had run away and word of her accusations reached Eufrasia, the doña started to regularly beat Isabel's twelve-year-old daughter in retaliation. These examples of cruelty that was sabido y notorio caused repugnance among the vecinos and contributed to their willingness to testify against Eufrasia.[62]

Eufrasia reacted with palpable shock when, instead of returning her property, the governor brought formal charges against her and sequestered her goods and chattels.[63] Wrapping herself in the narrative of righteous dominion, she described herself as an honorable Christian vecina of Mompós and repeatedly trotted out the tropes of Africans as lazy, ungrateful, violent, and dangerous brutes. She described her slaves as lazy and ungrateful and claimed that they had run away because they did not want to work. Not only did she treat them well, she genuinely loved them, and if she ever punished them it was only in response to their bad behavior. She explained that her slaves were chained up at night only to prevent their escape and beaten only moderately, commensurate with both law and custom, and only when they disobeyed her. She also vehemently denied ever forcing any of her slaves to eat excrement or imposing unusual or cruel punishments.[64]

Eufrasia marshaled a number of powerful people to support her claim that she was a good mistress. The testimonies of her well-born witnesses stand in stark contrast to the accounts of enslaved or lower-class witnesses for the prosecution.[65] In the standard historical understanding, testimonies given by elite witnesses should have offered the defendant an insurmountable advantage. However, in this case, a network of enslaved witnesses brought down a well-connected and powerful *vecina*. The judges relied heavily upon information given in slaves' testimonies to make this determination. Enslaved witnesses also played an important part in denouncing Eufrasia's attempts to hide evidence.[66] Because of the Spanish legal ecology and the demography of the Province of Cartagena, this outcome was not uncommon in criminal, civil, and religious cases.[67] The fact that slaves could bear witness and cooperate against social superiors anchored the system of checks and balances countering cruelty and abuse.

On September 15, 1639, five months after the initial raid on the palenque, the governor handed down a ruling in the case against Eufrasia Camargo. The sentence consisted of four parts. First, Eufrasia was fined four hundred pieces of eight as a penalty for the enslaved workers who had died in her house. Second, he ordered the sale of all hostile witnesses and Isabel's twelve-year-old daughter to good masters, with the stipulation that under no circumstances should Eufrasia buy back her slaves in person or through proxies. Third, he ordered local officials to monitor Eufrasia's treatment of her slaves to prevent continued cruelty or unusual punishments on pain of further fines and confiscations. Fourth, the governor ordered Eufrasia to pay all legal and administrative costs incurred by the crown in prosecuting the case against her. The sentence was exemplary but well deserved. The evidence against her was overwhelming. Not only did a broad swathe of local society make a wide range of declarations against her but also the judiciary found several damning pieces of physical evidence in her house, exposed by her victims despite her attempt to dissemble and hide it.[68]

Although enslaved people could testify against cruel owners in legal proceedings, royal officials did not usually take slave testimonies at face value. Nonetheless, this book documents several examples in which slave testimony carried enough legal weight to spark an investigation. Their testimony acquired greater weight in the final judgment as other witnesses or evidence confirmed and corroborated it. For example, physical evidence backed up the claims of abuse made by Eufrasia's slaves, giving their declarations greater power. The case documents repeatedly refer to the marks on the slaves' bodies demonstrating they had been severely beaten. The documents also frequently mention the various torture devices the investigators found in Eufrasia's possession, which she attempted to hide from them.[69]

The heavy preponderance of well-documented evidence necessary for an enslaved accuser to overcome a determined defense by their owner in court reminds us that a caveat is in order at this point in the narrative. It bears repeating that the protections Africans and their descendants could access through the legal ecology were of a lower order than those available to higher-class subjects of the Spanish crown.

An analogy to the American health insurance marketplace is useful here. Impoverished citizens' only alternative is basic policy plans, whose coverage costs little, comes without bells or whistles, and whose quality can fluctuate depending on political exigencies. However, all sectors of society benefit from these baseline structural protections—that is, basic minimum services that keep sick people from spreading diseases and dying on the streets. Elites, on the other hand, have access to luxury plans with much better service and broader ranges of options and perks. Throughout, the framework of the insurance marketplace remains universally important even though the market does not treat all its members equitably. So, too, with the Spanish legal ecology. On the one hand, the protections received by Africans and their descendants in the colonies were of inferior quality to those guaranteed the elites of Spanish America. On the other, those who sought to exclude the working poor from royal justice found a durable truth: taking services and rights away from communities at large and the vulnerable in particular could mobilize them and evoke the ire of the crown.[70]

PROPER RULE?

In the early modern idiom, the king was the theocratic father of his kingdom and people. This was a world where effective governance and what we would understand as religious zealotry were not contradictory. The mandate of heaven, as expressed through the language of good governance, was suffused with religiosity. As such, pious living, the destruction of heresy, effective defense against external enemies, the provision of royal justice, and the maintenance of the king's peace were the interwoven measures of a reign. Political classes forget at their peril that societal hierarchies must be justified by social utility. Law has always been the handmaiden to legitimacy. However, law without the institutions of rule is impotent. For laws and the institutions charged with implementing them to function, they need not only resources but also an ideological justification that resonates with the society in which they are embedded.[71]

Scholars of European history have argued that between the fourteenth and seventeenth centuries there was a military and bureaucratic "revolution," epitomized in the fiscal military state of the Dutch East India Company.[72] Similar narratives about the development of the fiscal military state in China during the Warring States period and Carthage before and during the Punic wars call into question the uniqueness of the Dutch East India Company.. Nonetheless, during the late medieval period the Holy Roman Empire, France, England, the Dutch, the Italian states, the Iberian kingdoms, and, eventually, the Ottomans danced to the ruinously costly tune of early modern wars. The exigencies of war led to innovations in state capacity and military technology.

Emblematic of this greater complexity were the exquisitely trained, massed English archers deployed so devastatingly at Agincourt by Henry V in 1415. The English state's ability to deliver large numbers of well-trained fighters across the channel allowed them, and their Iberian allies, to several times conquer great swathes of

France, the greatest nation in Christendom. Nonetheless, and despite strenuous efforts and some successes, the conquerors remained largely illegitimate in the eyes of the French and were eventually pushed out.

As the centuries of war ground on, successful leaders like Henry V and Isabel of Castile understood and adapted systems of thought along with military formations. With every turn of the wheel of innovation, it became brutally obvious that without legitimate governance and effective leadership no amount of money or military superiority was sufficient to achieve a durable victory. In contrast, legitimacy and good governance in the idiom of the people who are being ruled are essential for any political regime to have durability.[73]

In the optimistically named Age of Exploration (the first semipiratical global scramble), durable leadership and its concomitant rewards came to those groups that effectively balanced institutional capacity and ideological buy-in.[74] All complex states succeed inasmuch as they effectively balance the changing mix of popular support and violence necessary to generate the long-term cooperation necessary for the legal ecology to function. This mix lies on a spectrum where the obedience produced by violence can substitute for that of popular support (and vice versa) up to extremes illustrated by plantation colonies at the height of Atlantic slavery on one hand and the Nordic countries of today on the other.

All these threads came together when, in the face of the exponential rise in the cost of war, Spanish monarchs expanded the traditional expediency of selling offices. This tactic was clearly detrimental to good governance because politicians who had purchased their offices tended to prioritize recouping their investment over serving impartially. Critics in that era, echoed by modern scholars today, denounced this conflict of interest from the twelfth century onwards.[75] However, if we examine the sale of offices through an imperial lens, the sale of offices addresses not only the monarchy's fiscal exigencies, but also provides a mechanism through which royal authority can referee between different groups of powerful creole elites while at the same time extracting from them resources necessary for the maintenance of empire.

In Cartagena, the balancing factor between greed and good governance was the crown's need for legitimacy. For the Spanish Crown, maintaining a strong connection with the indigenous and the enslaved populations through the provision of royal justice was an essential counterbalance to the power of creole elites in the overseas kingdoms. Some scholars posit that the treatment of slaves in the New Kingdom of Granada focused on punishment to ensure compliance with an exploitative system that victimized them and provided no value.[76] This assessment is correct up to a point but incomplete. If governance and the law were not crucial, contemporaries would not have invested such enormous resources in controlling and affecting their course.

CONCLUSION

Shifting between the imperial and local levels of the Spanish Empire's legal ecology, we see that, despite many weaknesses, there were constant, structural incentives to deliver good justice. Despite struggles to reconcile the competing goals of the law, the case originating from the terrible abuse by Eufrasia Camargo shows royal officials who understood that, while punishing runaways helped enforce the law, as people they also required a minimum of protection to provide positive incentives for their cooperation.[77] People like Isabel Criolla were well aware that the law and social custom both gave and limited owners' ability to exploit and abuse their slaves. The majority of those captured by Spanish officials in the raid that sparked this case received harsh punishments; a minority that had suffered cruel and inhuman treatment from their owners received protection. Every subject within the empire was under the protection of the king's justice, which, though imperfectly enforced, explicitly included enslaved people. Eufrasia's exemplary punishment was as important for the maintenance of the emergent and motile social contract as the punishment applied to the cimarrones.

The ingenuity, tenacity, and bravery with which Africans and their descendants leveraged the legal ecology in their favor further contradicts the hypothesis that Spanish law was inconsequential to protecting the lives and rights of enslaved subjects.[78] Africans and their descendants faced risks, broke laws, disturbed the peace, and challenged the social order. In the records they show a keen understanding of their rights and responsibilities as residents and subjects of the Spanish Empire. Opportunity and knowledge created a matrix of pathways that they navigated to their benefit.

The strength and durability of the legal ecology depended on both its documentary depth and institutional and human interconnectedness. Each case in this chapter was affected in some way by the checks and balances built into the structure of the judicial system. However, this does not imply paralysis. Most appealed cases reached a resolution within four to eight months.

Audiencia judges, who in cases of frivolous litigation could make one side pay the legal costs for both parties, enabled this expeditiousness. As shown by the cases of García Mulato and Eufrasia Camargo, supervision of the enslaved population generally remained at the local level.[79] As a result, the largest groups of surviving cases involve serious crimes, because usually only sentences and/or punishments meted out for grave wrongdoings were appealed.

Nonetheless, a relatively large volume of heterogeneous cases survives in the archives of the Spanish Empire. Evidence of the courts' efforts to apply criminal law is compelling. More than 130 years of legal cases show a pattern of basic fairness within the contexts of the times. Furthermore, in most criminal cases against enslaved individuals, there is overwhelming evidence of guilt, meaning that the applied punishments were within the boundaries of justice as contemporaneously understood. The efforts of royal officials to uphold the law contributed to maintaining the social legitimacy of the institutions of Spanish rule. While abuses and cruelty certainly occurred, the system provided at least some protection and mercy for enslaved victims and criminals. Additionally, residents of the province, including both owners and slaves, suffered substantial penalties when prosecuted for crimes against enslaved people.

The acknowledged limitations of manpower and resources that constrained the delivery of royal justice were partially balanced by its exemplary nature. The public imprisonment and shaming of Eufrasia was a deliberate choice of admonitory justice. Verdicts at every level were deliberately made public. The sentences reached by the oidores were read on the steps of the Audiencia on an appointed day and reread in the town plaza whence the case originated. The convicted enslaved subjects were also whipped in the town plaza, and the time of their punishment was widely announced to enable spectators to attend.

While not all criminal acts received punishment, the justice system functioned as a signaling mechanism that indicated the boundaries of what were and were not tolerable deviations from imperial and societal norms. These cases show a social consensus, fortified by legal traditions, regarding the appropriate and expected levels of slaves' punishment and discipline. Social and legal checks and balances, many times potentiated by the actions of Africans and their descendants, reinforced this consensus, contributing to the legitimacy of royal justice.

Royal justice bound the Spanish Empire together in the face of internal and external threats.[80] The legal status of enslaved Afroiberians was buttressed by the Spanish Crown's conception of itself as a paternalistic and merciful interlocutor between the imperial elite and the monarch's humbler subjects. Judicial officials preserved social order by the paternalistic guarantee to slaves that (would or could) limit their owners' exploitation of them. Enslaved people, local officials, and other royal subjects who engaged with the judiciary generally appealed to and reinforced these ideas. The audiencia's design as a check on local officials and regional elites further legitimized the overarching judicial system, strengthening the crown's control while providing some protection to enslaved people.

Regardless of their roles—criminals, victims, witnesses—slaves actively engaged the full range of possibilities contained in Spanish customs, laws, and procedures. Without minimizing the formidable disadvantages inherent in their social and legal status, the women and men whose traces are preserved in the sources were far from passive victims in a system designed only to maximize their exploitation. By mastering the script, they strategically fortified Spanish governance to their benefit.

CONCLUSION

From the start, my understanding of slavery has been influenced by the debate surrounding the Tannenbaum hypothesis, wherein he argued that the differences in the laws of Iberoamerica and Angloamerica explained the differences in colonial and postcolonial outcomes. Alejandro de la Fuente reframed this debate, going beyond Tannenbaum's privileging of written law by positing that claims-making by enslaved Afroiberians was essential to triggering enforcement of the law. However, a crucial question remained: "Did slave owners have the institutional ability to define the surrounding social and legal environment according to their most immediate interests or was such capacity mediated, even obstructed, by an intrusive metropolitan government?"[1]

My examination of the role of enslaved people in the legal ecology of the Spanish Empire gets at the heart of this question. During the long seventeenth century, through a broad range of cases involving Africans and their descendants, laws, customs, and institutions checked and mediated the power of local elites. Facing structural exploitation and pervasive discrimination, enslaved Afroiberians under Spanish rule became fully engaged participants in shaping the legal ecology they inhabited. Amplifying their room to maneuver, Cartagena and its administrative hinterland served as a node of defense, commerce, and imperial administration, where different regional and local officials held intentionally mutually supervising jurisdictions.

For Africans and their children in Cartagena, becoming part of the community under royal protection meant they had to negotiate a definition of themselves that was only partially under their own control. In negotiating these trade-offs, enslaved people and those who claimed authority over them experienced the tensions between the human drive to cooperate with others and the equally human desire for control. At the local level, this tension was reflected in the gendered and culturally rooted identities deployed by unfree litigants. At the imperial level, there were consequential continuities in the legitimizing narratives that constrained and empowered the Spanish Empire, narratives which originated in the twelfth century Renaissance and continued through the Enlightenment.[2]

Inclusivity on hierarchical terms provided a space for royal power to position itself as a legitimate, benevolent, and irreplaceable protector of the crown's subjects. The archival evidence of mistreatment is often used as proof of the master class's untrammeled power and cruelty. However, it behooves us to ask why that evidence even exists. It is *because* Spanish authorities sometimes penalized cruelty toward the enslaved population that there is such abundant evidence of that cruelty in the archives.[3] Did this intervention provide full protection? Absolutely not, but to understand the experiences of enslaved Africans in the Spanish Empire, we have to engage the empire on its own terms.

Understanding the governing mindset characteristic of the leadership of the Spanish Empire in the long seventeenth century requires that we keep in mind the hard lessons learned by Christendom in the millennium after the fall of the western Roman Empire. This period was marked by an almost universal commitment to political stability and continuity among the leadership of Christendom, contextualized by a pervasively disordered and unstable political landscape. Respect for precedent was understood as a source of strength rather than as a limitation.[4] The stability and continuity of the western European legal ecology were neither rigidity nor stagnation. However, change was not pursued for its own sake. This was not the Enlightenment; hierarchy and tradition held comfortable legitimacy.[5]

The slow, incremental change favored by medieval European societies was tested by the chaos of the fourteenth century and by the accelerating pace of collective learning facilitated by the Age of Exploration. Systems that formed to slow and reverse the atomization of the post-Roman world were forced to adapt or succumb to ruin. In the Caribbean basin, the close proximity of European powers led to a Darwinian competition that spurred the development of economy, technology, and ideology, reaching an apotheosis of exploitation in the mature Atlantic slave trade.[6]

Globalization, amplified by printing, represented an information bonanza that put pressure on medieval identities. Compounding this for the Spanish, the tropical areas of the Americas contained an inestimable variety of indigenous groups. To this mélange they introduced Africans, with all their complexity, and Europeans drawn from across Christendom (figure C.1). Conquest, exploitation, miscegenation, recurrent catastrophic pandemics, and the resettlement of the survivors thereof in European-style towns further scrambled identities. The Caribbean basin, in particular, became a diverse and fluid region. Borders between empires, races, and classes were strenuously built up and maintained, and just as strenuously resisted, deconstructed, and subverted.

In the Caribbean, the epicenter of the indigenous demographic catastrophe, Africans and their descendants quickly became the majority of the population. As divided and inchoate as African American communities were, their attitudes toward the various Atlantic empires were a significant variable in imperial competition. Because slavery is a brutal system that is explicitly organized to extract unrecompensed labor from people through violence, it tends to provoke violent resistance

Figure C.1. Modern mixed-race Madonna and Child in Cartagena, 2011. Ricardo Raúl Salazar Rey.

from its victims. Effective leaders in all European empires were aware that the most dangerous elements in any conflict are young men who have lost hope in whatever system contains them. Furthermore, young men are frequently the most extreme elements in these conflicts, and in sufficient numbers they have the power to force everyone to operate on their level of brutality. This demographic group was over-represented in the transatlantic slave trade, for which the base unit of value was a *pieza de Indias*, defined as a healthy young man.[7]

From the sixteenth century onward, the Spanish Empire attempted to incorporate into itself hundreds of thousands of radicalization-prone would-be insurrectionists, even as Spain's rivals clamored to arm them. The success of those integration policies cannot be easily measured; however, a sense of their effectiveness can be gleaned from royal officials' use of temporary exile as a punishment for some enslaved convicts, as occurred in the case of Domingo Angola after he attacked Lorenzo Domínguez.[8]

Regardless of the morality of Iberian intentions, the paucity of metropolitan hard power made it essential for the Spanish Crown to divide, coopt, and arbitrate between its subjects in order to rule. Soft power, embodied in royal justice, was at the core of the legitimacy of royal authority among its Amerindian, European, and African subjects and their descendants. The "first mover" advantage that accrued to Spain in the Americas meant that rival polities could only capture and hold Iberoamerican territory through substantial defections from the local population. Awareness of this dynamic is reflected in the early charters of British mainland colonies, which proclaimed freedom for indigenes and slaves held in bondage by the Spanish who rebelled and joined them.

Counteracting their enemies' efforts and propaganda, Spanish monarchs presented themselves as just rulers defending the weak and protecting their subjects' property. Maintaining this image required a moral balancing act by royal agents charged with reconciling the conflicting interests of those who *had* property and those who *were* property.[9] Imperial authorities self-consciously understood their need to foster enough legitimacy so that when the days of reckoning came (as with the Dutch invasions of Brazil) enough of the population preferred to hold the empire together, rendering enemy invasion futile.[10]

With the growth of the slave-powered plantation complex in the contested lands at the edges of empire, economic integration and peripheralization occurred symbiotically with the racialization of colonial societies.[11] In this frame, race was a tool forged to serve the needs of European imperialism and its application was thoroughly profitable, exemplified by the self-interested permeation of racialized language throughout the legal ecology as in the Copete case.[12] The records from Cartagena complicate, and in some cases contradict, widely held assumptions about the solidity and pervasiveness of racial categories in colonial America. For the first century after 1492, physical location, work regime, and the level of socialization and an enslaved person's understanding of societal and legal norms generally affected the treatment he or she received more than what we today understand as race. Despite the illusion of permanence provided by its current social acceptance, it was difficult for early modern, mixed "race" empires to invest the energy needed to create enough of a social consensus for racial categories to be incorporated into their legal codes.

Frontline Spanish imperial functionaries generally opposed the racialization of social relations, faced as they were with the sustained opposition from those who would be disenfranchised and further exploited by the coagulation of a racialized society. As in the case of the death of Isabel Bran in chapter 3, the heterogeneity of witnesses called by plaintiffs, defendants, and royal officials largely reflected the makeup of the population, not the racial preferences of elite actors. Secular and ecclesiastical officials showed little detectable racial bias when evaluating the

testimony of Africans and their descendants. Despite attempts by elites like the Co-
petes to use race as a judicial cudgel, officials tended to follow procedure in adjudicating cases and generally heeded sentencing guidelines and local precedent in
assigning punishment. The ubiquity of the legal ecology in the Iberoamerican community's cultural imagination is reflected in the sophistication with which enslaved
subjects engaged with the law.[13]

This can be seen by returning to the case that opened this book. When we left
María Josefa and Lorenza Elena, they had managed to face down Francisco Copete
Jr.'s initial petition to have them declared his property, leading the judge to require
further evidence if the case was to proceed. As both sides gathered additional evidence, the sisters showed their legal acumen by delaying and obstructing the proceedings. In response, Francisco repeatedly petitioned to have them jailed. The alcalde handling the case did not grant Francisco's petition, but he did use the threat
of prison to encourage cooperation, move the case along, and prevent the sisters
from fleeing the city. María Josefa and Lorenza Elena riposted, negotiated with the
court, and obtained commitments of social and monetary capital from their social
network as surety for their freedom.

Despite all the efforts of María Josefa Copete, Lorenza Elena, and their allies to
delay and block the case from going forward, in April 1708 the lower court ren-
dered its judgment. In a catastrophe for the sisters and their children, alcalde ordinario Juan de Berrio ruled that they were rightfully Francisco and Juana María de
Copete's property.[14] They urgently requested an appeal but were blocked by Francisco's lawyer. Ratcheting up the pressure, he petitioned for them to be handed
over to him or to be jailed. At this critical juncture, María Josefa and Lorenza Elena
found a *letrado* (expert jurist) who worked as a *consultor* for the Inquisition but was
willing to evaluate their case. After another round of furious back-and-forth petitions the licenciado Francisco José de Madrigal Valdés gave a legal opinion that favored the sisters' right to appeal their case to the Audiencia de Santafé.[15] With an
almost audible sigh of relief the lower court judge Juan de Berrio accepted this and
allowed the appeal to proceed. To the great frustration of Francisco, appealing kept
María Josefa Copete and Lorenza Elena out of his clutches and out of jail.

Throughout, the conscious contest in which María Josefa Copete, parda, and
Lorenza, morena criolla, engaged for control of their racial and cultural descrip-
tors disrupts the pernicious idea of timeless race-based slavery and shows the importance and malleability of identity as a sign of acculturation and belonging. The
apparently slight, but fiercely contested, difference between "morena criolla" and
"negra" or "parda" and "mulata" gives us some idea of the importance of controlling
how race became part of common parlance. While our understanding of how slavery and race became intertwined is still incomplete, the multivalent meaning of
race is a central feature of early-modern Atlantic slavery, unlike its medieval an-
tecedents.[16] Indeed, it is during the long seventeenth century that modern racial

categories were broadly conceptualized and inhabited. Building on this intellectual groundwork after the War of Spanish Succession, the exploitation of the enslaved population in the Americas became increasingly racialized and violent, yielding ludicrous profits.

In the early Spanish Empire, royal and ecclesiastical officials taught enslaved Afroiberians the moral justification for their enslavement and the paths to manumission. They exhorted enslaved people to marry within the church and proclaimed that the liberation of exemplary captives would be pleasing to God, with little danger to royal authority. Manumission, in fact, strengthened the system by providing aspirational examples for other slaves, and marriage anchored captives in towns surrounded by an easily accessible frontier territory. In contrast, in the British island possessions that came to rely on plantation chattel slavery, for slaves to understand the economic and social system in which they lived increasingly represented an existential threat to the institution of slavery. Regional authorities in the British colonies viewed manumission as a problematic mechanism from the start; this perception hardened with the racialization of slavery. Responding to this, British colonial courts and legislatures increasingly defined black people as inhuman without rights under the law and erected barriers to manumission.[17] Parsing the experiences of enslaved people within different polities provides us with a deeper understanding of how European empires functioned, competed, and endured.[18]

Grasping the history of racial slavery is slippery; its broad extent begets a language of shared responsibility, and yet its specific inequality cries out for focused redress. We cannot move past the legacy of racialized slavery until we understand it.[19] This work is not concerned directly with race except in as much as it intrudes and complicates the legal ecology of Spanish America explored here. At the same time, even the most cursory examination of the creation of "race" and its coupling with the legal status of slavery shows that far from being a settled category as Aristotle philosophized, it was a messy and fiercely contested process.[20] As Alan Watson explains, ancient and medieval slavery largely did not depend on what now would be understood as a person's race.[21] The weight given to cultural versus phenotypical cues in making people enslavable changed during the long seventeenth century, with far-reaching consequences.[22] However, the clear racial and cultural divisions that we project backward onto the sixteenth and seventeenth centuries are largely artifacts of our desire to impose familiar labels on unfamiliar times.[23]

Scholars such as Bianca Premo provide a corrective to the tendency to overemphasize the core over the periphery in understanding empire. Her monograph *The Enlightenment on Trial* is set in a polycentric Atlantic, where the periphery has as much of an effect on the center as vice versa.[24] This matches what I have found in the records: "race," pushed by rent-seeking local elites, suffused practice, custom, and then, finally, entered the language of law with only the reluctant acceptance of metropolitan authorities.[25]

As the *Derecho Indiano* (the body of law regulating the overseas possessions of Spain) developed, Iberian jurists generally attempted to keep the legislative program regulating slavery grounded in the *Siete Partidas*.[26] This makes sense if we consider the operational rigidity of the legal ecology that bound the empire together. Changes to the rules of the game in holdings as vast and complex as those possessed by the Hapsburgs were self-limiting. The militarized, capital-intensive, and racialized slavery upon which the protoindustrial production of tropical commodities came to depend required a more robust and repressive state apparatus than the Spanish Empire possessed during the long seventeenth century.[27]

If there were a tipping point as race moved from being a part of the cultural imaginary toward its current hegemonic status, perhaps it was the discontinuity between medieval law codes and European colonial legislation.[28] For the Iberian, French, and British Empires the emergence of racialized chattel slavery led to dissonances between medieval law codes and colonial needs. In response, compilation codes like the Spanish *Recopilación de Leyes de las Indias* (1681) and the French *Code Noir* (1685) referenced precedent while innovating ties between race and servitude. The English state, wracked by civil war and then revolution (glorious and otherwise), proved unable to achieve consensus on regulations for slavery at an imperial level, leading to de facto delegation of this authority to regional legislatures and local microcosms.[29]

The dispensation of justice has always been seen as a crucial attribute of sovereignty, because it defines where and how the ruler can intervene in the lives of his subjects.[30] The Spanish Empire was expected to maintain order and provide retributive justice to those it governed. Therefore, despite the growing importance of African slavery to regional elites, they were not permitted either to independently write their own laws and regulations or directly appoint and instruct royal officials charged with applying the same.[31] Simultaneously, enslaved Afroiberians, freedpeople, and their descendants faced creeping oppression and exploitation from local elites, which they resisted, both collectively and individually. Established Afroiberian communities came to understand the necessity of collectively rejecting attempts to deprive them of legal standing or to infringe on their customary rights. Concurrently and interdependently, sabotage, conspiracy, self-harm, arson, murder, marronage, and outright rebellion never ceased. Detectable resistance provoked clumsy but unrelenting responses, constant reminders of both state and private violence bounding even "fractional freedoms."

Contextualizing the stick of state-sponsored violence, the carrot of integration and generational social mobility offered Africans, and their descendants, incentives to collaborate in the preservation of the status quo. Assimilation and social mobility, along with violence, ensured the durability of the institution of slavery in the Spanish Empire.[32] In a particularly interesting example of the myriad gradients of integration, Chloe Ireton has uncovered several hundred Afroiberians who received royal licenses to emigrate from Spain to the Indies as Old Christians, bringing needed skills while serving as cultural ambassadors.[33] Social proof that imperial guarantees would be respected was needed at each level of administration for Afroiberians to come forward and undertake risky intercontinental relocations.

The Spanish Empire under the Hapsburgs was a series of violently enforced but largely consensual trust networks, wherein the legal ecology molded relationships between freedpeople, enslaved subjects, slave owners, the law, imperial institutions, and the surrounding socioeconomic environment.[34] Vecinos suing for the annulment of the sale of a mistreated slave publicly committed themselves to a standard of righteous ownership, upholding the law by enforcing it on others. When troublemakers threw themselves on the mercy of the court, they vociferously committed to loyal Christian servitude. When parties in a redhibitoria lawsuit called enslaved witnesses to testify regarding ill treatment, they propagated and reinforced these norms. When owners defended themselves against charges of *sevicia* (cruel and unjustified treatment), professing their righteous mastery, they publicly endorsed the legal and societal underpinnings of Christian slavery. The law, even in the breach, provided a legitimate language of cooperation and mutual participation in society.[35]

In the final analysis, the Spanish Empire, as a global entity, possessed conflicting and mutually limiting motivations, of which its own survival was paramount. The need for social stability and dependable revenue sources demanded that Spanish law, mediated through imperial institutions, encourage Africans and their descendants to enmesh themselves into Iberoamerican society and pay their taxes. The need for inclusivity was reflected in a conception of social order that provided legitimate pathways for Africans to become assimilated Christians, subjects of the empire, and even vecinos of their towns. What I have described in no way excuses or minimizes people's morally indefensible (by the standards of the time)[36] participation in the institution of slavery. There is no simple narrative that can encompass the chimeric intersection of empire, race, and gender that enabled early modern Atlantic slavery.[37]

From Thomas Aquinas to Alonso de Sandoval, the Asiento through the Navigation Acts, Western philosophy and governance has been concerned with the construction, intellectual substantiation, and profiting from human differences. The rise and lingering death of racialized slavery is embedded in the global negotiations over terminology that began with the Age of Exploration.[38] One of the facets of these negotiations is reflected in the tenacity with which enslaved people worked to define themselves as righteous Christians or sought to control their names and social-racial identifiers. The emotional importance of these details and their real-life consequences in seventeenth century Iberoamerican society are hard for us to scan from this distance. However, the cases analyzed herein act like ice cores preserving delicate traces of the everyday strategies Afroiberians used to shape their identities.

A close reading of the documentation left behind by the four years of legal guer-
rilla warfare waged by the daughters of Juana de la Rosa shows how their self-
conception evolved. Toward the end of the file "María Josefa parda libre" dropped
the Copete surname she had so determinedly used at the beginning. She and "Lorenza Elena criolla libre" stopped calling themselves "residents of this town" and
began to identify themselves as "vecinas of this city" and were recorded as such
by royal officials. For a species as hypersensitive to identity politics as ours, their
names and identifiers affirmed their membership in their society and humanity. The
sisters, their community, some royal officials, and countless others of every status
resisted the spread of racialized chattel slavery, a system that depended on terror to
impose a broadly illegitimate regime.[39]

In their petition (prepared without an advocate) rejecting the ruling enslaving
them and arguing (successfully) that they be allowed to appeal their case to the Real
Audiencia in Santa Fe de Bogota, María Josefa and Lorenza Elena were in full command of both the form and the substance of their cause. Addressing lieutenant general José de Madrigal, "we ask your honor that we not be despoiled of our freedom,
in which we have been in possession for more than ten years." After crisply explaining the errors in Francisco's arguments, they write, "speaking with all due respect,
this (the judgment in favor of Francisco) contains nullities (an act that is legally
void) that have already been recognized, therefore your honor should amend your
writ, and order that the case file be returned to us *in integrum*, in the state in which
the case was when Alfonso de Guzmán (their last advocate) ceased to defend us."
Mastering the script provided them a medium through which they could defend
and define themselves. But effective as their defense was, we cannot say whether it
finally prevailed. Frustratingly, the case file is incomplete. It ends as it began, with
María Josefa and Lorenza Elena defending their "freedom which cannot be sold for
however much gold there is in the world."[40]

NOTES

Introduction

1. I date the long seventeenth century as having started in 1580 when, through the Union of Crowns, the Spanish and Portuguese empires came under the rule of Philip II, allowing for a sustained surge in the numbers of Africans forcibly transported from the Portuguese factories in Africa to the depopulated areas of the Americas. The era ended as the War of Spanish Succession (1700–1715) put an end to Hapsburg rule in the Americas. This conflict represented an inflection point after which a threshold was crossed, leading to an explosion in the volume of the Atlantic and inter-American slave trade.

2. Samuel Y. Edgerton, *Theaters of Conversion: Religious Architecture and Indian Artisans in Colonial Mexico* (Albuquerque: University of New Mexico Press, 2001); Gordon K. Lewis, *Main Currents in Caribbean Thought: The Historical Evolution of Caribbean Society in Its Ideological Aspects, 1492–1900* (Lincoln: University of Nebraska Press, 2004).

3. The standards of probity and wisdom aspired to by the people who made up imperial institutions and their many failings to live up to these standards are mercilessly depicted in early modern Iberian popular satire. See William Stanley Merwin, trans., *The Life of Lazarillo de Tormes: His Fortunes and Adversities* (New York: New York Review Books, 2005), 28.

4. Francisco Copete Jr. y Juan Ojeda, su cuñado; en pleito con María Josefa Copete y Lorenza Elena, esclavas que fueron de Manuela de Leiva, difunta, madre y suegra de ellos, respectivamente, las cuales habían pasado a la condición de libres, 1709. Fondo: Colonia. Grupo: Negros y esclavos de Bolívar, Legajo 2, Documento 1, Folios 1r–200v, Archivo General de la Nación (AGN), Bogota. Hereafter cited as Francisco Copete Jr. vs. María Josefa Copete y Lorenza Elena. The online catalogue of the AGN incorrectly lists the case under the Panama section. Despite herculean efforts by the staff of the archives, sometimes the digital and analogue catalogues can be uncertain in their classifications. I have attempted to present the most accurate information possible. Any mistakes are mine.

5. Francisco Copete Jr. vs. María Josefa Copete y Lorenza Elena, Folio 6r. All translations are mine except for the epigraph, translated by Mario Salazar Moran.

6. Francisco Copete Jr. vs. María Josefa Copete y Lorenza Elena, Folio 21v.

7. For our purposes, slavery is a legal condition—nothing more, nothing less. To accept anything else is to play into the hands of those for whom race is anything more than a social construct. So, then, for the purposes of this book, I will define a "slave" as a person who is owned by another person. As the ambiguous case that opens this book shows, proving you own someone can be a complex endeavor.

8. The need for popular and elite legitimacy created spaces where loyal opposition to imperial policy could be expressed. See Fray Francisco José de Jaca, *Resolución sobre la libertad de los negros y sus originarios, en estado de paganos y después ya cristianos: La primera condena de la esclavitud en el pensamiento hispano*, ed. Miguel Anxo Pena González (1645; repr., Madrid: CSIC, 2002).

9. Ann Swidler, "Culture in Action: Symbols and Strategies," *American Sociological Review* 51, no. 2 (1986): 273–86.

10. The early and continuous imperial competition is well illustrated by the story of Anthony Knivet in *The Admirable Adventures and Strange Fortunes of Master Anthony Knivet: An English Pirate in Sixteenth-Century Brazil*, ed. Vivien Kogut Lessa de Sá (New York: Cambridge University Press, 2015). See also Peter Linebaugh and Marcus Buford Rediker, *The Many-Headed Hydra: Sailors, Slaves, Commoners, and the Hidden History of the Revolutionary Atlantic* (Boston: Beacon Press, 2000).

11. Guillermo C. Barragán, *La obra legislativa de Alfonso el Sabio: Ensayo sobre su formación, promulgación, y transcendencia americana* (Buenos Aires: Abeledo-Perrot, 1983).

12. Francisco Copete Jr. vs. María Josefa Copete y Lorenza Elena, Folio 108r.

13. Francisco Copete Jr. vs. María Josefa Copete y Lorenza Elena, Folios 131r–v.

14. Frustratingly, nobody ever presented María Josefa Copete's birth certificate or explained what happened to it, even though her sister's birth certificate was found and presented as a key piece of evidence.

15. Francisco Copete Jr. vs. María Josefa Copete y Lorenza Elena, Folio 6r.

16. Francisco Copete Jr. vs. María Josefa Copete y Lorenza Elena, Folio 47r. A firsthand description of the destructive raid can be found in Jean-Bernard-Louis Desjean, baron de Pointis, *Monsieur de Pointi's expedition to Cartagena: Being a particular relation, I. Of the taking and plundering of that city, by the French, in the year 1697, II. Of their meeting with Admiral Nevil in their return, and the course they steer'd to get clear of him, III. Of their passing by Commadore Norris, at Newfound-Land, IV. Of their encounter with Capt. Harlow, at their going to Brest* (London: S. Buckley and A. Feltham, 1699).

17. Francisco Copete Jr. vs. María Josefa Copete y Lorenza Elena, Folios 170r–74v.

18. For a discussion of the importance of paper technology to Atlantic slavery, see Rebecca J. Scott and Jean M. Hébrard, *Freedom Papers: An Atlantic Odyssey in the Age of Emancipation* (Cambridge, MA: Harvard University Press, 2014), 3. See also Deborah Jenson, *Beyond the Slave Narrative: Politics, Sex, and Manuscripts in the Haitian Revolution* (Liverpool: Liverpool University Press, 2011) and Randolph Starn, "Truths in the Archives," *Common Knowledge* 8, no. 2 (2002): 387–401.

19. The whole discussion is essential reading. Judith Scheele et al., "Priorities of Law: A Conversation with Judith Scheele, Daniel Lord Smail, Bianca Premo, and Bhavani Raman," *Comparative Studies in Society and History*, January 8, 2018, https://cssh.lsa.umich.edu/2018/01/08/priorities-of-law/.

20. See the introduction in David Wheat, *Atlantic Africa and the Spanish Caribbean, 1570–1640* (Chapel Hill: University of North Carolina Press, 2016). See also Juan Carlos González Hernández, *Influencia del derecho español en América* (Madrid: Editorial MAPFRE, 1992).

21. The echoes in procedure and ideology are undeniable. See Debra Blumenthal, *Enemies and Familiars: Slavery and Mastery in Fifteenth-Century Valencia* (Ithaca: Cornell University Press, 2009).

22. See Gerardo A. Carlo Altieri, *El sistema legal y los litigios de esclavos en Indias: Puerto Rico siglo XIX* (Seville: CSIC, 2010); Patrick James Carroll, *Blacks in Colonial Veracruz: Race, Ethnicity, and Regional Development*, 2nd ed. (Austin: University of Texas Press, 2001).

23. Francisco Copete Jr. vs. María Josefa Copete y Lorenza Elena, Folios 157–59r.

24. See the examples in Solange Alberro and Diana Bonnett Vélez, *La Nueva Granada colonial: Selección de textos históricos* (Bogotá, Colombia: Universidad de Los Andes, 2005); Rina Cáceres Gómez, *Negros, mulatos, esclavos, y libertos en la Costa Rica del siglo XVII* (Mexico City: Instituto Panamericano de Geografía e Historia, 2000); Bernardino Bravo Lira, *Derecho común y derecho propio en el nuevo mundo* (Santiago de Chile: Editorial Jurídica de Chile, 1989); Sergio A. Mosquera, *La gente negra en la legislación colonial* (Medellín, Colombia: Editorial Lealon, 2004).

25. See "Voyages: The Transatlantic Slave Trade Database," Emory University, 2013. http://www.slavevoyages.org/.

26. See Linda Colley, *The Ordeal of Elizabeth Marsh: A Woman in World History* (New York: Anchor Books, 2008); Jason Oliver Chang, *Chino: Anti-Chinese Racism in Mexico, 1880–1940* (Champaign: University of Illinois Press, 2017).

27. Frank Tannenbaum, *Slave and Citizen: The Negro in the Americas* (New York: Random House, 1963), 61–69.

28. For example, Blumenthal, in *Enemies and Familiars*, shows how much custom and practice determined the functioning of the legal ecology in the Kingdom of Aragon.

29. An approach taken up by, for example, Herbert Klein, *Slavery in the Americas: A Comparative Study of Cuba and Virginia* (Chicago: University of Chicago Press, 1967).

30. Steven Mintz, "American Slavery in Comparative Perspective," The Gilder Lehrman Institute of American History, https://www.gilderlehrman.org/content/historical-context-american-slavery-comparative-perspective, n.d.

31. Alejandro de la Fuente, "Slave Law and Claims-Making in Cuba: The Tannenbaum Debate Revisited," *Law and History Review* 22, no. 2 (2004): 341–42.

32. See the seminal formulation in Orlando Patterson, *Slavery and Social Death: A Comparative Study* (Cambridge, MA: Harvard University Press, 1982).

33. Bianca Premo, "Before the Law: Women's Petitions in the Eighteenth-Century Spanish Empire," *Comparative Studies in Society and History* 53, no. 2 (2011): 261–89.

34. Liam Francis Horrigan, "Settling the Trade to Africa: The Anglo-African Trade, 1695–1715, and the Political and Economic Implications of 1698," Master of Arts by Research, University of Kent, 2016; Walter Johnson, "Resetting the Legal History of Slavery: Divination, Torture, Poisoning, Murder, Revolution, Emancipation, and Re-Enslavement," *Law and History Review* 29, no. 4 (2011): 1089–1095; Manuel Maza Miquel, *Esclavos, patriotas, y poetas a la sombra de la cruz: Cinco ensayos sobre catolicismo e historia cubana* (Santo Domingo: Centro de Estudios Sociales Padre Juan Montalvo, S.J, 1999).

35. John Huxtable Elliott, *Empires of the Atlantic World: Britain and Spain in America, 1492–1830* (New Haven, CT: Yale University Press, 2006).

36. Joyce E. Chaplin, *Round About the Earth: Circumnavigation from Magellan to Orbit* (New York: Simon and Schuster, 2012).

37. See Abbé Raynal, *A Philosophical and Political History of the Settlements and Trade of the Europeans in the East and West Indies*, 2nd ed., trans. J. O. Justamond (London: A. Strahan, 1798), chapter 1.

38. Wendy Warren lays out New Englanders' early integration of slavery into the region's economy, in *New England Bound: Slavery and Colonization in Early America* (New York: W. W. Norton & Company, 2016).

39. Abigail Leslie Swingen, *Competing Visions of Empire: Labor, Slavery, and the Origins of the British Atlantic Empire* (New Haven, CT: Yale University Press, 2015).

40. Trevor Burnard, *Planters, Merchants, and Slaves: Plantation Societies in British America, 1650–1820* (Chicago: University of Chicago Press, 2015).

41. Greg Grandin, *The Empire of Necessity: Slavery, Freedom, and Deception in the New World* (New York: Metropolitan Books, 2014).

42. Kristen Block, *Ordinary Lives in the Early Caribbean* (Athens: University of Georgia Press, 2012); Blumenthal, *Enemies and Familiars.*

43. Pedro Cardim et al., eds., *Polycentric Monarchies: How Did Early Modern Spain and Portugal Achieve and Maintain a Global Hegemony?* (Brighton: Sussex Academic Press, 2014).

44. Herman L. Bennett, *Africans in Colonial Mexico: Absolutism, Christianity, and Afro-Creole Consciousness, 1570–1640* (Bloomington: Indiana University Press, 2003); Nicole von Germeten, *Black Blood Brothers: Confraternities and Social Mobility for Afro-Mexicans* (Gainesville: University Press of Florida, 2006).

45. Jane G. Landers and Barry M. Robinson, eds., *Slaves, Subjects, and Subversives: Blacks in Colonial Latin America* (Albuquerque: University of New Mexico Press, 2006); Ben Vinson III, Sherwin K. Bryant, and Rachel Sarah O'Toole, eds., *Africans to Spanish America: Expanding the Diaspora* (Urbana: University of Illinois Press, 2012).

46. Linda Marinda Heywood and John Kelly Thornton, *Central Africans, Atlantic Creoles, and the Making of the Foundation of the Americas, 1585–1660* (New York: Cambridge University Press, 2007); Woody Holton and Omohundro Institute of Early American History & Culture, *Forced Founders: Indians, Debtors, Slaves, and the Making of the American Revolution in Virginia* (Chapel Hill: Published for the Omohundro Institute of Early American History and Culture by the University of North Carolina Press, 1999).

47. Marisa J. Fuentes, *Dispossessed Lives: Enslaved Women, Violence, and the Archive* (Philadelphia: University of Pennsylvania Press, 2016).

48. There seems to be an emergent consensus that understanding any section of European imperialism requires that we study it as a whole. The value of connecting parochial historiographies is exemplified by the scholars who contributed to Jorge Cañizares-Esguerra, ed., *Entangled Empires: The Anglo-Iberian Atlantic, 1500–1830* (Philadelphia: University of Pennsylvania Press, 2018).

49. Robert J. Cottrol, *The Long, Lingering Shadow: Slavery, Race, and Law in the American Hemisphere* (Athens: University of Georgia Press, 2013).

50. María del Carmen Borrego Plá, *Cartagena de Indias en el siglo XVI* (Seville: Escuela de Estudios Hispano-Americanos, 1983).

51. Sherwin K. Bryant, *Rivers of Gold, Lives of Bondage: Governing through Slavery in Colonial Quito* (Chapel Hill: University of North Carolina Press, 2014); Wheat, *Atlantic Africa and the Spanish Caribbean*; Michelle A. McKinley, *Fractional Freedoms: Slavery, Intimacy, and Legal Mobilization in Colonial Lima, 1600–1700* (New York: Cambridge University Press, 2016).

52. Wheat, *Atlantic Africa and the Spanish Caribbean*, 19.

53. Wheat, *Atlantic Africa and the Spanish Caribbean*, 3.

54. Linda Colley, *Captives: Britain, Empire, and the World, 1600–1850* (New York: Anchor Books, 2004).

55. Francisco Copete Jr. vs. María Josefa Copete y Lorenza Elena, Folios 149v–55r.

56. See Bryant, *Rivers of Gold, Lives of Bondage*, introduction.

57. Examples of a more limited view can be found in Leslie B. Rout, *The African Experience in Spanish America, 1502 to the Present Day* (New York: Cambridge University Press, 1976); Rolando R. Mellafe, *Negro Slavery in Latin America* (Berkeley: University of California Press, 1975); Miguel Acosta Saignes, Roger Bastide, and Julio Le Riverend, *Vida de los esclavos negros en Venezuela*, 3rd ed. (Valencia, Venezuela: Vadell, 1984).

58. Gabriel Paquette, *European Seaborne Empires: From the Thirty Years' War to the Age of Revolutions* (New Haven, CT: Yale University Press, 2019).

59. See Paquette, *European Seaborn Empires*.

60. Mariana L. R. Dantas, *Black Townsmen: Urban Slavery and Freedom in the Eighteenth-Century Americas* (New York: Palgrave Macmillan, 2008).

61. Felipe Fernández-Armesto, *The Canary Islands after the Conquest: The Making of a Colonial Society in the Early Sixteenth Century* (Oxford, UK: Clarendon Press, 1982).

62. Works that explore and explain the establishment of the Atlantic World include Franklin W. Knight and Peggy K. Liss, eds., *Atlantic Port Cities: Economy, Culture, and Society in the Atlantic World, 1650–1850* (Knoxville: University of Tennessee Press, 1991) and Lynne Guitar, "Criollos." Furthermore, James H. Sweet explores the role of African culture, kinship, and religion in the creations of Iberoamerica in *Recreating Africa: Culture, Kinship, and Religion in the African-Portuguese World, 1441–1770* (Chapel Hill: University of North Carolina Press, 2004).

63. During the War of Independence (1808–25), most of the original case files were destroyed. However, summaries of all ongoing cases were remitted regularly to the Office of the Inquisitor General in Spain and are now stored in the Archivo Histórico Nacional in Madrid. Invaluably, Splendiani, Sánchez, and Luque have transcribed and contextualized the first fifty years of cases. See Anna María Splendiani, José Enrique Sánchez Bohórquez, and Emma Cecilia Luque de Salazar, *Cincuenta años de Inquisición en el tribunal de Cartagena de Indias, 1610–1660* (Bogota: Pontificia Universidad Javeriana, Instituto Colombiano de Cultura Hispánica, 1997).

64. The way that I have chosen and engaged with the sources is inspired by the scholarship of James Lockhart, *Spanish Peru, 1532–1560: A Colonial Society* (Madison: University of Wisconsin Press, 1968); Carlo Ginzburg, *The Cheese and the Worms: The Cosmos of a Sixteenth-Century Miller* (New York: Penguin, 1992); Kyle Harper, *Slavery in the Late Roman World, AD 275–425* (New York: Cambridge University Press, 2011); and Kathryn Burns, *Into the Archive: Writing and Power in Colonial Peru* (Durham, NC: Duke University Press, 2010).

Chapter 1

Epigraph: Isabel was the queen of Castile who married Ferdinand of Aragon. The Empress Isabel of Portugal (October 24, 1503–May 1, 1539) was the wife of Ferdinand and Isabel's grandson Charles V.

1. Jorge Cañizares-Esguerra and Erik R. Seeman, eds., *The Atlantic in Global History: 1500–2000* (Oxford: Routledge, 2017); Jorge Cañizares-Esguerra, Matt D. Childs, and James Sidbury, eds., *The Black Urban Atlantic in the Age of the Slave Trade* (Philadelphia: University of Pennsylvania Press, 2013); Haroldo Calvo Stevenson and Adolfo Meisel Roca, *Cartagena de Indias y su historia* (Bogota: Universidad Jorge Tadeo Lozano, 1998).

2. Richard L. Kagan and Fernando Marías, *Urban Images of the Hispanic World, 1493–1793* (New Haven, CT: Yale University Press, 2000).

3. Julián Bautista Ruiz Rivera, *Los indios de Cartagena bajo la administración española en el Siglo XVII* (Bogota: Archivo General de la Nación, 1996).

4. Kenneth Pomeranz and Steven Topik, *The World that Trade Created: Society, Culture, and the World Economy, 1400 to Present*, 2nd ed. (Armonk, NY: M. E. Sharpe, Inc., 2006).

5. The Pacific coast of Colombia, for example. William Frederick Sharp, *Slavery on the Spanish Frontier: The Colombian Chocó, 1680–1810* (Norman: University of Oklahoma Press, 1976).

6. Lynne Guitar, "Criollos: The Birth of a Dynamic New Indo-Afro-European People and Culture on Hispaniola," *KACIKE: Journal of Caribbean Amerindian History and Anthropology* 1, no. 1 (2000): 2. In the 1530s, Spaniards were outnumbered by a minimum of six-and-a-half or eight-and-a-half to one by Indians, Africans, and "others."

7. See Enriqueta Vila Vilar, *Aspectos sociales en América colonial: De extranjeros, contrabando, y esclavos* (Bogota: Instituto Caro y Cuervo; Universidad Jorge Tadeo Lozano, 2001); and *Hispanoamérica y el comercio de esclavos* (Seville: Escuela de Estudios Hispano-Americanos, 1977).

8. The sense of distance comes through in Antonino Vidal Ortega and Álvaro Baquero Montoya, *De las Indias remotas: Cartas del cabildo de Santa Marta, 1529–1640* (Barranquilla: Ediciones Uninorte, 2007).

9. Guitar, "Criollos," 5.

10. Guitar, "Criollos," 44–62.

11. Borrego Plá, *Cartagena de Indias en el siglo XVI*, 381–87 (see introduction, n. 50) and David Ernesto Peñas Galindo, *Los bogas de Mompox: Historia del zambaje* (Bogota, Colombia: Tercer Mundo Editores, 1988).

12. Borrego Plá, *Cartagena de Indias en el siglo XVI*.

13. David Skerritt Gardner, *Una dinámica rural: Movilidad, cultura, y región en Veracruz* (Xalapa: Dirección Editorial, Universidad Veracruzana, 2008).

14. Examples of this can be found in Luis Querol Roso, "Negros y mulatos de Nueva España: Historia de su alzamiento en Méjico en 1612," *Anales de la Universidad de Valencia*, Año XII, Cuaderno 90 (Valencia: Imprenta Hijo F. Vives Mora, 1932); Reinaldo Rojas, *La rebelión del Negro Miguel y otros temas de africanía* (Barquisimeto, Venezuela: Fundación Buría, 2004).

15. Julia Herráez Sánchez de Escariche, *Don Pedro Zapata de Mendoza, Gobernador de Cartagena de Indias* (Seville: Publicaciones de la Escuela de Estudios Hispano-Americanos de Sevilla, 1946).

16. The monumental work by Manuel Lucena Salmoral contains a great number of examples. See *Leyes para esclavos: El ordenamiento jurídico sobre la condición, tratamiento, defensa, y represión de los esclavos en las colonias de la América española* (Madrid: Fundación MAPFRE TAVERA; Fundación Ignacio Larramendi, 2005). A clear and concise way of understanding the organization of the law is contained in Mary Ann Glynn and Lee Watkiss, "Exploring Cultural Mechanisms of Organizational Identity Construction," in *Constructing Identity in and Around Organizations*, ed. Majken Schultz et al., 63–88 (New York: Oxford University Press, 2012).

17. The consequences of this deep historical engagement can be seen in Marcela Echeverri, "Popular Royalists, Empire, and Politics in Southwestern New Granada, 1809–1819," *Hispanic American Historical Review* 91, no. 2 (2011): 267.

18. Bartolomé Moriano, vecino de Cartagena, su demanda contra Antón del Río, por una esclava que le había quitado y ocultado, 1630. Fondo: Colonia. Grupo: Negros y esclavos de Bolívar, Legajo 1, Documento 6, Folios 824r–971v, AGN, Bogota. Hereafter cited as Bartolomé Moriano vs. Antón del Río.

19. An exhaustive catalogue of slave marriages in Mexico City and the relevant imperial policy is provided by the work of Herman L. Bennett, based on extensive research in the Inquisition's archives. See *Africans in Colonial Mexico*; and *Colonial Blackness: A History of Afro-Mexico* (Bloomington: Indiana University Press, 2009). Father William Eugene Shiels wrote a classic explanation of the Patronato Real in *King and Church: The Rise and Fall of the Patronato Real* (Chicago: Loyola University Press, 1961).

20. A full description of the relevant law and a plethora of examples can be found in Bennett, *Africans in Colonial Mexico*, chapter 2.

21. See McKinley, *Fractional Freedoms*, especially chapter 2 (see introduction, n. 51).

22. Lucena Salmoral, *Leyes para esclavos*, 148.

23. The AGN preserves mostly civil and criminal suits. However, in the case of Catalina and Domingo, the archive includes all the evidence associated with the proceedings. The defense in the civil case submitted the religious case as evidence, hoping to engage overlapping imperial jurisdictions that generally tried to enforce the law cooperatively.

24. Felipe Verges, *Apuntes de derecho canónico* (Barcelona: Establecimiento Tipográfico de Jaime Jepús, 1867), 87–89.

25. Bartolomé Moriano vs. Antón del Río, Folios 931r–32v, 906r.

26. Bartolomé Moriano vs. Antón del Río, Folios 897–905.

27. "Christ our Lord . . . said, therefore they are no more twain, but one flesh; and straightway confirmed the firmness of that tie, proclaimed so long before by Adam, in these words; What therefore God hath joined together, let no man put asunder," Council of Trent, Session XXIV, 1563.

28. Bartolomé Moriano vs. Antón del Río, Folios 906r–907, 931r–32v.

29. Bartolomé Moriano vs. Antón del Río, Folio 826r.

30. Bartolomé Moriano vs. Antón del Río, Folio 831v.

31. See Massimo Livi-Bacci, "Return to Hispaniola: Reassessing a Demographic Catastrophe," *Hispanic American Historical Review* 83, no. 1 (February 2003): 3–52; and Jean-Pierre Tardieu, "Un proyecto utópico de manumisión de los cimarrones del palenque de los montes de Cartagena en 1682," in *Afrodescendientes en las Américas: Trayectorias sociales e identitarias: 150 años de la abolición de la esclavitud en Colombia*, ed. Claudia Mosquera, Mauricio Pardo, and Odile Hoffmann (Bogota: Universidad Nacional de Colombia, 2002), 169–80.

32. Bartolomé Moriano vs. Antón del Río, Folios 837v–38r.

33. Bartolomé Moriano vs. Antón del Río, Folios 828r–31v.

34. Bartolomé Moriano vs. Antón del Río, Folio 831v–33r.

35. Bartolomé Moriano vs. Antón del Río, Folios 833v–34v.

36. Bartolomé Moriano vs. Antón del Río, Folios 859v–60v.

37. Bartolomé Moriano vs. Antón del Río, Folio 877r.

38. Bartolomé Moriano vs. Antón del Río, Folios 877v–79r.

39. Bartolomé Moriano vs. Antón del Río, Folios 880r–81r.

40. Bartolomé Moriano vs. Antón del Río, Folio 909v.

41. Bartolomé Moriano vs. Antón del Río, Folios 913r–15v.

42. Bartolomé Moriano vs. Antón del Río, Folios 931r–32v.

43. Bartolomé Moriano vs. Antón del Río, Folios 957r–58v.

44. Bartolomé Moriano vs. Antón del Río, Folio 966r.

45. Recent historiography regarding the challenges of Spanish imperial administration is ably summarized by Max Deardorff, "Imperial Justice, Colonial Power: Pedro Vique y Manrique, the Galley Captain of Cartagena de Indias, 1578–1607," *CLAHR: Colonial Latin American Historical Review* 17, no. 2 (2008): 126–27.

46. This can be seen in the cases discussed by Kathryn Joy McKnight, "Gendered Declarations: Testimonies of Three Captured Maroon Women, Cartagena de Indias, 1634," *Colonial Latin American Historical Review* 12, no. 4 (Fall 2003): 499–527, as well as in the examples of resistance in Moisés Munive Contreras, "Resistencia estática. Los negros contra la esclavitude en Cartagena y Mompox. Siglo XVIII," *Tiempos Modernos: Revista Electrónica de Historia Moderna* 5, no. 14 (2006): 1–18.

47. This is comprehensively discussed in Alejandro de la Fuente, "From Slaves to Citizens? Tannenbaum and the Debates on Slavery, Emancipation, and Race Relations in Latin America," *International Labor and Working-Class History* 77, No. 1 (2010): 154–173; and "Slave Law and Claims-Making in Cuba," 341–42 (see introduction, n. 31).

48. See James Muldoon, ed., *The Spiritual Conversion of the Americas* (Gainesville: University Press of Florida, 2004); Martin Austin Nesvig, *Local Religion in Colonial Mexico* (Albuquerque: University of New Mexico, 2006); and Paul Edward Hedley Hair, "Heretics, Slaves, and Witches—As Seen by Guinea Jesuits c. 1610," *Journal of Religion in Africa* 28, no. 2 (1988): 131–44.

49. The lesser known crusades, especially those directed toward Eastern Europe, served for almost four hundred years (1147–1505) as a violent laboratory wherein Europeans perfected the theory and practice of expansive Christian imperialism. See William Urban, *The Baltic Crusades* (DeKalb: Northern Illinois University Press, 1975), 127–40. The application of this experience in Mesoamerica can be seen in Nancy M. Farriss, *Maya Society under Colonial Rule: The Collective Enterprise of Survival* (Princeton: Princeton University Press, 1984) and in Africa in Paul Edward Hedley Hair, *Africa Encountered: European Contacts and Evidence, 1450–1700* (Brookfield, VT: Variorum, 1997).

50. A seminal example is Alonso de Sandoval, *Un tratado sobre la esclavitud*, transcribed by Enriqueta Vila Vilar (Madrid: Alianza Universidad, 1987).

51. The complexity of the subject is well engaged by Alfonso Múnera, in *El fracaso de la nación: Región, clase, y raza en el Caribe colombiano (1717–1821)* (Bogota: Banco de la República; Ancora Editores, 1998).

52. The topic is beautifully introduced by Rebecca J. Scott, "Slavery and the Law in Atlantic Perspective: Jurisdiction, Jurisprudence, and Justice," *Law and History Review* 29, no. 4 (2011): 915–24.

53. Juan Manzano, *Recopilación de leyes de los reynos de las Indias* (Madrid: Ediciones Cultura Hispánica, 1973), 234.

54. A clear window into the endless and contested push for "reform" is presented by Liliana Regalado de Hurtado, "Denominadores comunes en las críticas y propuestas de 'Buen Gobierno' según las crónicas de los siglos XVI y XVII," in *International Congress of Americanists, América bajo los Austrias: Economía, cultura, y sociedad*, ed. Héctor Omar Noejovich (Lima: Pontificia Universidad Católica del Peru, 2001), 113–21; and Silvio Zavala, *The Defense of Human Rights in Latin America: Sixteenth to Eighteenth Centuries* (Paris: UNESCO, 1964).

55. A still useful classic is John Huxtable Elliott, *Imperial Spain, 1469–1716* (New York: The

New American Library, 1963). See also Majken Schultz et al., ed., *Constructing Identity in and Around Organizations*, vol. 2 (Oxford, UK: Oxford University Press, 2012).

56. This whole process is ably described in Bernard F. Reilly, *The Medieval Spains* (New York: Cambridge University Press, 1993).

57. The interconnectedness of the system is presented by Michael McCormick, *Origins of the European Economy: Communications and Commerce A.D. 300–900* (New York: Cambridge University Press, 2001).

58. The importance of this compilation and its impact on the legal ecology of the Spanish Empire is surveyed in Max Radin and Madaline W. Nichols, "Las Siete Partidas," *California Law Review* 20, no. 3 (March 1932): 260–85. Further perspective is provided by Robert I. Burns, ed., and Samuel Parsons Scott, trans., *The Medieval World of Law: Lawyers and their Work (Partida III)*. Volume 3 of *Las Siete Partidas* (Philadelphia: University of Pennsylvania Press, 2012).

59. At the base of much of our current understanding of medieval society is Mark Bloch, *Feudal Society* (Chicago: University of Chicago Press, 1964); the seminal work on military changes in the early modern period is Geoffrey Parker, *The Military Revolution: Military Innovation and the Rise of the West, 1500–1800*, 2nd ed. (New York: Cambridge University Press, 1996); the role of war in building state capacity is explained by Charles Tilly, "War Making and State Making as Organized Crime," in *Bringing the State Back In*, Peter B. Evans, Dietrich Rueschemeyer, and Theda Skocpol, ed. (New York: Cambridge University Press, 1985); the philosophy animating early modern state making efforts is surveyed by Bertrand de Jouvenel, *Sovereignty: An Inquiry into the Political Good* (Chicago: University of Chicago Press, 1957).

60. See Jean Bethke Elshtain, *Sovereignty: God, State, and Self* (Basic Books, 2008); F. H. Hinsley, *Sovereignty* (New York: Cambridge University Press, 1986); Thomas Hobbes, *Leviathan*, ed. Richard Tuck (New York: Cambridge University Press, 1996).

61. See Bernard F. Reilly, "The Chancery of Alfonso VII of León-Castilla: The Period 1116–35 Reconsidered," *Speculum* 51, no. 2 (April 1976): 243–61; Richard L. Kagan, *Lawsuits and Litigants in Castile, 1500–1700* (Chapel Hill: University of North Carolina Press, 1981), 234; Peter Denley, *Teachers and Schools in Siena (1357–1500)* (Siena: Betti Editrice, 2007).

62. Henry Kamen, *Empire: How Spain Became a World Power, 1492–1763* (New York: Perennial, 2004), 6.

63. Contemporary chroniclers who focused on Isabel's strict application of the law recognized her success. They portray Isabel as more inclined to justice than mercy and as far more rigorous and unforgiving than her husband—a fascinating contrast to standard medieval gender and royal roles.

64. In human history, only a few examples exist of a polity that can match or surpass the Spanish Empire's longevity and flexibility. In this vast enterprise, millions of enslaved subjects of the crown played a vital role. For a concise breakdown of some of the challenges faced, see John Lynch, *Spain under the Habsburgs: Spain and America 1598–1700*, 2nd ed., vol. 2 (Oxford, UK: Basil Blackwell, 1981), 1–13.

65. Kamen, *Empire*, xxi.

66. Chapter 2 of this book further explores how the Reconquista, the Reformation, and the discovery and conversion of new lands created a symbiotic relationship between the Catholic Church and the Spanish Crown.

67. For more, see Alberto de la Hera, "El regalismo indiano," *Ius Canonicum* 32, no. 64 (1992): 411–37.

68. Clarence Henry Haring, *The Spanish Empire in America* (New York: Harcourt, Brace, & World, 1963), 153.

69. Haring, *The Spanish Empire in America*, 147–51.

70. Chris Wickham, *Medieval Europe* (New Haven, CT: Yale University Press, 2016), 23.

71. Leslie Bethell, ed., *The Cambridge History of Latin America*, vol. 1, *Colonial Latin America* (New York: Cambridge University Press, 2008), 149.

72. Peter Marzahl, *Town in the Empire: Government, Politics, and Society in Seventeenth-Century Popayán* (Austin: University of Texas Press, 1978), 55–56.

73. For a more complete description of the institution of the cabildo, see Haring, *Spanish Empire in America*, chapter 9.

74. For a comprehensive description of a wide variety of cases in which judicial officials were called upon to mediate and adjudicate conflict dealing with imperial justice, see María Cristina Navarrete, *Génesis y desarrollo de la esclavitud en Colombia, siglos XVI y XVII* (Cali: Universidad del Valle, 2005), 276–93.

75. Although the alcaldes of the Santa Hermandad share a name, they are not related to the alcaldes of the cabildo. This case shows the Santa Hermandad in action in the New World. Francisco Trejo Atienza defiende tres esclavos suyos, condenados por cimarrones por el alcalde Alonso Cuadrado Cid, 1645. Fondo: Colonia. Grupo: Negros y esclavos de Bolívar, Legajo 9, Documento 13, Folios 894r–933v, AGN, Bogota. Hereafter cited as Francisco Trejo Atienza vs. Alonso Cuadrado Cid.

76. An example is the integration and subordination of Navarre, described in Kamen, *Empire*, 35–36.

77. The way that Spain negotiated the affirmation of its status with Charles V was symptomatic of the constant bargaining that allowed the Spanish Empire to function. The marriage of Isabel and Ferdinand, in a negotiated contract, united the core components of Spain. The conquistadors of the New World negotiated their charters with the crown. The cities and towns of the empire constantly negotiated with the crown for different terms. The development and nurturing of mechanisms for diffusing conflict and generating consensus reinforced the durability of the empire.

78. Haring, *Spanish Empire in America*, 2–19.

79. C. R. Boxer, *The Portuguese Seaborne Empire, 1415–1825* (London: Hutchinson, 1969).

80. The increased importation of Africans to the Indies was possible only because the structures of the slave trade were already in place when Europeans seriously entered the trade. In Africa, slavery and the slave trade were part of a long-standing tradition. The Central African kingdoms were especially prominent in the trade. However, even among the Muslim states, slavery was a major business, subject to legal and religious restraints, but still an important part of the economy. For an illuminating explanation, see Paul E. Lovejoy, "The Context of Enslavement in West Africa: Aḥmad Bābā and the Ethics of Slavery" in Landers and Robinson, *Slaves, Subjects, and Subversives*, 9–38 (see introduction, n. 45).

81. Burnard, *Planters, Merchants, and Slaves*, 22–52 (see introduction, n. 40).

82. Navarrete, *Génesis y desarrollo*, 33–40.

83. John K. Thornton and Linda M. Heywood, "'Canniball Negroes,' Atlantic Creoles, and the Identity of New England's Charter Generation African," *African Diaspora* 4, no. 1 (2011): 76–94.

84. Lynch, *Spain under the Habsburgs*, 1–13.

85. Echeverri, "Popular Royalists, Empire, and Politics," 241. "Both Indians and slaves were engaged with the Hispanic discourse of justice, and they appropriated monarchical values for individual and collective gains and empowerment."

86. Borrego Plá, *Cartagena de Indias en el siglo XVI*, 29; for a general survey of the indigenous residents of the area see Richard E. W. Adams and Murdo J. MacLeod, eds. *The Cambridge History of the Native Peoples of the Americas* Vol. 2. (New York: Cambridge University Press, 2000).

87. Jorge Orlando Melo, *Historia de Colombia: El establecimiento de la dominación española* (Bogota, Colombia: Presidencia de la República, 1996); Ignacio Avellaneda, *The Conquerors of the New Kingdom of Granada* (Albuquerque: University of New Mexico Press, 1995).

88. The establishment and development of the city is surveyed by María del Carmen Gómez Pérez, *Pedro de Heredia y Cartagena de Indias* (Seville: Escuela de Estudios Hispano-Americanos de Sevilla; CSIC, 1984).

89. Description of the defenses of the city are provided by Borrego Plá, *Cartagena de Indias en el siglo XVI*, 78–82; and Charles E. Nowell, "The Defense of Cartagena," *The Hispanic American Historical Review* 42, no. 4 (1962): 477–501.

90. The importance of imperial defense to the development of the region can be seen in Eduardo Lemaitre, *Breve historia de Cartagena* (Medellín, Colombia: Editorial Colina, 1993); Eduardo Lemaitre, Donaldo Bossa Herazo, and Francisco Sebá Patrón, *Historia general de Cartagena* (Bogotá: Banco de la República, 1983); and Sebastián de Eslava and Pedro de Mur, *Diario de todo lo ocurrido en la expugnacion de los fuertes de Bocachica, y sitio de la ciudad de Cartagena de las Indias; formado de los pliegos remitidos à Su Magestad (que Dios guarde) por el Virrey de Santa Fé Don Sebastian de Eslaba con d. Pedro de Mur, Su Ayudante General. Año 1741. De orden de Su Magestad* (Madrid: n.d., 1741).

91. The process that went into the planning of the city of Cartagena is introduced by Borrego Plá, *Cartagena de Indias en el siglo XVI*, 74; and further explained by Maruja Redondo Gómez, *Cartagena de Indias: Cinco siglos de evolución urbanística* (Bogota: Fundación Universidad de Bogotá Jorge Tadeo Lozano, 2004).

92. Deardorff provides a vivid description of the military development of the city and the varied efforts by imperial authorities to deal with enemy attacks and contraband in "Imperial Justice, Colonial Power," 117–42.

93. The interplay of local, regional, and imperial business practices can be seen in Anthony McFarlane, "Comerciantes y monopolio en la Nueva Granada: El consulado de Cartagena de Indias," *Anuario Colombiano de Historia Social y de la Cultura* 11 (1983): 43–69; and Lucas Fernández de Piedrahita, *Historia general del Nuevo Reino de Granada* (Bogotá: Impreso en la Editorial ABC, 1942).

94. Livi-Bacci, "Return to Hispaniola," 3–52.

95. The reasons for the high mortality rate suffered by native tribes in the New World are elegantly presented by Noble David Cook, *Born to Die: Disease and New World Conquest, 1492–1650* (New York: Cambridge University Press, 1998).

96. Jared Diamond, *Guns, Germs, and Steel* (New York: W.W. Norton & Company, 1997), 67–83.

97. The complexity of new social forms is explained in the introduction in Matthew Restall, *Beyond Black and Red: African-Native Relations in Colonial Latin America* (Albuquerque: University

of New Mexico Press, 2005); see also W. George Lovell and Christopher Lutz, *Demography and Empire: A Guide to the Population History of Spanish Central America, 1500–1821* (Boulder, CO: Westview Press, 1995), 190. Within the Caribbean basin, by the collapse of Spanish rule in 1825, there was an almost complete depopulation of the original indigenous people.

98. Marzahl, *Town in the Empire*, 75.

99. Barbara F. Weissberger, *Queen Isabel I of Castile: Power, Patronage, Persona* (Woodbridge, UK: Tamesis, 2008), 27–28.

100. David Abulafia, *The Discovery of Mankind: Atlantic Encounters in the Age of Columbus* (New Haven, CT: Yale University Press, 2008), 259.

101. See Germán Colmenares, *Los esclavos en la Gobernación de Popayán, 1680–1780* (Tunja: Publicaciones del Magister en Historia, Vice-Rectoría de Investigaciones Científicas y Extensión Universitaria, Universidad Pedagógica y Tecnológica de Colombia, 1991).

102. Herbert S. Klein and Ben Vinson III, *African Slavery in Latin America and the Caribbean*, 2nd ed. (New York: Oxford University Press, 2007), 19–21.

103. "Each of the three different groups of people—Indian, African and European—had its own complex multiethnic history. On Hispaniola, however, in the capital and in the other Spanish-dominated towns and cities, they all lived together, worked together, and forged closely linked networks of kinship and patronage together across all ethnic lines, creating a new people and a new culture that were outwardly 'Spanish' but very, very different from their pure Iberian counterparts." Guitar, "Criollos," 1.

104. PARES, Archivo General de Indias, Indiferente General, 418, Libro 1, fo. 101r. CO-DOIN II, V, 43–52.

105. Alan Watson, *Slave Law in the Americas* (Athens: University of Georgia Press, 1989), 30–35.

106. Watson, *Slave Law in the Americas*, 55–62.

107. The importance of the church fathers in shaping the legal structure of late Roman slavery is reviewed by S. Scott Bartchy, *[Mallon Chrēsai]: First-Century Slavery and the Interpretation of 1 Corinthians 7:21* (Eugene, OR: Wipf and Stock Publishers, 1973). *Las Siete Partidas* itself had roots in Roman law. Slaves in the Roman Empire possessed a legal personhood, although limited in many ways. As it was interpreted through the Visigothic codes, Catholic doctrine, and the medieval law codes, Roman legal structure added further rights and duties to enslaved people. For more background, see Pedro López Barja de Quiroga, "Manumisión y control de esclavos en la Antigua Roma," *Circe de Clásicos y Modernos* 16, no. 2 (2012): 63–67.

108. For example, as late as 1558, Turkish admiral Piyale Pasha captured the Balearic Islands, inflicting great damage on Minorca and enslaving many, while raiding the coasts of the Spanish mainland.

109. Debra Blumenthal's study of Valencia is a clear window into the day-to-day governance of a city with a large and active slave market and population. *Enemies and Familiars* (see introduction, n. 28). See also Jarbel Rodriguez, *Captives and their Saviors in the Medieval Crown of Aragon* (Washington, DC: Catholic University of America Press, 2007); the importance of people of color in Renaissance Europe is reviewed by T. F. Earle and K. J. P. Lowe, eds., *Black Africans in Renaissance Europe* (New York: Cambridge University Press, 2005).

110. The creation of these laws was partially due to the labor of many Spanish religious figures. Among these, Fray António de Montesinos stands out. In a homily that he delivered on

December 21, 1511, known as "the Christmas sermon," he advocated royal justice for indigenous subjects. Present at the time was Bartolomé de las Casas, who became the most famous of the Spanish defenders of the native residents of the Indies.

111. In response to demographic collapse during the sixteenth century there were repeated moral, juridical, and administrative arguments between those sounding the alarm over Spain's responsibility for the indigenous death rate and those who believed that these concerns were overblown. Indigenous depopulation provided a clear point of conflict between feudalists, who favored the encomienda system, and regalists, who sought to strengthen royal authority over the indigenous inhabitants of Spain's new empire. The crown allied itself firmly with those who, like Fray Antonio de Montesinos and Bartolomé de las Casas, believed that immoral and illegal actions by the Spanish settlers were directly responsible for the demographic collapse. While never putting in doubt the legitimacy of imperial rule, royal policy consistently reinforced the responsibilities and mutuality of its dominion over the Indies.

112. Manzano, *Recopilación de leyes*, 439.

113. Borrego Plá, *Cartagena de Indias en el siglo XVI*, 54. My translation.

114. José Luis Cortés López, *Esclavo y colono: Introducción y sociología de los negroafricanos en la América española del siglo XVI* (Salamanca: Ediciones Universidad de Salamanca, 2004), 241.

115. Manzano, *Recopilación de leyes*, 437.

116. Manzano, *Recopilación de leyes*, Ley 19, Título 5, Libro 7, 287, "Los Rancheadores no molesten a los morenos libres que estuvieren pacíficos."

117. The best descriptions of the way that the river transport network evolved are provided by Borrego Plá, *Cartagena de Indias en el siglo XVI*, 42–63 and 225–47.

118. Juan Bautista de Arrotigui, su demanda por robo contra el negro Alonso, piloto de canoa, 1621. Fondo: Colonia. Grupo: Negros y esclavos de Magdalena, Legajo 3, Documento 2, Folios 57r–72r, AGN, Bogota.

119. Manzano, *Recopilación de leyes*, Ley 17, Título 5, Libro 7, 287.

120. Lucena Salmoral, *Leyes para esclavos*, 650.

121. The downstream effects of variations in the legal ecology can be seen in Alejandro de la Fuente and Ariela J. Gross. "Comparative Studies of Law, Slavery and Race in the Americas." *University of Southern California Legal Studies Working Paper Series*, Working Paper 56 (February 2010).

122. The scholarly debate surrounding comparative studies of slavery is presented by de la Fuente, "Slave Law and Claims-Making in Cuba," 341–42; The consequences of these choices for the way forced labor functioned in Spanish America can be seen in Peter J. A Bakewell, *Miners of the Red Mountain: Indian Labor in Potosí, 1545–1650* (Albuquerque: University of New Mexico Press, 1984).

123. C. Velleius Paterculus, *Compendium of Roman History* (Cambridge, MA: Harvard University Press, Loeb Classical Library, 1924), 55.

124. Lucena Salmoral, *Leyes para esclavos*, 183.

125. The use of African slavery by the Spanish was both essential and contested from the start. See Orián Jiménez Meneses, "El Chocó: Vida negra, vida libre y vida parda, Siglos XVII y XVIII," *Historia y Sociedad* 7 (2000): 173–98; and Orián Jiménez Meneses, "Los amos y los esclavos en el Medellín del S. XVIII," *Historia y Sociedad* 5 (1998): 119–32. The ambiguous legacy of this history is still playing out: see Peter Wade, *Blackness and Race Mixture: The Dynamics of Racial Identity in Colombia* (Baltimore: Johns Hopkins University Press, 1995).

126. Manuel Jesús Izco Reina, *Amos, esclavos, y libertos: Estudios sobre la esclavitud en Puerto Real durante la edad moderna* (Cádiz: Universidad de Cádiz, Servicio de Publicaciones, 2002).

127. Lyman L. Johnson and Sonya Lipsett-Rivera, eds. *The Faces of Honor: Sex, Shame, and Violence in Colonial Latin America* (Albuquerque: University of New Mexico Press, 1998).

128. Examples of this can be found in José Ramón Jouve Martín, *Esclavos de la ciudad letrada: Esclavitud, escritura, y colonialismo en Lima (1650–1700)* (Lima: IEP, Instituto de Estudios Peruanos, 2005); Margarita González, *Ensayos de historia colonial colombiana*, 2nd ed. (Bogota: Ancora Editores, 1984); and Gregorio Hernández de Alba, *Libertad de los esclavos en Colombia* (Bogota: Editorial ABC, 1956).

129. Silvia Z. Mitchell, *Queen, Mother, and Stateswoman: Mariana of Austria and the Government of Spain* (University Park: Penn State University Press, 2019).

130. Manzano, *Recopilación de leyes*, Ley 9, Título 5, Libro 7, 286–87.

131. For a lucid discussion of such incentives, see Harper, *Slavery in the Late Roman World*, 220 (see introduction, n. 64). He in turn is elaborating on an "incentive model" first proposed by Stefano Fenoaltea, "Slavery and Supervision in Comparative Perspective: A Model," *Journal of Economic History* 44, no. 3 (1984): 635–68.

132. Even in the harshest plantation environments, there existed a mix of incentives. For example, food, religious celebrations, slave men's access to slave or free African or creole women, and better housing were often used to encourage hard work and good behavior. Klein and Vinson, *African Slavery in Latin America and the Caribbean*, 60–63.

133. Klein and Vinson, *African Slavery in Latin America and the Caribbean*, 19–23.

134. Robert Cooper West's *Colonial Placer Mining in Colombia* is still a relevant classic on this topic (Baton Rouge: Louisiana State University Press, 1952); for a comparative perspective see Peter J. Bakewell, *Silver Mining and Society in Colonial Mexico: Zacatecas, 1546–1700*, Cambridge Latin American Studies, 15 (Cambridge, MA: Cambridge University Press, 1971).

135. Borrego Plá, *Cartagena de Indias en el siglo XVI*, 140.

136. Barbara Bush, *Slave Women in Caribbean Society, 1650–1838* (Bloomington: Indiana University Press, 1990), 23–33.

137. Lucena Salmoral, *Leyes para esclavos*, 644.

138. See, for instance, Francisco Aguirre negro esclavo de Francisco Jiménez de Enciso, su pleito con este por obtener su libertad y pago de jornales, 1666. Fondo: Colonia. Grupo: Negros y esclavos de Bolívar, Legajo 14, Documento 2, Folios 25r–156v, AGN, Bogota. Hereafter cited as Francisco Aguirre negro esclavo vs. Francisco Jiménez de Enciso.

139. There is an expansive debate about the form of medieval social relations, and when and how they changed, aptly introduced in Keith Wrightson, "Mutualities and Obligations: Changing Social Relationships in Early Modern England," in *Proceedings of the British Academy*, vol. 139, *Lectures 2005*, ed. P. J. Marshall (London: British Academy, 2007).

140. Frederick P. Bowser, *The African Slave in Colonial Peru, 1524–1650* (Stanford: Stanford University Press, 1974), 79.

141. Abulafia, *The Discovery of Mankind*, 296.

142. The maximum expression of owners' control over enslaved families is laid out in Ned Sublette and Constance Sublette, *The American Slave Coast: A History of the Slave-Breeding Industry* (Chicago: Lawrence Hill Books, 2016).

143. Juana Patricia Pérez Munguía, "Derecho indiano para esclavos, negros, y castas: Integración, control, y estructura estamental," *Memoria y Sociedad* 7, no. 15 (2003): 196–97.

144. Munguía, "Derecho indiano para esclavos, negros, y castas," 198.

145. See María Cristina Navarrete, *Cimarrones y palenques en el siglo XVII* (Cali: Universidad del Valle, 2003). A specific example of the care warring military planners gave to the presence of potential Afroiberian allies may be found in Walter Bigges, Lieutenant Croftes, and Sir Thomas Gates, *A Summarie and True Discourse of Sir Francis Drakes West Indian Voyage: Wherein were Taken, the Townes of Saint Iago, Sancto Domingo, Cartagena & Saint Augustine: With Geographicall Mappes Exactly Describing each of the Townes with their Scituations, and the Manner of the Armies Approching to the Winning of them* (Imprinted at London: By Richard Field, dwelling in the Blacke-Friars by Ludgate, 1589).

146. See Jane Landers and Barry Robinson, "Cimarron and Citizen," in Landers and Robinson, *Slaves, Subjects, and Subversives*, 126–28.

147. McKinley paints a masterful picture of the myriad legal hustles that slaves used to exert control over their own lives in *Fractional Freedoms* (see introduction, n. 51).

148. David Armitage and Michael J. Braddick, eds., *The British Atlantic World, 1500–1800* (New York: Palgrave Macmillan, 2002).

149. "Unlike other New World settlers, the English had neither a law of slavery nor a tradition of slavery. The English, who arrived in Jamestown in 1607, came from a place where the legal institution of slavery was a relic of the past. Moreover, when the English came to Virginia, they saw themselves as potential liberators of the Indians and slaves, who were under the domination of the Spanish." Paul Finkelman, "Slavery in the United States: Persons or Property?" in *The Legal Understanding of Slavery: From the Historical to the Contemporary*, ed. Jean Allain (Oxford: Oxford University Press, 2012), 106.

150. Linda M. Rupert, "Marronage, Manumission, and Maritime Trade in the Early Modern Caribbean," *Slavery & Abolition* 30, no. 3 (2009): 361–82, 361. This article examines two sets of legal frameworks that were developed in the Dutch and Spanish orbits to deal with the movement of enslaved people in the context of contraband trade, as well as the impact and influence of these laws and the range of creative responses by enslaved people to the opportunities that the new legal systems created.

151. Rupert, "Marronage, Manumission, and Maritime Trade," 368; see also Natalie Zemon Davis, "Judges, Masters, Diviners: Slaves' Experience of Criminal Justice in Colonial Suriname," *Law and History Review* 29, no. 4 (2011): 925–84.

152. María Montera, negra horra, demandó a Alonso Peralta, por la devolución de una negra esclava que la negra Montera le había hipotecado. 1629, Fondo: Colonia. Grupo: Negros y Esclavos de Bolívar, Legajo 14, Documento 16, Folios 827r–918v, AGN, Bogota. Hereafter cited as María Montera negra horra vs. Alonso Peralta.

153. El Virrey aprueba los procedimientos empleados por don Manuel Díaz de Hoyos, alcalde de Santafé, para sofocar la insolencia de un esclavo de don Miguel Arteaga, tío del oidor don Juan Francisco Pey Ruíz, 1772. Fondo: Colonia. Grupo: Miscelánea, SC. 39, Legajo 116, Documento 78, Folios 531r–33v, AGN, Bogota.

154. Juan de Escanio contra Miguel de Gallas, defendiendo a unos negros suyos por ser acusados de robo, 1628. Fondo: Colonia. Grupo: Negros y esclavos de Bolívar, Legajo 2, Documento 6, Folios 661r–750v, AGN, Bogota. Among the principals and witnesses of this single case we find examples of all of the above.

155. María Montera negra horra vs. Alonso Peralta, Folios 827r–918v.

156. María Montera negra horra vs. Alonso Peralta, Folio 829r.

157. María Montera negra horra vs. Alonso Peralta, Folios 834v–36v.

158. María Montera negra horra vs. Alonso Peralta, Folios 831r–33r, 847r–48r, and 851v–52r.

159. María Montera negra horra vs. Alonso Peralta, Folios 897r–99r.

160. María Montera negra horra vs. Alonso Peralta, Folio 828r.

161. One of the effects of racism is the need to keep discovering Iberoamerica's African past. See Henry Louis Gates Jr., *Black in Latin America* (New York: New York University Press, 2011).

162. A good example of this can be found in Cottrol, *The Long, Lingering Shadow* (see introduction, n. 49). The importance of enslaved people's resistance in the creation of modernity is argued for by Eugene D. Genovese, *From Rebellion to Revolution: Afro-American Slave Revolts in the Making of the Modern World*, The Walter Lynwood Fleming Lectures in Southern History (Baton Rouge: Louisiana State University Press, 1979). The centrality of the way domesticity is conceived can be seen in Jack Goody, *Production and Reproduction: A Comparative Study of the Domestic Domain* (New York: Cambridge University Press, 1976). See also Annette Gordon-Reed and Peter S. Onuf, *"Most Blessed of the Patriarchs": Thomas Jefferson and the Empire of the Imagination* (New York: WW Norton & Company, 2016) and Martha S. Jones, "Time, Space, and Jurisdiction in Atlantic World Slavery: The Volunbrun Household in Gradual Emancipation New York," *Law and History Review* 29, no. 4 (2011): 1031–6060.

163. Malick W. Ghachem, "Prosecuting Torture: The Strategic Ethics of Slavery in Pre-Revolutionary Saint-Domingue (Haiti)," *Law and History Review* 29, no. 4 (2011): 985–1029.

164. Ghachem, "Prosecuting Torture," 985.

165. Kagan, *Lawsuits and Litigants in Castile, 1500–1700*, 113.

166. Excellent examples of this are provided throughout by Nicole von Germeten, *Violent Delights, Violent Ends: Sex, Race, and Honor in Colonial Cartagena de Indias* (Albuquerque: University of New Mexico Press, 2013).

167. Roger Pita Pico, "La 'esclavitud' de los sentimientos: Vida familiar y afectiva de la población esclava en el nororiente del Nuevo Reino de Granada, 1720–1819," *Revista de Indias* 72, no. 256 (2012): 651–86, 682.

168. Lucena Salmoral, *Leyes para esclavos*, 148.

Chapter 2

1. Bernal Díaz del Castillo, *The Conquest of New Spain*, trans. J. M. Cohen (Harmondsworth, UK: Penguin Books, 1963).

2. An effective overview is provided by John Edwards, *The Spanish Inquisition* (Stroud, Charleston, SC: Tempus, 1999).

3. For an excellent work that thickly describes the complexity and interconnected nature of religious trials, see Alison Rowlands, *Witchcraft Narratives in Germany: Rothenburg, 1561–1652* (Manchester, UK: Manchester University Press, 2003).

4. The understanding of the legitimacy that the Catholic Church had in places that became strongholds of Protestant power has been upended by the influential book by Eamon Duffy, *The Stripping of the Altars: Traditional Religion in England, 1400–1580* (New Haven, CT: Yale University Press, 2005).

5. Arab armies supplemented by Berber converts dealt Iberian forces a series of shattering blows, starting with the defeat of Roderic at Guadalete in 711. By the time any significant

pushback is recorded, Pelagius is "huddling" in Asturias, contemplating a no more certain future than that of the southern Franks. Within a few years, Muslim control over the Iberian Peninsula was almost absolute, leaving only a few semi-independent Christian polities that survived at the margins under the leadership of chieftains such as Theudemir, who cut an autonomy deal with the Muslims in Southeast Iberia.

6. The effects of expansion on the development of medieval society is explained by Robert Bartlett, *The Making of Europe: Conquest, Colonization, and Cultural Change, 950–1350* (Princeton: Princeton University Press, 1993).

7. Alex Novikoff, "Between Tolerance and Intolerance in Medieval Spain: A Historiographic Enigma," *Medieval Encounters* 11, nos. 1–2 (2005): 7–36. See also Marcelino Menéndez Pelayo, *Historia de los heterodoxos españoles* (Madrid: CSIC, 1992).

8. Both hostility and pragmatic toleration are reflected in popular imagination. See Mar Martínez Góngora, "El Magreb, pluralidad y memoria: Cervantes y las crónicas de Berbería en 'La historia del cautivo,'" *Cervantes: Bulletin of the Cervantes Society of America* 37, no. 2 (2017): 35–67.

9. Late medieval attitudes toward heterogeneity can be seen in Nora Berend, *At the Gate of Christendom: Jews, Muslims, and "Pagans" in Medieval Hungary, c. 1000–c. 1300*, Cambridge Studies in Medieval Life and Thought; 4th Ser., 50 (New York: Cambridge University Press, 2001); and John Arnold, *Inquisition and Power: Catharism and the Confessing Subject in Medieval Languedoc* (Philadelphia: University of Pennsylvania Press, 2001).

10. See Geoffrey Barraclough, *The Medieval Papacy* (London: Thames & Hudson, 1968).

11. The creation and endurance of this institution is expertly overviewed by Melvyn Bragg, "In Our Time: The Spanish Inquisition," BBC, June 2006, http://www.bbc.co.uk/programmes/p003c1bw.

12. The intensity of religiosity in medieval communities can be seen in David Nirenberg, *Communities of Violence: Persecution of Minorities in the Middle Ages* (Princeton: Princeton University Press, 1996); and Rudolph M. Bell, *Holy Anorexia* (Chicago: University of Chicago Press, 1987).

13. The complexity of this moment and its memory is introduced by Justin Stearns, "Representing and Remembering Al-Andalus: Some Historical Considerations Regarding the End of Time and the Making of Nostalgia," *Medieval Encounters* 15, nos. 2–4 (2009): 355–74.

14. For an overview of the extraordinary challenges faced by the Hapsburg dynasty see Patrick Balfour Kinross, *The Ottoman Centuries: The Rise and Fall of the Turkish Empire* (New York: Morrow, 1977); and Diarmaid MacCulloch, *Reformation: Europe's House Divided 1490–1700* (New York: Penguin Books, 2003).

15. Louise Milne, "Pieter Bruegel and Carlo Ginzburg: The Debatable Land of Renaissance Dreams," *Cosmos* 29 (2013): 59–126.

16. MacCulloch, *Reformation*.

17. Mary Elizabeth Perry and Anne J. Cruz, eds. *Cultural Encounters: The Impact of the Inquisition in Spain and the New World* (Berkeley: University of California Press, 1991), 155.

18. Silvio Arturo Zavala, *La filosofía política en la conquista de América* (Mexico City: Fondo de Cultura Económica, 1947), 70.

19. The structure of the supervision of Afroiberians is laid out by José Andrés-Gallego, *La esclavitud en la América española* (Madrid: Ediciones Encuentro; Fundación Ignacio Larramendi, 2005), 89–94. A useful comparison to the functioning of the Cartagena branch can be found in

Alberro, Solange, *La actividad del Santo Oficio de la Inquisición en Nueva España, 1571–1700* (Colección Científica, México: Instituto Nacional de Antropología e Historia, Departamento de Investigaciones Históricas, Seminario de Historia de las Mentalidades y Religión en el México Colonial, 1981).

20. Rina Cáceres Gómez, *Rutas de la esclavitud en África y América Latina* (San Jose, Costa Rica: Editorial de la Universidad de Costa Rica, 2001).

21. Borrego Plá, *Cartagena de Indias en el siglo XVI*, 126.

22. Margaret M. Olsen, *Slavery and Salvation in Colonial Cartagena de Indias* (Gainesville: University Press of Florida, 2004), 56.

23. Alex Borucki, David Eltis, and David Wheat, "Atlantic History and the Slave Trade to Spanish America," *American Historical Review* 120, no. 2 (2015): 434.

24. See, for example, Ana E. Schaposchnik, *The Lima Inquisition: The Plight of Crypto-Jews in Seventeenth-Century Peru* (Madison: University of Wisconsin Press, 2015).

25. For example, Bowser's *African Slave in Colonial Peru* is vastly useful and detailed (see chapter 1, n. 140). However, even though he utilizes inquisitorial sources throughout his book, Bowser dedicates only two pages to the structure, interests, and institutional culture of the Holy Office. Another example of this is the similarly useful Heather Rachelle White, "Between the Devil and the Inquisition: African Slaves and the Witchcraft Trials in Cartagena de Indies," *The North Star* 8, no. 2 (2005): 1–15. White, however, paints the Inquisition as an institution oppressive toward slaves and does not interrogate the manner in which testimony was produced before the tribunal.

26. Diana Luz Ceballos Gómez, *Hechicería, brujería, e inquisición en el Nuevo Reino de Granada: Un duelo de imaginarios* (Bogotá, Colombia: Editorial Universidad Nacional, 1994).

27. See Germán Colmenares, *Historia económica y social de Colombia: Popayán, una sociedad esclavista, 1680–1800* (Bogotá: La Carreta, 1979).

28. The persistent engagement of Spanish governance with the institution of slavery is illustrated by Tatiana Seijas and Pablo Miguel Sierra Silva, "The Persistence of the Slave Market in Seventeenth-Century Central Mexico," *Slavery & Abolition* 37, no. 2 (2016): 307–33.

29. Vinson, Bryant, and O'Toole, *Africans to Spanish America* (see introduction, n. 45); Rachel Sarah O'Toole, *Bound Lives: Africans, Indians, and the Making of Race in Colonial Peru* (Pittsburgh: University of Pittsburgh Press, 2012).

30. Catalina, negra esclava de Beatriz de Quintanilla, procesada en Cartagena como hechicera y herbolaria, y sentenciada a muerte. 1566, Fondo: Colonia. Grupo: Negros y esclavos de Bolívar, Legajo 6, Documento 3, Folios 273r–356v. AGN, Bogota. Hereafter cited as Catalina, esclava procesada por brujería.

31. Catalina, esclava procesada por brujería, Folios 278r–80r.

32. Catalina, esclava procesada por brujería, Folios 284v–85r.

33. Catalina, esclava procesada por brujería, Folios 284r–88v.

34. Catalina, esclava procesada por brujería, Folios 309v–310r.

35. Poignant examples of this torture can be found in Catalina, esclava procesada por brujería, Folios 291r, 292r, 297v299r, and 307r.

36. Catalina, esclava procesada por brujería, Folios 308v–28v.

37. Catalina, esclava procesada por brujería, Folio 321r.

38. Catalina, esclava procesada por brujería, Folios 331v–33r.

39. Catalina, esclava procesada por brujería, Folios 334r–41r.

40. Catalina, esclava procesada por brujería, Folios 340v–55r.

41. Catalina, esclava procesada por brujería, Folio 320r.

42. Splendiani, Sánchez Bohórquez, and Luque de Salazar, *Cincuenta años de Inquisición*, 87 (see introduction, n. 63).

43. See Kathryn Joy McKnight, "Performing Double-Edged Stories: The Three Trials of Paula de Eguiluz," *Colonial Latin American Review* 25, no. 2 (2016): 154–74.

44. The institutional sophistication of the Spanish Inquisition is brought home by comparison. See, for example, Alison Rowlands, "Father Confessors and Clerical Intervention in Witch-Trials in Seventeenth-Century Lutheran Germany: The Case of Rothenburg, 1692," *The English Historical Review* 131, no. 552 (2016): 1010–42.

45. Splendiani, Sánchez Bohórquez, and Luque de Salazar, *Cincuenta años de Inquisición*, 88. This Spanish phrase is difficult to elegantly render in English, but was used to refer to people who were "excessively rude" (in the sense of being unsophisticated, uncultured) and uncouth in expression.

46. Excomunión, 1633, Inquisición 4816, Expediente 19, Folios 1r–197r, AHN, Madrid.

47. Proceso criminal contra Juan López de Medina por homicidio del negro Domingo Folupo, esclavo de don Gregorio Vanquesel, 1668. Inquisición 1617, Expediente 7, Folio 1r–124v, AHN, Madrid. Hereafter cited as Gregorio Vanquesel vs. Juan López de Medina.

48. This policy was applied across the board in Cartagena, regardless of the race or servile condition of the accused. In 1680 Santiago Peregrino, a recently arrived and converted Turk, was accused of practicing "sortileges." The inquisitors absolved him because of his ignorance and sent him to the local priest to be instructed in the faith. See Fermina Álvarez Alonso, *La Inquisición en Cartagena de Indias durante el siglo XVII* (Madrid: Fundación Universitaria Española, 1999), 219.

49. As yet, no single monograph deals comprehensively with this interaction, although some books examine this issue in particular regions and a growing body of articles and dissertations examine singular cases. See, for example, Ana María Díaz Burgos, *Fisuras inquisitoriales, voces femeninas, y hechicería en Cartagena de Indias* (PhD diss., Emory University, 2011). Burgos focuses on the case of Doña Lorenzana, the wife of the royal scribe of Cartagena de Indias, whose charges and subsequent sentence seem to contradict her social position, status as wife and mother, age, and lineage. Although Doña Lorenzana may ultimately have been condemned, it is Burgos's contention that the voluminous case, 106 pages front and back, reveals in its fissures the incomplete hegemony and even subversion of inquisitorial law, socioeconomic stratification, and racial codes in this auto-da-fé. Her approach, based on extensive archival research in Spain, Colombia, and the United States, opens up an interdisciplinary reading of these documents based on history, rhetorical analysis, and gender studies.

50. Contextualizing the extraordinary life of Paula de Eguiluz, McKnight provides a succinct survey of the historiography of slaves and witch trials. See "Performing Double-Edged Stories."

51. Splendiani, Sánchez Bohórquez, and Luque de Salazar, *Cincuenta años de Inquisición*, 31. See also Andrés Roncancio Parra, Indices de documentos de la Inquisición de Cartagena de Indias: Programa de recuperación, sistematización, y divulgación de archivos (Bogota: Instituto Colombiano de Cultura Hispánica, Ministerio de Cultura, 2000), xi.

52. The process through which the Catholic Church made orthodox Christians out of

enslaved Africans is explored in depth in Joan Cameron Bristol, *Christians, Blasphemers, and Witches: Afro-Mexican Ritual Practice in the Seventeenth Century* (Albuquerque: University of New Mexico Press, 2007), 63–91.

53. Álvarez Alonso, *La Inquisición en Cartagena de Indias*, 212.

54. Domingo Martínez contra Francisco de Llerena y Juan Domingo, niño negro esclavo, por la muerte de Manuel Melgarejo. 1685, Inquisición 1618, Expediente 4, Folios 1r–293v, AHN, Madrid. Hereafter cited as Domingo Martínez vs. Francisco de Llerena y Juan Domingo niño negro esclavo.

55. Domingo Martínez vs. Francisco de Llerena y Juan Domingo niño negro esclavo, Folio 116r.

56. Richard Price, *Maroon Societies: Rebel Slave Communities in the Americas*, 3rd ed. (Baltimore, MD: Johns Hopkins University Press, 1996). See also David M. Davidson, "Negro Slave Control and Resistance in Colonial Mexico, 1519–1650," *The Hispanic American Historical Review* 46, no. 3 (1966): 235–53; and María del Carmen Borrego Plá, *Palenques de negros en Cartagena de Indias a fines del siglo XVII* (Seville: Escuela de Estudios Hispano-Americanos, 1973).

57. See the examples in Luz Adriana Maya Restrepo, *Brujería y reconstrucción de identidades entre los africanos y sus descendientes en la Nueva Granada, Siglo XVII* (Bogota: Ministerio de Cultura, 2005).

58. Bowser, *African Slave in Colonial Peru*, 260 (see chapter 1, n. 140).

59. See Bennett, *Africans in Colonial Mexico* (see ch. 1, n. 19).

60. O'Toole, "To be Free and Lucumí: Ana de la Calle and Making African Diaspora Identities in Colonial Peru," in Vinson, Bryant, and O'Toole, *Africans to Spanish America*, 73–92 (see introduction, n. 45); O'Toole, *Bound Lives*; Douglas Walter Bristol, *Knights of the Razor: Black Barbers in Slavery and Freedom* (Baltimore: Johns Hopkins University Press, 2009); Frank T. Proctor, *Damned Notions of Liberty: Slavery, Culture, and Power in Colonial Mexico, 1640–1769* (Albuquerque: University of New Mexico Press, 2010); Javier Villa-Flores, *Dangerous Speech: A Social History of Blasphemy in Colonial Mexico* (Tucson: University of Arizona Press, 2006); Bowser, *African Slave in Colonial Peru*; Bennett, *Africans in Colonial Mexico*.

61. Although some can be found; see Jaime Humberto Borja Gómez, *Inquisición, muerte, y sexualidad en el Nuevo Reino de Granada* (Bogota: Editorial Ariel; CEJA, 1996).

62. Proceso criminal contra Pedro de Angola, esclavo negro del capitán Antonio Núñez de Gramajo, por lesiones a Diego, esclavo negro de la viuda de Luis Blanco de Salcedo. 1627, Inquisición 1616, Expediente 10, Folios 2r–2v, AHN, Madrid. Hereafter cited as Juan de Ortíz vs. Pedro de Angola negro esclavo.

63. Juan de Ortíz vs. Pedro de Angola negro esclavo, Folio 15v.

64. Juan de Ortíz vs. Pedro de Angola negro esclavo, Folio 2v.

65. Brian P. Levack, *The Witch-Hunt in Early Modern Europe* (London: Longman, 1987).

66. See the introduction in Henry Kamen, *The Spanish Inquisition: A Historical Revision* (New Haven, CT: Yale University Press, 1998).

67. Navarrete, *Génesis y desarrollo*, 58–60 (see chapter 1, n. 74).

68. For a good example of this, see the beautiful description of the first auto-da-fé carried out in Cartagena de Indias in Álvarez Alonso, *La Inquisición en Cartagena de Indias*, Appendix 3.

69. Gregorio Vanquesel vs. Juan López de Medina, Folio 24v.

70. Gregorio Vanquesel vs. Juan López de Medina, Folios 3r–120r.

71. Gregorio Vanquesel vs. Juan López de Medina, Folios 3r–14r.

72. Gregorio Vanquesel vs. Juan López de Medina, Folios 57r–99r.

73. Franklin E. Zimring, *The Great American Crime Decline* (New York: Oxford University Press, 2007), 12.

74. Splendiani, Sánchez Bohórquez, and Luque de Salazar, *Cincuenta años de Inquisición*, 239.

75. Splendiani, Sánchez Bohórquez, and Luque de Salazar, 297.

76. Splendiani, Sánchez Bohórquez, and Luque de Salazar, 298.

77. While canon law was broadly the same in the Portuguese Empire as in the Spanish Empire, Brazil lacked a permanent branch of the Inquisition, allowing greater deviance from accepted dogma. The proximity of the Spanish Inquisition increased the riskiness of supernatural aid in any endeavor. See Laura de Mello E. Souza, *The Devil and the Land of the Holy Cross: Witchcraft, Slavery, and Popular Religion in Colonial Brazil* (Austin: University of Texas Press, 2003).

78. Splendiani, Sánchez Bohórquez, and Luque de Salazar, *Cincuenta años de Inquisición*, 299.

79. See Andrés-Gallego, *La esclavitud en la América española*, 111.

80. See chapter 6 of von Germeten, *Violent Delights*, in which she discusses Paula de Eguiluz (see chapter 1, n. 166).

81. Splendiani, Sánchez Bohórquez, and Luque de Salazar, *Cincuenta años de Inquisición*, 195.

82. *Cincuenta años de Inquisición*, 237.

83. Splendiani, Sánchez Bohórquez, and Luque de Salazar, *Cincuenta años de Inquisición*, 306.

84. *Cincuenta años de Inquisición*, 49. The title *mohan* was actually an indigenous term that had been transformed to include African healers.

85. *Cincuenta años de Inquisición*, 335.

86. *Cincuenta años de Inquisición*, 336.

87. *Cincuenta años de Inquisición*, 334.

88. *Cincuenta años de Inquisición*, 335.

89. Splendiani, Sánchez Bohórquez, and Luque de Salazar, *Cincuenta años de Inquisición*, 336.

90. Kathryn Joy McKnight, "'En su tierra lo aprendió': An African Curandero's Defense before the Cartagena Inquisition," *Colonial Latin American Review* 12, no. 1 (2003): 63. Interestingly, the use of herbs wherever it was learned of was perfectly acceptable to the Inquisition. Perhaps McKnight did not know this, which led her to underestimate the multilayered and sophisticated defense presented by Mateo Arará.

91. *Cincuenta años de Inquisición*, 336.

92. Álvarez Alonso, *La Inquisición en Cartagena de Indias*, 205–6.

93. Splendiani, Sánchez Bohórquez, and Luque de Salazar, *Cincuenta años de Inquisición*, 318.

94. The awareness of the Inquisition of its need to keep different stakeholders across the global Hapsburg empires on board with their mission while navigating the intrigues of the court is ably introduced by Kimberly Lynn, *Between Court and Confessional: The Politics of Spanish Inquisitors* (New York: Cambridge University Press, 2013).

95. In Cartagena the Jesuits arrived late in comparison with the different mendicant orders. They rapidly distinguished themselves by taking on the ministry among enslaved Africans with great devotion. See José del Rey Fajardo, *Los jesuitas en Cartagena de Indias, 1604–1767* (Bogota: Centro Editorial Javeriano, 2004).

96. A picture of the complexity of local religiosity can be found in María Piedad Quevedo Alvarado, *Un cuerpo para el espíritu: Mística en la Nueva Granada, el cuerpo, el gusto, y el asco,*

1680–1750 (Bogota: Instituto Colombiano de Antropología e Historia, 2007); and Kathryn Joy McKnight, "Confronted Rituals: Spanish Colonial and Angolan 'Maroon' Executions in Cartagena de Indias (1634)," *Journal of Colonialism & Colonial History* 5, no. 3 (2004): 1–19.

97. Liam Matthew Brockey, *Journey to the East: The Jesuit Mission to China, 1579–1724* (Cambridge, MA: Harvard University Press, 2007); C. R. Boxer, ed., *South China in the Sixteenth Century* (Bangkok: Orchid Press, 2006); Timothy Brook, *Vermeer's Hat: The Seventeenth Century and the Dawn of the Global World* (London: Profile Books, 2008).

98. José Toribio Medina, *La Inquisición en Cartagena de Indias*, 2nd ed. (Bogota: Carlos Valencia Editores, 1978).

Chapter 3

1. M. I. Finley, *Ancient Slavery and Modern Ideology* (London: Chatto & Windus, 1980), 142.

2. Elliott, *Empires of the Atlantic World*, 131 (see introduction, n. 35).

3. The complex, contested, and changing nature of honor is succinctly summarized by Ann Twinam, "The Negotiation of Honor" in *The Faces of Honor: Sex, Shame, and Violence in Colonial Latin America*, ed. Lyman L. Johnson and Sonya Lipsett-Rivera, 68–102 (Albuquerque: University of New Mexico Press, 1998).

4. E. G. Bourne, ed., *The Northmen, Columbus, and Cabot, 985–1503: The Voyages of the Northmen* (New York: Charles Scribner's Sons, 1906), 270.

5. The difficulty of projecting transatlantic military power against entrenched and determined opposition is demonstrated by John Gabriel Stedman, *Narrative of a Five Years Expedition against the Revolted Negroes of Surinam*, Richard Price and Sally Price, eds. (Baltimore: Johns Hopkins University Press, 1988).

6. Ably introduced by Antonio Benítez Rojo and James E. Maraniss, *The Repeating Island: The Caribbean and the Postmodern Perspective* (Durham: Duke University Press, 1996).

7. Jack D. Forbes, *Africans and Native Americans: The Language of Race and the Evolution of Red-Black Peoples*, 2nd ed. (Urbana: University of Illinois Press, 1993).

8. Stephanie E. Smallwood, *Saltwater Slavery: A Middle Passage from Africa to American Diaspora* (Cambridge, MA: Harvard University Press, 2007); Linda M. Rupert, "Contraband Trade and the Shaping of Colonial Societies in Curaçao and Tierra Firme." *Itinerario* 30, no. 3 (2006): 35; Rebecca J. Scott, "Paper Thin: Freedom and Re-Enslavement in the Diaspora of the Haitian Revolution," *Law and History Review* 29, no. 4 (2011): 1061–87; Manisha Sinha, *The Slave's Cause: A History of Abolition* (New Haven, CT: Yale University Press, 2016); Jalil Sued-Badillo, "Facing Up to Caribbean History." *American Antiquity* 57, no. 4 (1992): 599–607; Hermes Tovar Pinzón, *La estación del miedo o la desolación dispersa: El Caribe colombiano en el siglo XVI* (Bogotá: Editorial Ariel, 1997).

9. See David Brion Davis, *Inhuman Bondage: The Rise and Fall of Slavery in the New World* (New York: Oxford University Press, 2006); and Ira Berlin and Leslie M. Harris, ed., *Slavery in New York* (New York: New Press, 2005).

10. Horacio Bernardo, *Libres y esclavos* (Montevideo: Ediciones La Gotera, 2005); Alex Borucki, Karla Chagas, and Natalia Stalla, *Esclavitud y trabajo: Un estudio sobre los afrodescendientes en la frontera uruguaya (1835–1855)* (Montevideo: Pulmón Ediciones, 2004).

11. Consejo de Indias, *Recopilación de leyes de los Reinos de las Indias*, 5th ed. (Madrid: Boix, 1841).

12. A good explanation of the theoretical basis of and consequences of this policy is provided by José de la Puente Brunke, "Codicia y bien público: Los ministros de la Audiencia en la Lima seiscentista," *Revista de Indias* 66, no. 236 (2006): 137; and Jorge L. Esquirol, *Excessive Legalism, Lawlessness and Other Stories about Latin American Law* (Doctor of Juridical Science (SJD) dissertation, Harvard Law School, 2001).

13. Knowledgeable people could use the grey zones that developed in the legal ecology to shape the outcome to their benefit. Such was the case of Diego Gómez Hidalgo, demanda que presentó en Cartagena contra José, su negro esclavo, por robo; dicha demanda originó una competencia de jurisdicción entre Diego Durango de Maza, alcalde, y Pedro Martínez de Montoya, teniente de gobernador, 1695. Fondo: Colonia. Grupo: Negros y esclavos de Bolívar, Legajo 1, Documento 2, Folios 235r–441v, AGN, Bogota.

14. For a detailed history of the kingdom and its administration, see Lucas Fernández de Piedrahita, *Historia general del Nuevo Reino de Granada* (Biblioteca Popular De Cultura Colombiana. Historia; v. 4–7. Bogota: Impreso en la Editorial ABC, 1942).

15. A broad overview of the development of Spanish imperium is presented by Richard L. Garner and William B. Taylor, eds., *Iberian Colonies, New World Societies: Essays in Memory of Charles Gibson* (University Park, PA: R. L. Garner, 1985); and J. H. Parry, *The Spanish Seaborne Empire*, Berkeley: University of California Press, 1990.

16. The same pattern can be seen in the work of Aquiles Escalante, *El negro en Colombia* (Barranquilla: Corporación Educativa Mayor del Desarrollo Simón, 2002); and María Elena Díaz, *The Virgin, the King, and the Royal Slaves of El Cobre: Negotiating Freedom in Colonial Cuba, 1670–1780* (Stanford: Stanford University Press, 2000).

17. The work of de la Fuente does an exemplary job of showing the development of an Atlantic port city. See Alejandro de la Fuente, *Havana and the Atlantic in the Sixteenth Century* (Chapel Hill: University of North Carolina Press, 2008).

18. Francisco Aguirre negro esclavo de Francisco Jiménez de Enciso, su pleito con este por obtener su libertad y pago de jornales, 1666. Fondo: Colonia. Grupo: Negros y esclavos de Bolívar, Legajo 14, Documento 2, Folios 25r–156v, AGN, Bogota. Hereafter cited as Francisco Aguirre negro esclavo vs. Francisco Jiménez de Enciso, su amo.

19. Mark A. Burkholder and Lyman L. Johnson, *Colonial Latin America*, 8th ed. (New York: Oxford University Press, 2012), 338–39.

20. For a classic but limited monograph on Spanish institutions and enslaved people see Bowser, *African Slave in Colonial Peru*, chapter 7 (see chapter 1, n. 140).

21. For recent archaeological evidence supporting the sprawl of pre-Columbian settlements, see Meritt Kennedy, "'Game Changer': Maya Cities Unearthed in Guatemalan Forest Using Lasers," NPR, February 2, 2018. Generally speaking, the process of Spanish urbanization in the New World has been widely misunderstood. See also Abdón Yaranga Valderrama, "Las 'reducciones': Uno de los instrumentos del etnocidio," *Revista Complutense de Historia de América*, no. 21 (1995): 241–62.

22. For a general overview, see Noble David Cook, *Born to Die: Disease and New World Conquest, 1492–1650* (Cambridge, UK: Cambridge University Press, 1998); a more focused examination of tropical demography is provided by Livi-Bacci, "Return to Hispaniola" (see chapter 1, n. 31).

23. Francisco negro esclavo de Manuel Bautista, pide su liberación por medio de un pleito

que promueve para ello, 1615. Fondo: Colonia. Grupo: Negros y esclavos de Bolívar, Legajo 13, Documento 9, Folio 868r, AGN, Bogota. A young black slave recently arrived from Africa, Francisco, brought a suit against his owner Manuel Bautista Pérez, resident of Cartagena, to gain his freedom. He won the suit, and the Audiencia in Santa Fe confirmed his freedom. Hereafter cited as Francisco negro esclavo vs. Manuel Bautista, su amo.

24. Francisco negro esclavo vs. Manuel Bautista, su amo, Folio 872v.

25. In 1540, the king issued another *cédula real* reiterating the obligation to daily indoctrinate all the Indians and blacks both free and slave. Lucena Salmoral, *Leyes para esclavos*, 647 (see chapter 1, n. 16).

26. Alonso de Sandoval, *Treatise on Slavery: Selections from De Instauranda Aethiopum Salute*, ed. Nicole von Germeten (Indianapolis: Hackett, 2008), x–xv.

27. A good example of the uncertain, long-running, and expensive litigation that could ensue when a slave died soon after purchase is provided by the case of Francisco Rosas, a resident of Cartagena, who brought suit against Cristóbal García and Cristóbal de Herrera, after María, a slave he had recently purchased from them, died of disease. The court found against the sellers, who were sentenced to pay back the two hundred pesos Rosas had paid for María. Francisco Rosas contra Cristóbal García y Cristóbal de Herrera, por la propiedad de unos negros esclavos, 1577. Fondo: Colonia. Grupo: Negros y esclavos de Bolívar, Legajo 13, Documento 11, Folio 1020r, AGN, Bogota. Hereafter cited as Francisco Rosas vs. Cristóbal García y Cristóbal de Herrera.

28. Ordinances in Spanish port cities took pains to determine the reputation of acculturated slaves in order to evaluate their importability. See the ordinances of Santo Domingo in Lucena Salmoral, "Leyes para esclavos," 592.

29. The witnesses in this case and the way that they supported Francisco show the different stages of socialization common to enslaved Afroiberians in the Province of Cartagena. Francisco negro esclavo vs. Manuel Bautista, su amo, Folios 865–925.

30. The range of applicable legal procedures is presented in Carlos Eduardo Valencia Villa, *Alma en boca y huesos en costal: Una aproximación a los contrastes socio-económicos de la esclavitud: Santafé, Mariquita, y Mompox, 1610–1660* (Bogota: Instituto Colombiano de Antropología e Historia, 2003).

31. See, for example, Francisco Rosas vs. Cristóbal García y Cristóbal de Herrera, Folios 1019r–61v. Another case is the one Matías Suarez de Melo, canon of the cathedral of Cartagena, brought against Juana González and Antonio de Villalobos for the return of the money that he paid for Isabel Bran, who died in his home. He testified that Isabel Bran died under his care due to a serious illness that she contracted in the service of her previous masters, who treated her cruelly and inhumanely. In the end, the courts absolved the previous owners of cruelty but still found them liable for her death and ordered them to return the money received as payment for Isabel. This case is explored in more detail later in the chapter. See Matías Suarez de Melo, canónigo de la catedral de Cartagena, su relación sobre la venta que le hicieron Antonio de Villalobos y Juana González, de una negra esclava que falleció en su poder, debido a grave enfermedad, por crueles tratamientos, 1653. Fondo: Colonia. Grupo: Negros y esclavos de Bolívar, Legajo 15, Documento 3, Folios 48r–230v, AGN, Bogota. Hereafter cited as Matías Suarez de Melo, canónigo de la catedral de Cartagena, vs. Antonio de Villalobos y Juana González.

32. An in-depth investigation into a consortium of slave traffickers can be found in Marisa

Vega Franco, *El tráfico de esclavos con América: Asientos de grillo y lomelín, 1663–1674* (Seville: Escuela de Estudios Hispano-Americanos de Sevilla, 1984).

33. A general investigation of the narratives animating Iberoamerican society can be found in Ann Twinam, *Public Lives, Private Secrets: Gender, Honor, Sexuality, and Illegitimacy in Colonial Spanish America* (Stanford: Stanford University Press, 1999); the specific case of Cartagena is explored in ManuelTejado Fernández, *Aspectos de la vida social en Cartagena de Indias durante el seiscientos* (Seville: Escuela de Estudios Hispano-Americanos, 1954).

34. Francisco Gutiérrez de Jereda contra Josefa Melgarejo, por la redhibitoria de la venta de una esclava, 1665. Fondo: Colonia. Grupo: Negros y esclavos de Bolívar, Legajo 14, Documento 10, Folio 590r–91v, AGN, Bogota. Hereafter cited as Francisco Gutiérrez de Jereda vs. Josefa Melgarejo.

35. An overview of this is presented by Navarrete, *Génesis y desarrollo*, 145–91 (see chapter 1, n. 74).

36. The role of enslaved artisans is forcefully presented in Bowser, *African Slave in Colonial Peru*, chapter 6.

37. Navarrete, *Génesis y desarrollo*, 211–47. See also Jennifer L. Morgan, *Laboring Women: Reproduction and Gender in New World Slavery* (Philadelphia: University of Pennsylvania Press, 2004).

38. In 1653 Cristóbal de Bustamante and other heirs of Magdalena Esquivel, vecina of Cartagena, took Juana Bran and Ana Biojó, two of her former slaves, to court. The enslaved women had been living in freedom for three years since Magdalena Esquivel's death, and claimed that she had freed them in her will. Cristóbal de Bustamante argued that this had not been the case, and therefore that Juana Bran and Ana Biojó belonged to Magdalena Esquivel's heirs. As such, he petitioned the court to have them re-enslaved. As the final will and testament of Magdalena Esquivel could not be located, the judges of the Real Audiencia gave the slave women a term of two years to pay 325 patacones each, and if they did so, they would forever after be free. See Magdalena Esquivel, vecina que fue de Cartagena, cuyos herederos, encabezados por Cristóbal Bustamante, sostienen pleito con las esclavas de ella, a quienes por póstuma disposición testamentaria concedía su libertad, 1653. Fondo: Colonia. Grupo: Negros y esclavos de Bolívar, Legajo 14, Documento 4, Folio 186r, AGN, Bogota.

39. Lawsuit between Catalina Pimienta Pacheco, vecina of Cartagena, widow of *capitán* Julio Evangelista, and her slave Juana Zamba, who requested that the courts grant her freedom. Catalina Pimiento Pacheco, vecina de Cartagena, viuda del capitán Julio Evangelista, tiene un pleito con Juana, su negra esclava, quien pedía carta de libertad, 1634. Fondo: Colonia. Grupo: Negros y esclavos de Bolívar, Legajo 9, Documento 1, Folios 1–136, AGN, Bogota. Hereafter cited as Juana negra esclava vs. Catalina Pimiento Pacheco, su ama.

40. The ability of some of the enslaved Afroiberians to acquire their freedom, and in some cases become part of the slave owning class, is demonstrated by the case of María Montera, a former slave woman who prospered to the point where she had acquired several slaves of her own. María Montera negra horra vs. Alonso Peralta, Folios 827r–918v.

41. Linda M. Rupert, "Marronage, Manumission, and Maritime Trade in the Early Modern Caribbean," *Slavery & Abolition* 30, no. 3 (2009): 361–82.

42. "As dozens of cases in the Venezuelan archives attest, these immigrants were as much running toward something known and attractive—the promise of legal freedom, land, and economic opportunities—as they were fleeing away from an oppressive slave society. Like

immigrants throughout history, their journeys were based on calculated, carefully informed decisions." Rupert, "Marronage, Manumission, and Maritime Trade," 374.43. Enslaved people constantly negotiated and renegotiated the deals they made, the work they could get away with not doing, their relationships with each other and their master. In common with slaves in the Roman Empire much of the power of slave owners in Cartagena de Indias came from the negation of *otium* (leisure) to the people under their power.

44. Francisco Aguirre negro esclavo vs. Francisco Jiménez de Enciso, su amo, Folios 25r–156v.

45. Francisco Aguirre negro esclavo vs. Francisco Jiménez de Enciso, su amo, Folio 27r.

46. Francisco Aguirre negro esclavo vs. Francisco Jiménez de Enciso, su amo, Folio 30r.

47. Francisco Aguirre negro esclavo vs. Francisco Jiménez de Enciso, su amo, Folio 27v.

48. In a succinct and readable monograph, Schmidt-Nowara perhaps undervalues the role of enslaved people in the courts. See Christopher Schmidt-Nowara, *Slavery, Freedom, and Abolition in Latin America and the Atlantic World* (Albuquerque: University of New Mexico Press, 2011); conversely, the work of von Germeten extensively and sensitively uses slaves' testimony. See von Germeten, *Violent Delights* (see chapter 1, n. 166).

49. Fernando Mayorga García, *La Audiencia de Santafé en los siglos XVI y XVII* (Bogota: Instituto Colombiano de Cultura Hispánica, 1991), 601.

50. Enslaved people were also key witnesses in criminal cases. This aspect is discussed in detail in the next chapter using the case brought against Eufrasia Camargo for cruelty against her slaves. Eufrasia Camargo, se le sigue causa por sevicia con un esclavo y muerte de otros esclavos suyos, 1639. Fondo: Colonia. Grupo: Negros y esclavos de Bolívar, Legajo 1, Documento 1, Folios 1r–234v, AGN, Bogota. Hereafter cited as Eufrasia Camargo se le sigue causa por sevicia con sus esclavos.

51. Matías Suarez de Melo, canónigo de la catedral de Cartagena, vs. Antonio de Villalobos y Juana González, Folio 48r.

52. Matías Suarez de Melo, canónigo de la catedral de Cartagena, vs. Antonio de Villalobos y Juana González, Folio 55v.

53. Matías Suarez de Melo, canónigo de la catedral de Cartagena, vs. Antonio de Villalobos y Juana González, Folio 83v.

54. Matías Suarez de Melo, canónigo de la catedral de Cartagena, vs. Antonio de Villalobos y Juana González, Folio 83v.

55. Matías Suarez de Melo, canónigo de la catedral de Cartagena, vs. Antonio de Villalobos y Juana González, Folios 89–90.

56. Matías Suarez de Melo, canónigo de la catedral de Cartagena, vs. Antonio de Villalobos y Juana González, Folio 135v.

57. Matías Suarez de Melo, canónigo de la catedral de Cartagena, vs. Antonio de Villalobos y Juana González, Folio 48r.

58. Matías Suarez de Melo, canónigo de la catedral de Cartagena, vs. Antonio de Villalobos y Juana González, Folio 79v.

59. Matías Suarez de Melo, canónigo de la catedral de Cartagena, vs. Antonio de Villalobos y Juana González, Folio 55v.

60. Matías Suarez de Melo, canónigo de la catedral de Cartagena, vs. Antonio de Villalobos y Juana González, Folio 164v.

61. Matías Suarez de Melo, canónigo de la catedral de Cartagena, vs. Antonio de Villalobos y Juana González, Folio 48r.

62. Francisco de León Teleche contra Juan de Cáceres por una negra esclava llamada Manuela, que dice le pertenece a Francisco de León, 1664. Fondo: Colonia. Grupo: Negros y Esclavos de Tolima, Legajo 2, Documento 6, Folios 88r–184v, AGN, Bogota. Hereafter cited as Francisco de León Teleche vs. Juan de Cáceres.

63. Francisco de León Teleche vs. Juan de Cáceres, Folio 91r.

64. Francisco de León Teleche vs. Juan de Cáceres, Folios 99r–104r.

65. Francisco de León Teleche vs. Juan de Cáceres, Folio 133r.

66. Francisco de León Teleche vs. Juan de Cáceres, Folio 127r.

67. Francisco de León Teleche vs. Juan de Cáceres, Folio 150r.

68. Francisco de León Teleche vs. Juan de Cáceres, Folio 175r.

69. Francisco de León Teleche vs. Juan de Cáceres, Folio 112r.

70. Francisco de León Teleche vs. Juan de Cáceres, Folio 175r.

71. Gonzalo de Herrera contra Francisca de los Santos, esclava que fue de Isabel de Moya, pide su liberación, porque su ama así lo dispuso en su testamento, 1671. Fondo: Colonia. Grupo: Negros y esclavos de Bolívar, Legajo 10, Documento 3, Folios 536r–639v, AGN, Bogota.

72. Rupert, "Marronage, Manumission, and Maritime Trade," 374–76. Enrique Dussel, and Comisión de Estudios de Historia de la Iglesia en Latinoamérica, eds., *The Church in Latin America, 1492–1992*, vol. 1 of *A History of the Church in the Third World* (Maryknoll, NY: Orbis Books, 1992).

73. We can see clearly the tradeoffs between profit and integration in the poignant stories recounted throughout Edward E. Baptist, *The Half Has Never Been Told: Slavery and the Making of American Capitalism* (2014; repr., New York: Basic Books, 2016).

74. Silvio Arturo Zavala, *Servidumbre natural y libertad cristiana, según los tratadistas españoles de los siglos XVI y XVII* (Mexico City: Editorial Porrúa, 1975), 20.

75. Alexander de la Fuente, "Slaves and the Creation of Legal Rights in Cuba: Coartación and Papel," *Hispanic American Historical Review* 87, no. 4 (2007): 659–92.

76. Francisco Aguirre negro esclavo vs. Francisco Jiménez de Enciso, su amo, Folio 25r.

77. Bowser, *African Slave in Colonial Peru*, 329.

78. The following cases illustrate the tight relationship between honor, family patrimony, dowries, and enslaved people. In 1632 Francisca Domínguez, vecina of Cartagena, wife of Melchor de los Reyes, sued Gabriel Arenas over the sale of her slave María Arará. Francisca Domínguez asked the court to invalidate the sale, claiming her husband illegally took María Arará from her dowry. She lost her case in the first review but the Real Audiencia ruled in her favor upon appeal. The oidores ordered Gabriel Arenas to return the enslaved woman to Francisca Domínguez and pay her 200 pesos for lost labor. Francisca Domínguez, esposa de Melchor de los Reyes contra Gabriel de Arenas por una negra esclava perteneciente a la dote de la señora Domínguez, y que su marido se la vendió a Arenas, 1632. Fondo: Colonia. Grupo: Negros y esclavos de Bolívar, Legajo 10, Documento 4, Folio 640r–90v, AGN, Bogota. The following incomplete case contains several petitions by Juan López de Cañizares, inquiring about the reason for the imprisonment of Sebastián Negro, his slave. In these petitions Juan López de Cañizares denounces the imprisonment of his slave and requests swift justice based on the significant investment, of both social and monetary capital, that Sebastián Negro represented. He

argues that the imprisonment of his slave is causing him to lose honor. Juan López de Cañizares inquiriendo la causa de la prisión de un negro suyo llamado Sebastián, 1611. Fondo: Colonia. Grupo: Negros y esclavos de Bolívar, Legajo 6, Documento 8, Folio 634r–644v, AGN, Bogota.

79. Stephanie Gail Wood, *Transcending Conquest: Nahua Views of Spanish Colonial Mexico* (Norman: University of Oklahoma Press, 2003), 83.

80. Kris Lane, "Captivity and Redemption: Aspects of Slave Life in Early Colonial Quito and Popayán," *The Americas* 57, no. 2, *The African Experience in Early Spanish America* (2000): 225–46.

81. Claudio Moisés Ogass Bilbao, "Por mi precio o mi buen comportamiento: Oportunidades y estrategias de manumisión de los esclavos negros y mulatos en Santiago de Chile, 1698–1750," *Historia* 42, no. 1 (2009): 141–84.

82. Munguía, "Derecho indiano" (see chapter 1, n. 143).

83. Juana negra esclava vs. Catalina Pimiento Pacheco, su ama, Folio 26r.

84. Francisco Copete Jr. vs. María Josefa Copete y Lorenza Elena, Folios 1r–200v.

85. Bianca Premo, "Before the Law: Women's Petitions in the Eighteenth-Century Spanish Empire," *Comparative Studies in Society and History* 53, no. 2 (2011): 261–89.

86. Se le sigue causa a Lorenzo negro esclavo de Francisco Marmolejo, por haber cortado la cara del capitán Pedro Pérez en la procesión de los disciplinantes, 1572. Fondo: Colonia. Grupo: Negros y esclavos de Bolívar, Legajo 7, Documento 3, Folios 724r–898v, AGN, Bogota. Hereafter cited as Pedro Pérez vs. Francisco Marmolejo y su negro esclavo Lorenzo.

87. Pedro Pérez vs. Francisco Marmolejo y su negro esclavo Lorenzo, Folio 792r.

88. Pedro Pérez vs. Francisco Marmolejo y su negro esclavo Lorenzo, Folio 725r.

89. A good example of this narrative is presented by María Cristina Navarrete, "Los avatares de la mala vida: La trasgresión a la norma entre la población negra, libre y esclava," *Historia y Espacio* 19, no. 1 (2002): 12–42, 26.

90. The structure and importance of both indigenous and African slavery can be seen when mainland Europeans arrived in the Canary Islands as described by Manuel Lobo Cabrera, Ramón López Caneda, and Elisa Torres Santana, *La "otra" población: Expósitos, ilegítimos, esclavos: Las Palmas de Gran Canaria, Siglo XVIII* (Las Palmas: Universidad de Las Palmas de Gran Canaria, 1993); took shape in the Carribbean, Antonio Núñez Jiménez, *Los esclavos negros* (Havana: Fundación de la Naturaleza y el Hombre/ Editorial Letras Cubanas, 1998); spread into mainland South America, Miguel Angel Ortega, *La Esclavitud En El Contexto Agropecuario Colonial: Siglo XVIII* (Caracas: Editorial APICUM, 1992); and eventually reached all the way to the other side of the world, Rolando R. Mellafe, *La introducción de la esclavitud negra en Chile: Tráfico y rutas* (Santiago, Chile: Editorial Universitaria, 1984).

91. Moisés Munive, "Blanco seguro: El maltrato a los esclavos en Cartagena y Mompox durante el siglo XVIII," *Procesos Históricos*, no. 13 (2008): 97–116, 112. See also Andrew Jackson O'Shaughnessy, "As Historical Subjects: The African Diaspora in Colonial Latin American History," *History Compass* 11, no. 12 (2013): 1094–1110; and Franklin W. Knight, *The African Dimension in Latin American Societies* (New York: Macmillan, 1974).

92. Lynne Guitar, "Boiling it Down: Slavery on the First Commercial Sugarcane Ingenios in the Americas (Hispaniola, 1530–45)," in Landers and Robinson, *Slaves, Subjects, and Subversives*, 39–82 (see introduction, n. 38).

93. Guitar, "Boiling it Down," 50–53.

94. In the spring and summer of 1788, a master was prosecuted for the torture of two female

slaves in the French Caribbean colony of Saint-Domingue (present-day Haiti). The exceptional nature of the case was immediately obvious to the participants who lived through it. The governor and intendant of Saint-Domingue—in essence, the colony's chief military and administrative officers, respectively—described it as a "unique opportunity to arrest, by means of a single example, the course of so many cruelties." In 1788, the most recent victims of this long eighteenth-century history of cruelties included two slaves known only as Zabeth and Marie-Rose, ostensibly tortured because they were suspected of having administered poison to their master and fellow slaves. This article tells the story of the prosecution of the master who tortured them: Ghachem, "Prosecuting Torture" (see chapter 1, n. 163).

95. See the section "Disciplining Cuadrado" in chapter 4 of this book. Francisco Trejo Atienza vs. Alonso Cuadrado Cid, Folios 894r–933v.

96. See chapter 4 of this book.

Chapter 4

1. Arturo Rodríguez-Bobb, *Historia del negro en el Caribe (Cartagena, Colombia): Políticas monárquicas, transgresiones, exclusión, estrategias, poderes, esclavitud, violencia, y derechos suprimidos* (Berlin: WVB, Wissenschaftlicher Verlag Berlin, 2007).

2. See Laurent Dubois, *Avengers of the New World: The Story of the Haitian Revolution* (Cambridge, MA: Harvard University Press, 2004).

3. Gregory E. O'Malley, *Final Passages: The Intercolonial Slave Trade of British America, 1619–1807* (Chapel Hill: University of North Carolina Press, 2014); Andrew Jackson O'Shaughnessy, *An Empire Divided: The American Revolution and the British Caribbean* (Philadelphia: University of Pennsylvania Press, 2000).

4. Agustín Liniers de Estrada, *Manual de historia del derecho (español, indiano, argentino)* (Buenos Aires: Abeledo-Perrot, 1993).

5. De la Fuente, "Slave Law and Claims-Making in Cuba" (see introduction, n. 31).

6. Miguel Luque Talaván, *Un universo de opiniones: La literatura jurídica indiana* (Madrid: CSIC, 2003); also, Guillermo Floris Margadant S., *Introducción al derecho indiano y novohispano*, (Mexico City: Colegio de México, 2000).

7. Olga Portuondo Zúñiga, *Entre esclavos y libres de Cuba colonial* (Santiago de Cuba: Editorial Oriente, 2003).

8. Rushforth explores these same issues in a different but resonant geographic and historical context. Brett Rushforth, *Bonds of Alliance: Indigenous and Atlantic Slaveries in New France* (Chapel Hill: University of North Carolina Press, 2012).

9. Juan Díaz, vecino de Mompós, dueño del esclavo Domingo Angola, su apelación de la sentencia de Antonio del Castillo, teniente de gobernador de Cartagena, por la cual condenó a dicho siervo, a pena de azotes y destierro, por desacatos al alcalde, 1645. Fondo: Colonia. Grupo: Negros y esclavos de Bolívar, Legajo 14, Documento 1, Folios 1–24, AGN, Bogota. Hereafter cited as Juan Díaz appeal.

10. A selection of scholars who seem to take the position that enslaved people are usually assumed to be guilty includes Bennett, *Colonial Blackness* (see chapter 1, n. 19); Bennett, *Africans in Colonial Mexico*) (see chapter 1, n. 19); Sweet, *Recreating Africa* (see chapter 1, n. 62).

11. Guevara Jaramillo provides a good example of the relentlessly negative narrative about slaves being powerless before the brutality of their society, slave owners, and the state. Nathalia

Guevara Jaramillo, *Delito y resistencia esclava: Hurtos, homicidios y agresiones en la Nueva Granada, 1750–1800* (PhD diss., Universidad Nacional de Colombia, 2010): 153–56.

12. For an in-depth examination of these types of ploys, see von Germeten, *Violent Delights* (see chapter 1, n. 166).

13. Juan Díaz appeal, Folio 8v.

14. Juan Díaz appeal, Folio 8v.

15. Juan Díaz appeal, Folio 17v.

16. Causa hecha por Benito Maldonado contra Juan Salinas negro esclavo, por los escándalos hechos en la ciudad de Cartagena, 1622. Fondo: Colonia. Grupo: Miscelánea, SC. 39, Legajo 122, Documento 14, Folio 84r, AGN, Bogota. Hereafter cited as Benito Maldonado vs. Juan Salinas negro esclavo.

17. See, for example, Juan Díaz appeal, Folios 1r–24v.

18. Juan Díaz appeal, Folio 20r.

19. Watson, *Slave Law in the Americas*, 40 (see chapter 1, n. 105). The regulation, transformation, and transmission of slavery from the Roman Empire to Iberoamerica can be seen in William D. Phillips, *Slavery from Roman Times to the Early Transatlantic Trade* (Manchester, UK: Manchester University Press, 1985); William D. Phillips, *Slavery in Medieval and Early Modern Iberia* (Philadelphia: University of Pennsylvania Press, 2013); and José Antonio Piqueras, *La esclavitud en las Españas: Un lazo transatlántico* (Madrid: Libros de la Catarata, 2012).

20. For royal officials charged with dispensing justice to maintain the legitimacy of their office, they could not allow themselves to become beholden to any one group. "Power is the ability to determine and enforce differentiations between what is true and false. Thus, there are many possible codifications and recodifications of power relations." Kimberly Gauderman, "Father Fiction: A Comparison of English, Spanish and Andean Gender Norms," *UCLA Historical Journal* (Special Issue), vol. 12 (1992), 122 – 51.

21. Laura Foner and Eugene D. Genovese, *Slavery in the New World: A Reader in Comparative History* (Englewood Cliffs, NJ: Prentice-Hall, 1969), 113–37.

22. A good explanation of this is given by A. Leon Higginbotham and Anne F. Jacobs, "The 'Law Only as an Enemy': The Legitimization of Racial Powerlessness through the Colonial and Antebellum Criminal Laws of Virginia," *The North Carolina Law Review* 70 (1992): 969–1070.

23. Lucena Salmoral, *Leyes para esclavos*, 729.

24. For a classic explanation of this process, see Peter Marzahl, *Town in the Empire: Government, Politics, and Society in Seventeenth-Century Popayán* (Austin: University of Texas Press, 1978), 59.

25. Lucena Salmoral, *Leyes para esclavos*, 731.

26. The scholarly position that posits that enslaved people are especially victimized by the legal system of the Spanish Empire is illustrated by Navarrete, "Los avatares de la mala vida," 16 (see chapter 3, n. 89).

27. Manuel Lucena Salmoral, *Los códigos negros de la América española* (Spain: Ediciones UNESCO: Universidad Alcalá, 2000).

28. Juan Núñez de Villegas, vecino de Cartagena, su proceso por el homicidio de un negro, su esclavo, 1600. Fondo: Colonia. Grupo: Negros y esclavos de Bolívar, Legajo 11, Documento 2, Folios 171r–229v, AGN, Bogota.

29. Cuadrado Solanilla, Fiscal Real, su vista fiscal en la causa seguida al mulato Francisco

Segura, por el homicidio de Francisco Salud, negro esclavo de las galeras de Cartagena, 1610. Fondo: Colonia. Grupo: Negros y esclavos de Bolívar, Legajo 10, Documento 9, Folios 1005–1038, AGN, Bogota.

30. For the best explanation and contextualization of Sandoval's work, see Nicole von Germeten's introduction in Sandoval, *Treatise on Slavery*, ix–xxx (see chapter 3, n. 26).

31. Francisco Trejo Atienza vs. Alonso Cuadrado Cid, Folio 897r.

32. Francisco Trejo Atienza vs. Alonso Cuadrado Cid, Folios 894r–933v.

33. Ironically, "*capitán* Cuadrado" translates as "Captain Square."

34. Francisco Trejo Atienza vs. Alonso Cuadrado Cid, Folio 906r.

35. For a good description and explanation of petit marronage, see Price, *Maroon Societies*, 3 (see chapter 2, n. 56).

36. Francisco Trejo Atienza vs. Alonso Cuadrado Cid, Folio 904r.

37. See Borrego Plá, *Palenques de negros* (see chapter 2, n. 56).

38. Francisco Trejo Atienza vs. Alonso Cuadrado Cid, Folios 907r–v.

39. Francisco Trejo Atienza vs. Alonso Cuadrado Cid, Folio 895r.

40. Francisco Trejo Atienza vs. Alonso Cuadrado Cid, Folios 898v–99r.

41. Francisco Trejo Atienza vs. Alonso Cuadrado Cid, Folio 896v.

42. Francisco Trejo Atienza vs. Alonso Cuadrado Cid, Folio 896r.

43. See María Montera negra horra vs. Alonso Peralta, Folios 827r–918v.

44. Throughout the royal Spanish judiciary, following proper procedure was the rule rather than the exception. Kagan, *Lawsuits and Litigants*, 112–13 (see chapter 1, n. 62).

45. Benito Maldonado vs. Juan Salinas negro esclavo, Folios 67r–122v.

46. Benito Maldonado vs. Juan Salinas negro esclavo, Folio 70v.

47. Benito Maldonado vs. Juan Salinas negro esclavo, Folio 72v.

48. Benito Maldonado vs. Juan Salinas negro esclavo, Folio 75v.

49. Benito Maldonado vs. Juan Salinas negro esclavo, Folio 88r.

50. Benito Maldonado vs. Juan Salinas negro esclavo, Folio 95r.

51. Benito Maldonado vs. Juan Salinas negro esclavo, Folio 99v.

52. See Borrego Plá, *Cartagena de Indias*, chapter 2.

53. A thorough discussion of inland slave prices can be found in Rafael Antonio Díaz Díaz, *Esclavitud, region, y ciudad: El sistema esclavista urbano-regional en Santafé de Bogota, 1700–1750* (Bogota: Centro Editorial Javeriano CEJA, 2001), 90–109.

54. Eufrasia Camargo, se le sigue causa por sevicia con sus esclavos, Folios 1r–234v.

55. Francisco Gutiérrez de Jereda vs. Josefa Melgarejo, Folios 587r–693v.

56. Bartolomé Moriano vs. Antón del Río, Folios 824r–971v.

57. Eufrasia Camargo, se le sigue causa por sevicia con sus esclavos, Folio 6v.

58. Eufrasia Camargo, se le sigue causa por sevicia con sus esclavos, Folio 7v.

59. Eufrasia Camargo, se le sigue causa por sevicia con sus esclavos, Folios 8r–24v.

60. Eufrasia Camargo, se le sigue causa por sevicia con sus esclavos, Folio 9r.

61. Eufrasia Camargo, se le sigue causa por sevicia con sus esclavos, Folio 44v.

62. Eufrasia Camargo, se le sigue causa por sevicia con sus esclavos, Folios 51r–79v.

63. Eufrasia Camargo, se le sigue causa por sevicia con sus esclavos, Folio 67r.

64. Eufrasia Camargo, se le sigue causa por sevicia con sus esclavos, Folios 130r–37v.

65. Eufrasia Camargo, se le sigue causa por sevicia con sus esclavos, Folios 125r–156v.

66. Eufrasia Camargo, se le sigue causa por sevicia con sus esclavos, Folio 97v.

67. Another good example of this can be found in the 1653 case that Matías Suarez de Melo, the *canónigo* of the cathedral of Cartagena de Indias initiated against Antonio de Villalobos and Juana Gonzáles over the death of Isabel Bran, as discussed in chapter 3. Thanks to a large group of enslaved witnesses, de Melo recovered his investment. Matías Suarez de Melo vs. Antonio de Villalobos y Juana González, Folios 48r–230v.

68. Eufrasia Camargo, se le sigue causa por sevicia con sus esclavos, Folio 220r.

69. Eufrasia Camargo, se le sigue causa por sevicia con sus esclavos, Folio 97r.

70. The regulation, transformation, and transmission of slavery from the Roman Empire to Iberoamerica can be seen in William D. Phillips, *Slavery from Roman Times to the Early Transatlantic Trade* (Manchester, UK: Manchester University Press, 1985); William D. Phillips, *Slavery in Medieval and Early Modern Iberia* (Philadelphia: University of Pennsylvania Press, 2013); and José Antonio Piqueras, *La esclavitud en las Españas: Un lazo transatlántico* (Madrid: Libros de la Catarata, 2012).

71. See Sergio Serulnikov, *Subverting Colonial Authority: Challenges to Spanish Rule in Eighteenth-Century Southern Andes* (Durham: Duke University Press, 2003), chapter 1.

72. See Mark Knights, *Fiscal-Military State: Oxford Bibliographies Online Research Guide* (New York: Oxford University Press, 2010).

73. Mainstream historians seldom engage with the complexities inherent in stabilizing military conquest. This despite the fact that, even with the growth in modern states' military capacity, conquest remains a very difficult proposition. For example, overwhelming military power devoid of legitimacy crippled Napoleon's efforts to install his brother on the throne of Spain in 1808 and bedevils the United States in Afghanistan in 2019 (currently the longest war in US history).

74. Elliott, *Empires of the Atlantic World* (see introduction, n. 35).

75. Kenneth J. Andrien, "The Sale of Fiscal Offices and the Decline of Royal Authority in the Viceroyalty of Peru, 1633–1700," *The Hispanic American Historical Review* 62, no. 1 (1982): 49–71.

76. Guevara Jaramillo, *Delito y resistencia esclava*, 161–71.

77. Eufrasia Camargo, se le sigue causa por sevicia con sus esclavos, Folio 7v.

78. See John Herbert Roper and Lolita G. Brockington, "Slave Revolt, Slave Debate: A Comparison," *Phylon* 45, no. 2 (1984): 98–110.

79. In both these cases, several codefendants were initially condemned. Those condemned for lesser crimes did not appeal their sentences.

80. The durability of the legitimacy that Spanish royal justice acquired in Iberoamerica can be seen in Juan Carlos González Hernández, *Influencia del derecho español en América*, Colección Relaciones entre España y América 9 (Madrid: Editorial MAPFRE, 1992).

Conclusion

1. De la Fuente, "Slave Law and Claims-Making in Cuba," 343 (see introduction, n. 31).

2. Theodore Vial, *Modern Religion, Modern Race* (New York: Oxford University Press, 2016); von Germeten, *Violent Delights* (see chapter 1, n. 166).

3. Munive, "Blanco seguro," 101 (see chapter 3, n. 91).

4. For the roles that women and tradition play in deciding which customs and practices

become established, see Heath Dillard, *Daughters of the Reconquest: Women in Castilian Town Society, 1100–1300* (New York: Cambridge University Press, 1984).

5. See Thomas F. X. Noble and John van Engen eds., *European Transformations: The Long Twelfth Century* (Notre Dame, IN: University of Notre Dame Press, 2013); and Robert Swanson, *The Twelfth-Century Renaissance* (Manchester, UK: Manchester University Press, 1999).

6. Wim Klooster, *The Dutch Moment: War, Trade, and Settlement in the Seventeenth-Century Atlantic World* (Ithaca: Cornell University Press, 2016); Eric Williams, *Capitalism and Slavery* (Chapel Hill: University of North Carolina Press, 1944); Baptist, *The Half Has Never Been Told* (see chapter 3, n. 73).

7. See the definition of *pieza de indias* in Junius P. Rodríguez, ed., *The Historical Encyclopedia of World Slavery* (Santa Barbara, CA: ABC-CLIO, 1997).

8. See "The Passion of Domingo Angola" in chapter 4 of this book. This form of punishment has not been explored because it seems so counter-intuitive to modern conceptions of slavery. However, in the records of Cartagena, I have found numerous examples of exile being imposed on and exile being resisted by the slaves. This punishment superseded owners' rights to their slave and is another example of state interest overpowering individual property rights.

9. Spanish imperial authorities had to contend with the common challenge presented by businesspeople willing to relocate their capital in order to secure a more favorable regulatory framework regardless of the long-term damage to their home governments. See Vicente Ribes Iborra, *Comerciantes, esclavos, y capital sin patria* (Valencia: Generalitat Valenciana, 1993).

10. The development of a mixed-race society in Brazil is explored in Oswaldo de Oliveira Riedel, *Perspectiva Antropológica do Escravo no Ceará* (Fortaleza: Universidade Federal do Ceará, 1988). The social contradictions and conflicts that ripped Colombia asunder after the stabilizing hand of Spanish metropolitan power was withdrawn can be seen in Frank Safford and Marco Palacios, *Colombia: Fragmented Land, Divided Society* (New York: Oxford University Press, 2002).

11. The theory expressed by Manfred Kühn, "Peripheralization: Theoretical Concepts Explaining Socio-Spatial Inequalities," *European Planning Studies* 23, no. 2 (2015): 367–78, may be seen in practice in John Huxtable Elliott, *The Count-Duke of Olivares: The Statesman in an Age of Decline* (New Haven, CT: Yale University Press, 1986).

12. The downstream effects of these social and economic processes can be seen in Peter James Hudson, *Bankers and Empire: How Wall Street Colonized the Caribbean* (Chicago: University of Chicago Press, 2017).

13. Stuart Hall, *Representation: Cultural Representations and Signifying Practices* (London: Sage Publications, 1997); Benedict Anderson, *Imagined Communities* (London: Verso, 2006); Alicia R. Schmidt Camacho, *Migrant Imaginaries: Latino Cultural Politics in the US-Mexico Borderlands* (New York: New York University Press, 2008).

14. Francisco Copete Jr. vs. María Josefa Copete y Lorenza Elena, Folio 140v.

15. Francisco Copete Jr. vs. María Josefa Copete y Lorenza Elena, Folios 157r–86r.

16. Karen Y. Morrison, "Whitening Revisited: Nineteenth-Century Cuban Counterparts," in Vinson, Bryant, and O'Toole, *Africans to Spanish America*, 163–85 (see introduction, n. 45).

17. Finkelman, "Slavery in the United States," 105–34 (see chapter 1, n. 149).

18. A great academic model for tracking the effects of the Caribbean collapse of French power in the Caribbean through the Atlantic world is provided by David P. Geggus, ed., *The Impact of the Haitian Revolution in the Atlantic World* (Columbia: University of South Carolina Press, 2001).

19. At every level of Americas and throughout the Atlantic world there is a strong push by academics to reset the parameters of history to include the effects of racialized slavery. See Julia McClure, "Making Waves in the Historicised Atlantic," *Traversea: Journal of Transatlantic History* 2 (2012): 45–59; Nikhil Pal Singh, *Race and America's Long War* (Berkeley: University of California Press, 2017); and Henry Louis Gates Jr., *Black in Latin America* (New York: New York University Press, 2011).

20. Robert C. Schwaller, "Defining Difference in Early New Spain" (PhD diss., Pennsylvania State University, 2010).

21. Watson, *Slave Law in the Americas* (see chapter 1, n. 105).

22. The notion that even "one drop of black blood" renders a person and a family ineluctably black—imprinted in the US's popular consciousness by racialized slavery—is brought home by the video for Jay Z, "The Story of OJ," performed by Jay Z (New York City: Roc Nation Records, 2017). Video: https://www.youtube.com/watch?v=RM71w00vzq0.

23. Morrison, "Whitening Revisited."

24. Bianca Premo, *The Enlightenment on Trial: Ordinary Litigants and Colonialism in the Spanish Empire* (New York: Oxford University Press, 2017).

25. The breakdown of the Spanish Empire was intertwined with the racialization of customs and the law. See the introduction and chapter 1 of Jeremy Adelman, *Sovereignty and Revolution in the Iberian Atlantic* (Princeton: Princeton University Press, 2006).

26. Javier Barrientos Grandon, *Historia del derecho indiano: Del descubrimiento colombino a la codificación* (Rome: Il Cigno Galileo Galilei, 2000).

27. Peter J. Bakewell, *A History of Latin America: C. 1450 to the Present*, The Blackwell History of the World, 2nd ed. (Malden, MA: Blackwell Publishing, 2004); Federico Brito Figueroa, *El problema tierra y esclavos en la historia de Venezuela* (Caracas: Ediciones Teoría y Praxis, 1973).

28. See Trevor Burnard and John Garrigus, *The Plantation Machine: Atlantic Capitalism in French Saint-Domingue and British Jamaica* (Philadelphia: University of Pennsylvania Press, 2016).

29. The Enlightenment author Abbé Raynal declared in 1770 that the labors of colonists in these "long-scorned islands" brought such profit to Europe that "they can be regarded as the principal cause of the rapid movement which stirs the universe." *A Philosophical and Political History*, 6 (see introduction, n. 37).

30. Jean Bodin, *On Sovereignty*, Julian H. Franklin, ed. (New York: Cambridge University Press, 1992); Richard Bourke and Quentin Skinner, eds., *Popular Sovereignty in Historical Perspective* (Cambridge, MA: Cambridge University Press, 2016).

31. Compare this with Higginbotham and Jacobs, "The 'Law Only as an Enemy'" (see chapter 4, n. 22).

32. Consuelo Maqueda Abreu, *El Virreinato de Nueva Granada (1717–1780): Estudio Institucional* (Madrid: Dykinson; Puertollano, Spain: Ediciones Puertollano, 2007); and Aline Helg, *Liberty and Equality in Caribbean Colombia, 1770–1835* (Chapel Hill: University of North Carolina Press, 2004).

33. Chloe Ireton, "'They Are Blacks of the Caste of Black Christians': Old Christian Black Blood in the Sixteenth- and Early Seventeenth-Century Iberian Atlantic," *Hispanic American Historical Review* 97, no. 4 (2017): 579–612.

34. Linda A. Newson and Susie Minchin, *From Capture to Sale: The Portuguese Slave Trade to Spanish South America in the Early Seventeenth Century* (Leiden: Brill, 2007).

35. The effects of the legal ecology on all aspects of life can be seen in Cem Karayalcin, "Property Rights and the First Great Divergence: Europe 1500–1800," *International Review of Economics and Finance* 42 (2016); and Robert C. Allen, "The Great Divergence in European Wages and Prices from the Middle Ages to the First World War," *Explorations in Economic History* 38, no. 4 (2001): 44–47.

36. See the letter to the king from Friar Alonso de Montúfar, archbishop of Mexico (1551–1572) in Lucena Salmoral, *Leyes para esclavos*, 721.

37. The Atlantic slave trade knit together trends and locations that we do not usually assemble in that way. New England was a place with no cash crops. It was also a place that became known for its strong antislavery sentiment during the nineteenth century. Nonetheless, New Englanders practiced and profited from slavery as far back as the region's past goes. See Warren, *New England Bound* (see introduction, n. 38).

38. The conflict over terminology and its legal consequences can be seen in Jeremy D. Popkin, *You are all Free: The Haitian Revolution and the Abolition of Slavery* (New York: Cambridge University Press, 2010); and José de la Riva-Agüero, *La emancipación y la república*, vol. 7 of Obras Completas de José de la Riva-Agüero (Lima: Pontificia Universidad Católica del Peru, 1971).

39. Ultimately, it took a united (enough) black majority and cataclysmic violence to end plantation slavery. See Trevor Burnard, *Planters, Merchants, and Slaves* (introduction, n. 40).

40. Francisco Copete Jr. vs. María Josefa Copete y Lorenza Elena, Folios 176r–80.

BIBLIOGRAPHY

Archives and Printed Primary Sources

Archivo General de la Nación, Bogota, Colombia (AGN).

Archivo General de Indias, Seville, Spain (AGI).

Archivo Histórico Nacional, Madrid, Spain (AHN).

Archivo Notarial de Xalapa, Fernando Winfield Capitaine, and Universidad Veracruzana.

Biblioteca Central. Esclavos en el archivo notarial de Xalapa, Veracruz. Xalapa: Universidad Veracruzana, Museo de Antropología, 1984.

Bigges, Walter, Lieutenant Croftes, and Sir Thomas Gates. *A Summarie and True Discourse of Sir Francis Drakes West Indian Voyage: Wherein were Taken, the Townes of Saint Iago, Sancto Domingo, Cartagena & Saint Augustine: With Geographicall Mappes Exactly Describing each of the Townes with their Scituations, and the Manner of the Armies Approching to the Winning of them.* Imprinted at London: By Richard Field, dwelling in the Blacke-Friars by Ludgate, 1589.

Consejo de Indias. *Recopilación de leyes de los Reinos de las Indias.* 5th ed. Madrid: Boix, 1841.

Eslava, Sebastián de, and Pedro de Mur. *Diario de todo lo ocurrido en la expugnacion de los fuertes de Bocachica, y sitio de la ciudad de Cartagena de las Indias; formado de los pliegos remitidos à Su Magestad (que Dios guarde) por el Virrey de Santa Fé Don Sebastian de Eslaba con d. Pedro de Mur, Su Ayudante General. Año 1741. De orden de Su Magestad.* Madrid: n.d., 1741.

Jaca, Fray Francisco José de, [1645]. *Resolución sobre la libertad de los negros y sus originarios, en estado de paganos y después ya cristianos: La primera condena de la esclavitud en el pensamiento hispano.* Edited by Miguel Anxo Pena González. Madrid: CSIC, 2002.

Splendiani, Anna María, José Enrique Sánchez Bohórquez, and Emma Cecilia Luque de Salazar. *Cincuenta años de Inquisición en el tribunal de Cartagena de Indias, 1610–1660.* Bogota: Pontificia Universidad Javeriana, Instituto Colombiano de Cultura Hispánica, 1997.

Secondary Sources

Abulafia, David. *The Discovery of Mankind: Atlantic Encounters in the Age of Columbus.* New Haven, CT: Yale University Press, 2008.

Acosta Saignes, Miguel, Roger Bastide, and Julio Le Riverend. *Vida de los esclavos negros en Venezuela.* 3rd ed. Valencia, Venezuela: Vadell, 1984.

Adams, Richard E. W., and Murdo J. MacLeod, eds. *Mesoamerica: The Cambridge History of the Native Peoples of the Americas.* Vol. 2. New York: Cambridge University Press, 2000.

Adelman, Jeremy. *Sovereignty and Revolution in the Iberian Atlantic.* Princeton: Princeton University Press, 2006.

Alberro, Solange. *La actividad del Santo Oficio de la Inquisición en Nueva España, 1571–1700.* Colección Científica, México: Instituto Nacional de Antropología e Historia, Departamento de Investigaciones Históricas, Seminario de Historia de las Mentalidades y Religión en el México Colonial, 1981.

Alberro, Solange, and Diana Bonnett Vélez. *La Nueva Granada colonial: Selección de textos históricos.* Bogota, Colombia: Universidad de Los Andes, 2005.

Allen, Robert C. "The Great Divergence in European Wages and Prices from the Middle Ages to the First World War." *Explorations in Economic History* 38, no. 4 (2001): 411–47.

Álvarez Alonso, Fermina. *La Inquisición en Cartagena de Indias durante el siglo XVII.* Madrid: Fundación Universitaria Española, 1999.

Anderson, Benedict. *Imagined Communities.* London: Verso, 2006.

Andrés-Gallego, José. *La esclavitud en la América española.* Madrid: Ediciones Encuentro; Fundación Ignacio Larramendi, 2005.

Andrien, Kenneth J. "The Sale of Fiscal Offices and the Decline of Royal Authority in the Viceroyalty of Peru, 1633–1700." *The Hispanic American Historical Review* 62, no. 1 (1982): 49–71.

Armitage, David, and Michael J. Braddick, eds. *The British Atlantic World, 1500–1800.* New York: Palgrave Macmillan, 2002.

Arnold, John. *Inquisition and Power: Catharism and the Confessing Subject in Medieval Languedoc.* Philadelphia: University of Pennsylvania Press, 2001.

Avellaneda, Ignacio. *The Conquerors of the New Kingdom of Granada.* Albuquerque: University of New Mexico Press, 1995.

Bakewell, Peter J. *A History of Latin America: C. 1450 to the Present.* The Blackwell History of the World. 2nd ed. Malden, MA: Blackwell Publishing, 2004.

———. *Miners of the Red Mountain: Indian Labor in Potosí, 1545–1650.* Albuquerque: University of New Mexico Press, 1984.

———. *Silver Mining and Society in Colonial Mexico: Zacatecas, 1546–1700.* Cambridge Latin American Studies, 15. Cambridge, UK: Cambridge University Press, 1971.

Barraclough, Geoffrey. *The Medieval Papacy.* London: Thames & Hudson, 1968.

Barragán, Guillermo C. *La obra legislativa de Alfonso el Sabio: Ensayo sobre su formación, promulgación y transcendencia americana.* Buenos Aires: Abeledo-Perrot, 1983.

Barrientos Grandon, Javier. *Historia del derecho indiano: Del descubrimiento colombino a la codificación.* Rome: Il Cigno Galileo Galilei, 2000.

Bartchy, S. Scott. *[Mallon Chrēsai]: First-Century Slavery and the Interpretation of 1 Corinthians 7:21.* Eugene, OR: Wipf and Stock Publishers, 1973.

Bartlett, Robert. *The Making of Europe: Conquest, Colonization, and Cultural Change, 950–1350.* Princeton: Princeton University Press, 1993.

Baptist, Edward E. *The Half Has Never Been Told: Slavery and the Making of American Capitalism.* New York: Basic Books, 2016. First published 2014 by Basic Books.

Bell, Rudolph M. *Holy Anorexia.* Chicago: University of Chicago Press, 1987.

Benítez Rojo, Antonio, and James E. Maraniss. *The Repeating Island: The Caribbean and the Postmodern Perspective.* Durham: Duke University Press, 1996.

Bennett, Herman L. *Africans in Colonial Mexico: Absolutism, Christianity, and Afro-Creole Consciousness, 1570–1640.* Bloomington: Indiana University Press, 2003.

———. *Colonial Blackness: A History of Afro-Mexico.* Bloomington: Indiana University Press, 2009.

Berend, Nora. *At the Gate of Christendom: Jews, Muslims, and "Pagans" in Medieval Hungary, c. 1000–c. 1300*. Cambridge Studies in Medieval Life and Thought; 4th Ser., 50. New York: Cambridge University Press, 2001.

Berlin, Ira, and Leslie M. Harris, eds. *Slavery in New York*. New York: New Press, 2005.

Bernardo, Horacio. *Libres y esclavos*. Montevideo: Ediciones La Gotera, 2005.

Bethell, Leslie, ed. *The Cambridge History of Latin America*. Vol. 1, *Colonial Latin America*. New York: Cambridge University Press, 2008.

Block, Kristen. *Ordinary Lives in the Early Caribbean*. Athens: University of Georgia Press, 2012.

Bloch, Mark. *Feudal Society*. Chicago: University of Chicago Press, 1964.

Blumenthal, Debra. *Enemies and Familiars: Slavery and Mastery in Fifteenth-Century Valencia*. Ithaca: Cornell University Press, 2009.

Bodin, Jean. *On Sovereignty*. Edited by Julian H. Franklin. New York: Cambridge University Press, 1992.

Borja Gómez, Jaime Humberto. *Inquisición, muerte, y sexualidad en el Nuevo Reino de Granada*. Bogota: Editorial Ariel; CEJA, 1996.

Borrego Plá, María del Carmen. *Cartagena de Indias en el siglo XVI*. Seville: Escuela de Estudios Hispano-Americanos; CSIC, 1983.

———. *Palenques de negros en Cartagena de Indias a fines del siglo XVII*. Seville: Escuela de Estudios Hispano-Americanos de Sevilla, 1973.

Borucki, Alex, Karla Chagas, and Natalia Stalla. *Esclavitud y trabajo: Un estudio sobre los afrodescendientes en la frontera uruguaya (1835–1855)*. Montevideo: Pulmón Ediciones, 2004.

Borucki, Alex, David Eltis, and David Wheat. "Atlantic History and the Slave Trade to Spanish America." *The American Historical Review* 120, no. 2 (2015): 433–61.

Bourke, Richard and Quentin Skinner, eds. *Popular Sovereignty in Historical Perspective*. Cambridge, UK: Cambridge University Press, 2016.

Bourne, E. G., ed. *The Northmen, Columbus, and Cabot, 985–1503: The Voyages of the Northmen*. New York: Charles Scribner's Sons, 1906.

Bowser, Frederick P. *The African Slave in Colonial Peru, 1524–1650*. Stanford, CA: Stanford University Press, 1974.

Boxer, C. R., ed. *The Portuguese Seaborne Empire, 1415–1825*. London: Hutchinson, 1969.

———. *South China in the Sixteenth Century*. Bangkok: Orchid Press, 2006.

Bragg, Melvyn. "In Our Time: The Spanish Inquisition." BBC, June 2006, http://www.bbc.co.uk/programmes/p003c1bw.

Bravo Lira, Bernardino. *Derecho común y derecho propio en el nuevo mundo*. Santiago de Chile: Editorial Jurídica de Chile, 1989.

Bristol, Douglas Walter. *Knights of the Razor: Black Barbers in Slavery and Freedom*. Baltimore: Johns Hopkins University Press, 2009.

Bristol, Joan Cameron. *Christians, Blasphemers, and Witches: Afro-Mexican Ritual Practice in the Seventeenth Century*. Albuquerque: University of New Mexico Press, 2007.

Brito Figueroa, Federico. *El problema tierra y esclavos en la historia de Venezuela*. Caracas: Ediciones Teoría y Praxis, 1973.

Brockey, Liam Matthew. *Journey to the East: The Jesuit Mission to China, 1579–1724*. Cambridge, MA: Harvard University Press, 2007.

Brook, Timothy. *Vermeer's Hat: The Seventeenth Century and the Dawn of the Global World*. London: Profile Books, 2008.

Bryant, Sherwin K. *Rivers of Gold, Lives of Bondage: Governing through Slavery in Colonial Quito*. Chapel Hill: University of North Carolina Press, 2014.

Burkholder, Mark A., and Lyman L. Johnson. *Colonial Latin America*. 8th edition. New York: Oxford University Press, 2012.

Burnard, Trevor. *Planters, Merchants, and Slaves: Plantation Societies in British America, 1650–1820*. Chicago: University of Chicago Press, 2015.

Burnard, Trevor, and John Garrigus. *The Plantation Machine: Atlantic Capitalism in French Saint-Domingue and British Jamaica*. Philadelphia: University of Pennsylvania Press, 2016.

Burns, Kathryn. *Into the Archive: Writing and Power in Colonial Peru*. Durham: Duke University Press, 2010.

Burns, Robert I., ed., and Samuel Parsons Scott, trans. *The Medieval World of Law: Lawyers and their Work (Partida III)*. Volume 30 of *Las Siete Partidas*. Philadelphia: University of Pennsylvania Press, 2012.

Bush, Barbara. *Slave Women in Caribbean Society, 1650–1838*. Bloomington: Indiana University Press, 1990.

Cáceres Gómez, Rina. *Rutas de la esclavitud en Africa y América Latina*. San José: Editorial de la Universidad de Costa Rica, 2001.

———. *Negros, mulatos, esclavos, y libertos en la Costa Rica del siglo XVII*. Mexico City: Instituto Panamericano de Geografía e Historia, 2000.

Calvo Stevenson, Haroldo, and Adolfo Meisel Roca. *Cartagena de Indias y su historia*. Bogota: Universidad Jorge Tadeo Lozano, 1998.

Cañizares-Esguerra, Jorge, ed. *Entangled Empires: The Anglo-Iberian Atlantic, 1500–1830*. Philadelphia: University of Pennsylvania Press, 2018.

Cañizares-Esguerra, Jorge, and Erik R. Seeman, eds. *The Atlantic in Global History: 1500–2000*. Oxford: Routledge, 2017.

Cañizares-Esguerra, Jorge, Matt D. Childs, and James Sidbury, eds. *The Black Urban Atlantic in the Age of the Slave Trade*. Philadelphia: University of Pennsylvania Press, 2013.

Cardim, Pedro, Tamar Herzog, José Javier Ruiz Ibáñez, and Gaetano Sabatini, eds. *Polycentric Monarchies: How Did Early Modern Spain and Portugal Achieve and Maintain a Global Hegemony?* Brighton: Sussex Academic Press, 2014.

Carlo Altieri, Gerardo A. *El sistema legal y los litigios de esclavos en Indias: Puerto Rico siglo XIX*. Vol. 16. Seville: CSIC, 2010.

Carroll, Patrick James. *Blacks in Colonial Veracruz: Race, Ethnicity, and Regional Development*. 2nd ed. Austin: University of Texas Press, 2001.

Castillo, Otto René. *Vámonos patria a caminar*. Guatemala: Editorial Landívar, 1965.

Ceballos Gómez, Diana Luz. *Hechicería, brujería, e inquisición en el Nuevo Reino de Granada: Un duelo de imaginarios*. Bogota, Colombia: Editorial Universidad Nacional, 1994.

Chang, Jason Oliver. *Chino: Anti-Chinese Racism in Mexico, 1880–1940*. Champaign: University of Illinois Press, 2017.

Chaplin, Joyce E. *Round About the Earth: Circumnavigation from Magellan to Orbit*. New York: Simon and Schuster, 2012.

Colley, Linda. *Captives: Britain, Empire, and the World, 1600–1850*. New York: Anchor Books, 2004.

———. *The Ordeal of Elizabeth Marsh: A Woman in World History*. New York: Anchor Books, 2008.

Colmenares, Germán. *Los esclavos en la Gobernación de Popayán, 1680–1780*. Tunja: Publicaciones del Magister en Historia, Vice-Rectoría de Investigaciones Científicas y Extensión Universitaria, Universidad Pedagógica y Tecnológica de Colombia, 1991.

―――. *Historia económica y social de Colombia: Popayán, una sociedad esclavista, 1680–1800*. Bogota: La Carreta, 1979.

Cook, Noble David. *Born to Die: Disease and New World Conquest, 1492–1650*. New York: Cambridge University Press, 1998.

Cortés López, José Luis. *Esclavo y colono: Introducción y sociología de los negroafricanos en la América española del siglo XVI*. Salamanca: Ediciones Universidad de Salamanca, 2004.

Cottrol, Robert J. *The Long, Lingering Shadow: Slavery, Race, and Law in the American Hemisphere*. Athens: University of Georgia Press, 2013.

Dantas, Mariana L. R. *Black Townsmen: Urban Slavery and Freedom in the Eighteenth-Century Americas*. New York: Palgrave Macmillan, 2008.

Davidson, David M. "Negro Slave Control and Resistance in Colonial Mexico, 1519–1650." *The Hispanic American Historical Review* 46, no. 3 (1966): 235–53.

Davis, David Brion. *Inhuman Bondage: The Rise and Fall of Slavery in the New World*. New York: Oxford University Press, 2006.

Davis, Natalie Zemon. "Judges, Masters, Diviners: Slaves' Experience of Criminal Justice in Colonial Suriname." *Law and History Review* 29, no. 4 (2011): 925–84.

Denley, Peter. *Teachers and Schools in Siena, 1357–1500*. Siena: Betti Editrice, 2007.

Deardorff, Max. "Imperial Justice, Colonial Power: Pedro Vique y Manrique, the Galley Captain of Cartagena de Indias, 1578–1607." *CLAHR: Colonial Latin American Historical Review* 17, no. 2 (2008): 117–42.

Diamond, Jared. *Guns, Germs, and Steel*. New York: W. W. Norton & Company, 1997.

Díaz, María Elena. *The Virgin, the King, and the Royal Slaves of El Cobre: Negotiating Freedom in Colonial Cuba, 1670–1780*. Stanford, CA: Stanford University Press, 2000.

Díaz Burgos, Ana María. "Fisuras inquisitoriales, voces femeninas, y hechicería en Cartagena de Indias." PhD diss., Emory University, 2011.

Díaz del Castillo, Bernal. *The Conquest of New Spain*. Translated by J. M. Cohen. Harmondsworth, UK: Penguin Books, 1963.

Díaz Díaz, Rafael Antonio. *Esclavitud, región, y ciudad: El sistema esclavista urbano-regional en Santafé de Bogotá, 1700–1750*. Bogota: Centro Editorial Javeriano CEJA, 2001.

Dillard, Heath. *Daughters of the Reconquest: Women in Castilian Town Society, 1100–1300*. New York: Cambridge University Press, 1984.

Dubois, Laurent. *Avengers of the New World: The Story of the Haitian Revolution*. Cambridge, MA: Belknap Press of Harvard University Press, 2004.

Duffy, Eamon. *The Stripping of the Altars: Traditional Religion in England, 1400–1580*. New Haven, CT: Yale University Press, 2005.

Dussel, Enrique, and Comisión de Estudios de Historia de la Iglesia en Latinoamérica, eds. *The Church in Latin America, 1492–1992*. Vol. 1 of *A History of the Church in the Third World*. Maryknoll, NY: Orbis Books, 1992.

Earle, T. F., and K. J. P. Lowe, eds. *Black Africans in Renaissance Europe*. New York: Cambridge University Press, 2005.

Echeverri, Marcela. "Popular Royalists, Empire, and Politics in Southwestern New Granada, 1809–1819." *Hispanic American Historical Review* 91, no. 2 (2011): 237–69.

Edgerton, Samuel Y. *Theaters of Conversion: Religious Architecture and Indian Artisans in Colonial Mexico*. Albuquerque: University of New Mexico Press, 2001.

Edwards, John. *The Spanish Inquisition*. Charleston, SC: Tempus, 1999.

Elliott, John Huxtable. *The Count-Duke of Olivares: The Statesman in an Age of Decline*. New Haven, CT: Yale University Press, 1986.

———. *Empires of the Atlantic World: Britain and Spain in America, 1492–1830*. New Haven, CT: Yale University Press, 2006.

———. *Imperial Spain, 1469–1716*. New York: New American Library, 1963.

Elshtain, Jean Bethke. *Sovereignty: God, State, and Self*. New York: Basic Books, 2008.

Escalante, Aquiles. *El negro en Colombia*. Barranquilla: Corporación Educativa Mayor del Desarrollo Simón Bolívar, 2002.

Esquirol, Jorge L. "Excessive Legalism, Lawlessness, and Other Stories about Latin American Law." PhD diss., Harvard Law School, 2001.

Farriss, Nancy M. *Maya Society under Colonial Rule: The Collective Enterprise of Survival*. Princeton: Princeton University Press, 1984.

Fenoaltea, Stefano. "Slavery and Supervision in Comparative Perspective: A Model." *Journal of Economic History* 44, no. 3 (1984): 635–68.

Fernández de Piedrahita, Lucas. *Historia general del Nuevo Reino de Granada*. Biblioteca Popular De Cultura Colombiana. Historia; v. 4–7. Bogota: Impreso en la Editorial ABC, 1942.

Fernández-Armesto, Felipe. *The Canary Islands after the Conquest: The Making of a Colonial Society in the Early Sixteenth Century*. Oxford: Clarendon Press, 1982.

Finkelman, Paul. "Slavery in the United States: Persons or Property?" In *The Legal Understanding of Slavery: From the Historical to the Contemporary*, edited by Jean Allain, 105–34. New York: Oxford University Press, 2012.

Finley, M. I. *Ancient Slavery and Modern Ideology*. London: Chatto & Windus, 1980.

Foner, Laura, and Eugene D. Genovese. *Slavery in the New World: A Reader in Comparative History*. Englewood Cliffs, NJ: Prentice-Hall, 1969.

Forbes, Jack D. *Africans and Native Americans: The Language of Race and the Evolution of Red-Black Peoples*. 2nd ed. Urbana: University of Illinois Press, 1993.

Fuente, Alejandro de la. "From slaves to citizens? Tannenbaum and the debates on slavery, emancipation, and race relations in Latin America." *International Labor and Working-Class History* 77, no. 1 (2010): 154–73.

———. *Havana and the Atlantic in the Sixteenth Century*. Chapel Hill: University of North Carolina Press, 2008.

———. "Slave Law and Claims-Making in Cuba: The Tannenbaum Debate Revisited." *Law and History Review* 22, no. 2 (2004): 339–69.

———. "Slaves and the Creation of Legal Rights in Cuba: Coartación and Papel." *Hispanic American Historical Review* 87, no. 4 (2007): 659–92.

Fuente, Alejandro de la, and Ariela J. Gross. "Comparative Studies of Law, Slavery, and Race in the Americas." *University of Southern California Legal Studies Working Paper Series*. Working Paper 56 (February 2010).

Fuentes, Marisa J. *Dispossessed Lives: Enslaved Women, Violence, and the Archive*. Philadelphia: University of Pennsylvania Press, 2016.

García, Fernando Mayorga. *La Audiencia de Santafé en los siglos XVI y XVII*. Bogota: Instituto Colombiano de Cultura Hispánica, 1991.

Garrigus, John D. *Before Haiti: Race and Citizenship in French Saint-Domingue.* New York: Palgrave Macmillan, 2006.

Gates Jr., Henry Louis. *Black in Latin America.* New York: New York University Press, 2011.

Gauderman, Kimberly. "Father Fiction: A Comparison of English, Spanish, and Andean Gender Norms." *UCLA Historical Journal* (Special Issue), 12 (1992): 122–51.

Geggus, David P., ed. *The Impact of the Haitian Revolution in the Atlantic World.* Columbia: University of South Carolina Press, 2001.

Genovese, Eugene D. *From Rebellion to Revolution: Afro-American Slave Revolts in the Making of the Modern World.* The Walter Lynwood Fleming Lectures in Southern History, Louisiana State University. Baton Rouge: Louisiana State University Press, 1979.

Ghachem, Malick W. "Prosecuting Torture: The Strategic Ethics of Slavery in Pre-Revolutionary Saint-Domingue (Haiti)." Special Issue on Law, Justice, and Slavery, *Law and History Review* 29, no. 4 (2011): 985–1029.

Garner, Richard L., and William B. Taylor, eds. *Iberian Colonies, New World Societies: Essays in Memory of Charles Gibson.* University Park, PA: R. L. Garner: 1985.

Germeten, Nicole von. *Black Blood Brothers: Confraternities and Social Mobility for Afro-Mexicans.* Gainesville: University Press of Florida, 2006.

———. *Violent Delights, Violent Ends: Sex, Race, and Honor in Colonial Cartagena de Indias.* Albuquerque: University of New Mexico Press, 2013.

Ginzburg, Carlo. *The Cheese and the Worms: The Cosmos of a Sixteenth-Century Miller.* London: Penguin, 1992.

Glynn, Mary Ann, and Lee Watkiss. "Exploring Cultural Mechanisms of Organizational Identity Construction." In *Constructing Identity in and Around Organizations*, edited by Majken Schultz, Steve Maguire, Ann Langley, and Haridimos Tsoukas, 63–88: New York: Oxford University Press, 2012.

Gómez Pérez, María del Carmen. *Pedro de Heredia y Cartagena de Indias.* Seville: Escuela de Estudios Hispano-Americanos de Sevilla; CSIC, 1984.

González, Margarita. *Ensayos de historia colonial colombiana.* 2nd ed. Bogotá: Ancora Editores, 1984.

González Hernández, Juan Carlos. *Influencia del derecho español en América.* Colección Relaciones entre España y América 9. Madrid: Editorial MAPFRE, 1992.

Goody, Jack. *Production and Reproduction: A Comparative Study of the Domestic Domain.* New York: Cambridge University Press, 1976.

Gordon-Reed, Annette, and Peter S. Onuf. *"Most Blessed of the Patriarchs": Thomas Jefferson and the Empire of the Imagination.* New York: W. W. Norton & Company, 2016.

Grandin, Greg. *The Empire of Necessity: Slavery, Freedom, and Deception in the New World.* New York: Metropolitan Books, 2014.

Guevara Jaramillo, Nathalia. *Delito y resistencia esclava: Hurtos, homicidios, y agresiones en la Nueva Granada, 1750–1800.* PhD diss., Universidad Nacional de Colombia, 2010.

Guitar, Lynne. "Boiling it Down: Slavery on the First Commercial Sugarcane Ingenios in the Americas (Hispaniola, 1530–45)." In Landers and Robinson, *Slaves, Subjects, and Subversives*, 39–82. Albuquerque: University of New Mexico Press, 2006.

———. "Criollos: The Birth of a Dynamic New Indo-Afro-European People and Culture on Hispaniola." *KACIKE: Journal of Caribbean Amerindian History and Anthropology* 1, no. 1 (2000): 1–17.

Hair, Paul Edward Hedley. *Africa Encountered: European Contacts and Evidence, 1450–1700*. Brookfield, VT: Variorum, 1997.

———. "Heretics, Slaves, and Witches—As Seen by Guinea Jesuits c. 1610," *Journal of Religion in Africa* 28, 2 (1988): 131–44.

Hall, Stuart. *Representation: Cultural Representations and Signifying Practices*. London: Sage Publications, 1997.

Haring, Clarence Henry. *The Spanish Empire in America*. New York: Harcourt, Brace, & World, 1963.

Harper, Kyle. *Slavery in the Late Roman World, AD 275–425*. New York: Cambridge University Press, 2011.

Helg, Aline. *Liberty and Equality in Caribbean Colombia, 1770–1835*. Chapel Hill: University of North Carolina Press, 2004.

Hera, Alberto de la. "El regalismo indiano." *Ius Canonicum* 32, no. 64 (1992): 411–37.

Hernández de Alba, Gregorio. *Libertad de los esclavos en Colombia*. Bogota: Editorial ABC, 1956.

Herráez Sánchez de Escariche, Julia. *Don Pedro Zapata de Mendoza, Gobernador de Cartagena de Indias*. Seville: Publicaciones de la Escuela de Estudios Hispano-Americanos de Sevilla, 32, serie 1, 13, 1946.

Heywood, Linda Marinda, and John Kelly Thornton. *Central Africans, Atlantic Creoles, and the Making of the Foundation of the Americas, 1585–1660*. New York: Cambridge University Press, 2007.

Higginbotham, A. Leon, and Anne F. Jacobs. "The 'Law Only as an Enemy': The Legitimization of Racial Powerlessness through the Colonial and Antebellum Criminal Laws of Virginia." *The North Carolina Law Review* 70 (1992): 969–1070.

Hinsley, F. H. *Sovereignty*. New York: Cambridge University Press, 1986.

Hobbes, Thomas. *Leviathan*. Edited by Richard Tuck. New York: Cambridge University Press, 1996.

Holton, Woody, and Omohundro Institute of Early American History & Culture. *Forced Founders: Indians, Debtors, Slaves, and the Making of the American Revolution in Virginia*. Chapel Hill: Omohundro Institute of Early American History and Culture; University of North Carolina Press, 1999.

Horrigan, Liam Francis. "Settling the Trade to Africa: The Anglo-African Trade, 1695–1715, and the Political and Economic Implications of 1698." Master of Arts by Research, University of Kent, 2016.

Hudson, Peter James. *Bankers and Empire: How Wall Street Colonized the Caribbean*. Chicago: University of Chicago Press, 2017.

Ireton, Chloe. "'They Are Blacks of the Caste of Black Christians:' Old Christian Black Blood in the Sixteenth- and Early Seventeenth-Century Iberian Atlantic." *Hispanic American Historical Review* 97, no. 4 (2017): 579–612.

Izco Reina, Manuel Jesús. *Amos, esclavos, y libertos: Estudios sobre la esclavitud en Puerto Real durante la edad moderna*. Cádiz: Universidad de Cádiz, Servicio de Publicaciones, 2002.

Jay Z. "The Story of OJ." Performed by Jay Z. New York City: Roc Nation Records, 2017. Video: https://www.youtube.com/watch?v=RM71w00vzq0.

Jenson, Deborah. *Beyond the Slave Narrative: Politics, Sex, and Manuscripts in the Haitian Revolution*. Liverpool: Liverpool University Press, 2011.

Jiménez Meneses, Orián. "El Chocó: Vida negra, vida libre, y vida parda, Siglos XVII y XVIII." *Historia y Sociedad* 7 (2000): 173–98.

———. "Los amos y los esclavos en el Medellín del S. XVIII." *Historia y Sociedad* 5 (1998): 119–32.

Johnson, Lyman L., and Sonya Lipsett-Rivera, eds. *The Faces of Honor: Sex, Shame, and Violence in Colonial Latin America*. Albuquerque: University of New Mexico Press, 1998.

Johnson, Walter. "Resetting the Legal History of Slavery: Divination, Torture, Poisoning, Murder, Revolution, Emancipation, and Re-Enslavement." *Law and History Review* 29, no. 4 (2011): 1089–95.

Jones, Martha S. "Time, Space, and Jurisdiction in Atlantic World Slavery: The Volunbrun Household in Gradual Emancipation New York." *Law and History Review* 29, no. 4 (2011): 1031–60.

Jouve Martín, José Ramón. *Esclavos de la ciudad letrada: Esclavitud, escritura, y colonialismo en Lima (1650–1700)*. Lima: IEP, Instituto de Estudios Peruanos, 2005.

Jouvenel, Bertrand de. *Sovereignty: An Inquiry into the Political Good*. Chicago: University of Chicago Press, 1957.

Kagan, Richard L. *Lawsuits and Litigants in Castile, 1500–1700*. Chapel Hill: University of North Carolina Press, 1981.

Kagan, Richard L., and Fernando Marías. *Urban Images of the Hispanic World, 1493–1793*. New Haven, CT: Yale University Press, 2000.

Kamen, Henry. *Empire: How Spain Became a World Power, 1492–1763*. New York: Perennial, 2004.

———. *The Spanish Inquisition: A Historical Revision*. New Haven, CT: Yale University Press, 1998.

Karayalcin, Cem. "Property Rights and the First Great Divergence: Europe 1500–1800." *International Review of Economics and Finance* 42 (2016): 484–98.

Kennedy, Meritt. "'Game Changer': Maya Cities Unearthed in Guatemalan Forest Using Lasers." NPR. February 2, 2018.

Kinross, Patrick Balfour. *The Ottoman Centuries: The Rise and Fall of the Turkish Empire*. New York: Morrow, 1977.

Klein, Herbert. *Slavery in the Americas: A Comparative Study of Cuba and Virginia*. Chicago: University of Chicago Press, 1967.

Klein, Herbert S., and Ben Vinson III. *African Slavery in Latin America and the Caribbean*. 2nd ed. Oxford: Oxford University Press, 2007.

Klooster, Wim. *The Dutch Moment: War, Trade, and Settlement in the Seventeenth-Century Atlantic World*. Ithaca, NY: Cornell University Press, 2016.

Knight, Franklin W. *The African Dimension in Latin American Societies*. New York: Macmillan, 1974.

Knight, Franklin W., and Peggy K. Liss, eds. *Atlantic Port Cities: Economy, Culture, and Society in the Atlantic World, 1650–1850*. Knoxville: University of Tennessee Press, 1991.

Knights, Mark. *Fiscal-Military State: Oxford Bibliographies Online Research Guide*. New York: Oxford University Press, 2010.

Knivet, Anthony. *The Admirable Adventures and Strange Fortunes of Master Anthony Knivet: An English Pirate in Sixteenth-Century Brazil*. Edited by Vivien Kogut Lessa de Sá. New York: Cambridge University Press, 2015.

Kühn, Manfred. "Peripheralization: Theoretical Concepts Explaining Socio-Spatial Inequalities." *European Planning Studies* 23, no. 2 (2015): 367–78.

Landers, Jane G., and Barry Robinson, eds. *Slaves, Subjects, and Subversives: Blacks in Colonial Latin America*. Albuquerque: University of New Mexico Press, 2006.

Lane, Kris. "Captivity and Redemption: Aspects of Slave Life in Early Colonial Quito and Popayán." *The Americas* 57, no. 2 (2000): 225–46.

Lemaitre, Eduardo. *Breve historia de Cartagena*. Medellín, Colombia: Editorial Colina, 1993.

Lemaitre, Eduardo, Donaldo Bossa Herazo, and Francisco Sebá Patrón. *Historia general de Cartagena*. Bogota: Banco de la República, 1983.

Levack, Brian P. *The Witch-Hunt in Early Modern Europe*. London: Longman, 1987.

Lewis, Gordon K. *Main Currents in Caribbean Thought: The Historical Evolution of Caribbean Society in its Ideological Aspects, 1492–1900*. Lincoln: University of Nebraska Press, 2004.

Linebaugh, Peter, and Marcus Buford Rediker. *The Many-Headed Hydra: Sailors, Slaves, Commoners, and the Hidden History of the Revolutionary Atlantic*. Boston: Beacon Press, 2000.

Liniers de Estrada, Agustín. *Manual de historia del derecho (español, indiano, argentino)*. Buenos Aires: Abeledo-Perrot, 1993.

Livi-Bacci, Massimo. "Return to Hispaniola: Reassessing a Demographic Catastrophe." *Hispanic American Historical Review* 83, no. 1 (February 2003): 3–52.

Lobo Cabrera, Manuel, Ramón López Caneda, and Elisa Torres Santana. *La "otra" población: Expósitos, ilegítimos, esclavos (Las Palmas de Gran Canaria, Siglo XVIII)*. Las Palmas: Universidad de Las Palmas de Gran Canaria, 1993.

Lockhart, James. *Spanish Peru, 1532–1560: A Colonial Society*. Madison: University of Wisconsin Press, 1968.

López Barja de Quiroga, Pedro. "Manumisión y control de esclavos en la Antigua Roma." *Circe de Clásicos y Modernos* 16, no. 2 (2012): 57–71.

Lovejoy, Paul E. "The Context of Enslavement in West Africa: Aḥmad Bābā and the Ethics of Slavery." In Landers and Robinson, *Slaves, Subjects, and Subversives*, 9–38.

Lovell, W. George, and Christopher Lutz. *Demography and Empire: A Guide to the Population History of Spanish Central America, 1500–1821*. Boulder: Westview Press, 1995.

Lucena Salmoral, Manuel. *Leyes para esclavos: El ordenamiento jurídico sobre la condición, tratamiento, defensa y represión de los esclavos en las colonias de la América española*. Madrid: Fundación MAPFRE TAVERA; Fundación Ignacio Larramendi, 2005.

Luque Talaván, Miguel. *Un universo de opiniones: La literatura jurídica indiana*. Biblioteca de Historia de América, 26. Madrid: CSIC, 2003.

Lynch, John. *Spain under the Habsburgs: Spain and America 1598–1700*. 2nd ed., Vol. 2. Oxford: Basil Blackwell, 1981.

Lynn, Kimberly. *Between Court and Confessional: The Politics of Spanish Inquisitors*. New York: Cambridge University Press, 2013.

MacCulloch, Diarmaid. *Reformation: Europe's House Divided 1490–1700*. New York: Penguin Books, 2003.

Manzano, Juan. *Recopilación de leyes de los reynos de las Indias*. Madrid: Ediciones Cultura Hispánica, 1973.

Maqueda Abreu, Consuelo. *El Virreinato de Nueva Granada (1717–1780): Estudio Institucional*. Madrid: Dykinson; Puertollano, Spain: Ediciones Puertollano, 2007.

Margadant S., Guillermo Floris. *Introducción al derecho indiano y novohispano*. Mexico City: Colegio de México, 2000.

Martínez Góngora, Mar. "El Magreb, pluralidad, y memoria: Cervantes y las crónicas de Berbería en 'La historia del cautivo.'" *Cervantes: Bulletin of the Cervantes Society of America* 37, no. 2 (2017): 35–67.

Marzahl, Peter. *Town in the Empire: Government, Politics, and Society in Seventeenth-Century Popayán*. Austin: University of Texas Press, 1978.

Maya Restrepo, Luz Adriana. *Brujería y reconstrucción de identidades entre los africanos y sus descendientes en la Nueva Granada, Siglo XVII*. Bogota: Ministerio de Cultura, 2005.

Maza Miquel, Manuel. *Esclavos, patriotas, y poetas a la sombra de la cruz: Cinco ensayos sobre catolicismo e historia cubana*. Santo Domingo: Centro de Estudios Sociales Padre Juan Montalvo, S. J., 1999.

McFarlane, Anthony. "Comerciantes y monopolio en la Nueva Granada. El Consulado de Cartagena de Indias." *Anuario Colombiano de Historia Social y de la Cultura* 11 (1983): 43–69.

McClure, Julia. "Making Waves in the Historicised Atlantic." *Traversea: Journal of Transatlantic History* 2 (2012): 45–59.

McCormick, Michael. *Origins of the European Economy: Communications and Commerce A.D. 300–900*. New York: Cambridge University Press, 2001.

McKinley, Michelle A. *Fractional Freedoms: Slavery, Intimacy, and Legal Mobilization in Colonial Lima, 1600–1700*. New York: Cambridge University Press, 2016.

McKnight, Kathryn Joy. "Confronted Rituals: Spanish Colonial and Angolan 'Maroon' Executions in Cartagena de Indias (1634)." *Journal of Colonialism & Colonial History* 5, no. 3 (2004): 1–19.

———. "'En su tierra lo aprendió:' An African Curandero's Defense before the Cartagena Inquisition." *Colonial Latin American Review* 12, no. 1 (2003): 63–84.

———. "Gendered Declarations: Testimonies of Three Captured Maroon Women, Cartagena de Indias, 1634." *Colonial Latin American Historical Review* 12, no. 4 (2003): 499–527.

———. "Performing Double-Edged Stories: The Three Trials of Paula de Eguiluz." *Colonial Latin American Review* 25, no. 2 (2016): 154–74.

Medina, José Toribio. *La Inquisición en Cartagena de Indias*. 2nd ed. Bogota: Carlos Valencia Editores, 1978.

Mellafe, Rolando R. *La introducción de la esclavitud negra en Chile: Tráfico y rutas*. Santiago, Chile: Editorial Universitaria, 1984.

———. *Negro Slavery in Latin America*. Berkeley: University of California Press, 1975.

Melo, Jorge Orlando. *Historia de Colombia: El establecimiento de la dominación española*. Bogota, Colombia: Presidencia de la República, 1996.

Menéndez Pelayo, Marcelino. *Historia de los heterodoxos españoles*. 3 Vol. Madrid: CSIC, 1992.

Merwin, William Stanley, trans. *The Life of Lazarillo de Tormes: His Fortunes and Adversities*. New York: New York Review Books, 2005.

Milne, Louise. "Pieter Bruegel and Carlo Ginzburg: The Debatable Land of Renaissance Dreams." *Cosmos* 29 (2013): 59–126.

Mintz, Steven. "American Slavery in Comparative Perspective." The Gilder Lehrman Institute of American History, https://www.gilderlehrman.org/content/historical-context-american-slavery-comparative-perspective.

Mitchell, Silvia Z. *Queen, Mother, and Stateswoman: Mariana of Austria and the Government of Spain.* University Park: Penn State University Press, 2019.

Morgan, Jennifer L. *Laboring Women: Reproduction and Gender in New World Slavery.* Philadelphia: University of Pennsylvania Press, 2004.

Morrison, Karen Y. "Whitening Revisited: Nineteenth-Century Cuban Counterparts." In Vinson, Bryant, and O'Toole, *Africans to Spanish America: Expanding the Diaspora*, 163–85.

Mosquera, Sergio A. *La gente negra en la legislación colonial.* Medellín, Colombia: Editorial Lealon, 2004.

Muldoon, James, ed. *The Spiritual Conversion of the Americas.* Gainesville: University Press of Florida, 2004.

Múnera, Alfonso. *El fracaso de la nación: Región, clase, y raza en el Caribe colombiano (1717–1821).* Bogota: Banco de la República; Ancora Editores, 1998.

Munguía, Juana Patricia Pérez. "Derecho indiano para esclavos, negros, y castas. Integración, control, y estructura estamental." *Memoria y Sociedad* 7, no. 15 (2003): 193–205.

Munive, Moisés. "Blanco seguro: El maltrato a los esclavos en Cartagena y Mompox durante el siglo XVIII." *Procesos Históricos*, no. 13 (2008): 97–116.

Munive Contreras, Moisés. "Resistencia estática. Los negros contra la esclavitude en Cartagena y Mompox. Siglo XVIII." *Tiempos Modernos: Revista Electrónica de Historia Moderna* 5, no. 14 (2006): 1–18.

Navarrete, María Cristina. "Los avatares de la mala vida: La trasgresión a la norma entre la población negra, libre y esclava." *Historia y Espacio* 19, no. 1 (2002): 12–42.

———. *Cimarrones y palenques en el siglo XVII.* Cali: Universidad del Valle, 2003.

———. *Génesis y desarrollo de la esclavitud en Colombia, siglos XVI y XVII.* Cali: Universidad del Valle, 2005.

Nesvig, Martin Austin. *Local Religion in Colonial Mexico.* Albuquerque: University of New Mexico, 2006.

Newson, Linda A., and Susie Minchin. *From Capture to Sale: The Portuguese Slave Trade to Spanish South America in the Early Seventeenth Century.* Leiden: Brill, 2007.

Nirenberg, David. *Communities of Violence: Persecution of Minorities in the Middle Ages.* Princeton: Princeton University Press, 1996.

Noble, Thomas F. X., and John van Engen, eds. *European Transformations: The Long Twelfth Century.* Notre Dame, IN: University of Notre Dame Press, 2013.

Novikoff, Alex. "Between Tolerance and Intolerance in Medieval Spain: A Historiographic Enigma." *Medieval Encounters* 11, nos. 1–2 (2005): 7–36.

Nowell, Charles E. "The Defense of Cartagena." *The Hispanic American Historical Review* 42, no. 4 (1962): 477–501.

Núñez Jiménez, Antonio. *Los esclavos negros.* Havana: Fundación de la Naturaleza y el Hombre/ Editorial Letras Cubanas, 1998.

Ogass Bilbao, Claudio Moisés. "Por mi precio o mi buen comportamiento: Oportunidades y estrategias de manumision de los esclavos negros y mulatos en Santiago de Chile, 1698– 1750." *Historia* 42, no. 1 (2009): 141–84.

Olsen, Margaret M. *Slavery and Salvation in Colonial Cartagena de Indias.* Gainesville: University Press of Florida, 2004.

O'Malley, Gregory E. *Final Passages: The Intercolonial Slave Trade of British America, 1619–1807.*

Chapel Hill: University of North Carolina Press, 2014.

Ortega, Miguel Angel. *La esclavitud en el contexto agropecuario colonial: Siglo XVIII*. Caracas: Editorial APICUM, 1992.

O'Shaughnessy, Andrew Jackson. *An Empire Divided: The American Revolution and the British Caribbean*. Philadelphia: University of Pennsylvania Press, 2000.

———. "As Historical Subjects: The African Diaspora in Colonial Latin American History." *History Compass* 11, no. 12 (2013): 1094–1110.

O'Toole, Rachel Sarah. *Bound Lives: Africans, Indians, and the Making of Race in Colonial Peru*. Pittsburgh: University of Pittsburgh Press, 2012.

———. "To be Free and Lucumí: Ana de la Calle and Making African Diaspora Identities in Colonial Peru." In Bryant, Vincent, and O'Toole, *Africans to Spanish America*, 73–92.

Paquette, Gabriel. *European Seaborne Empires: From the Thirty Years' War to the Age of Revolutions*. New Haven, CT: Yale University Press, 2019.

Parker, Geoffrey. *The Military Revolution: Military Innovation and the Rise of the West, 1500–1800*. 2nd ed. New York: Cambridge University Press, 1996.

Parry, J. H. *The Spanish Seaborne Empire*. Berkeley: University of California Press, 1990.

Paterculus, C. Velleius. *Compendium of Roman History*. Cambridge, MA: Harvard University Press, Loeb Classical Library, 1924.

Patterson, Orlando. *Slavery and Social Death: A Comparative Study*. Cambridge, MA: Harvard University Press, 1982.

Peñas Galindo, David Ernesto. *Los bogas de Mompox: Historia del zambaje*. Bogota, Colombia: Tercer Mundo Editores, 1988.

Perry, Mary Elizabeth, and Anne J. Cruz, eds. *Cultural Encounters: The Impact of the Inquisition in Spain and the New World*. Berkeley: University of California Press, 1991.

Phillips, William D. *Slavery from Roman Times to the Early Transatlantic Trade*. Manchester, UK: Manchester University Press, 1985.

———. *Slavery in Medieval and Early Modern Iberia*. Philadelphia: University of Pennsylvania Press, 2013.

Piqueras, José Antonio. *La esclavitud en las Españas: Un lazo transatlántico*. Madrid: Libros de la Catarata, 2012.

Pita Pico, Roger. "La 'esclavitud' de los sentimientos: Vida familiar y afectiva de la población esclava en el nororiente del Nuevo Reino de Granada, 1720–1819." *Revista de Indias* 72, no. 256 (2012): 651–86.

Pointis, Jean-Bernard-Louis Desjean, baron de. *Monsieur de Pointi's expedition to Cartagena: being a particular relation, I. Of the taking and plundering of that city, by the French, in the year 1697, II. Of their meeting with Admiral Nevil in their return, and the course they steer'd to get clear of him, III. Of their passing by Commadore Norris, at Newfound-Land, IV. Of their encounter with Capt. Harlow, at their going to Brest*. London, Sold by S. Crouch, R. Mount: S. Buckley and A. Feltham, 1699.

Pomeranz, Kenneth, and Steven Topik. *The World that Trade Created: Society, Culture, and the World Economy, 1400 to Present*. 2nd edition. Armonk, NY: M. E. Sharpe, 2006.

Popkin, Jeremy D. *You Are All Free: The Haitian Revolution and the Abolition of Slavery*. New York: Cambridge University Press, 2010.

Portuondo Zúñiga, Olga. *Entre esclavos y libres de Cuba colonial*. Santiago de Cuba: Editorial Oriente, 2003.

Premo, Bianca. "Before the Law: Women's Petitions in the Eighteenth-Century Spanish Empire." *Comparative Studies in Society and History* 53, no. 2 (2011): 261–89.

———. *The Enlightenment on Trial: Ordinary Litigants and Colonialism in the Spanish Empire*. New York: Oxford University Press, 2017.

Price, Richard. *Maroon Societies: Rebel Slave Communities in the Americas*. 3rd ed. Baltimore: Johns Hopkins University Press, 1996.

Proctor, Frank T. *Damned Notions of Liberty: Slavery, Culture, and Power in Colonial Mexico, 1640–1769*. Albuquerque: University of New Mexico Press, 2010.

Puente Brunke, José de la. "Codicia y bien público: Los ministros de la Audiencia en la Lima seiscentista." *Revista de Indias* 66, no. 236 (2006): 133–48.

Querol Roso, Luis. "Negros y mulatos de Nueva España: Historia de su alzamiento en Méjico en 1612." *Anales de la Universidad de Valencia*. Año XII. Cuaderno, 90. Valencia: Imprenta Hijo F. Vives Mora, 1932.

Quevedo Alvarado, María Piedad. *Un cuerpo para el espíritu: Mística en la Nueva Granada, el cuerpo, el gusto y el asco, 1680–1750*. Bogota: Instituto Colombiano de Antropología e Historia, 2007.

Radin, Max, and Madaline W. Nichols. "Las Siete Partidas." *California Law Review* 20, no. 3 (1932): 260–85.

Raynal, abbé Guillaume-Thomas-François. *A Philosophical and Political History of the Settlements and Trade of the Europeans in the East and West Indies*. Translated by J. O. Justamond. 2nd edition. London: A. Strahan, 1798.

Redondo Gómez, Maruja. *Cartagena de Indias: Cinco siglos de evolución urbanística*. Bogota: Fundación Universidad de Bogotá Jorge Tadeo Lozano, 2004.

Regalado de Hurtado, Liliana. "Denominadores comunes en las críticas y propuestas de 'Buen Gobierno' según las crónicas de los Siglos XVI y XVII." In *International Congress of Americanists, América Bajo Los Austrias: Economía, Cultura, y Sociedad*, edited by Héctor Omar Noejovich. Lima: Pontificia Universidad Católica del Peru, 2001.

Reilly, Bernard F. "The Chancery of Alfonso VII of León-Castilla: The Period 1116–35 Reconsidered." *Speculum* 51, no. 2 (1976): 243–61.

———. *The Medieval Spains*. New York: Cambridge University Press, 1993.

Restall, Matthew. *Beyond Black and Red: African-Native Relations in Colonial Latin America*. Albuquerque: University of New Mexico Press, 2005.

Rey Fajardo, José del. *Los jesuitas en Cartagena de Indias, 1604–1767*. Bogota: Centro Editorial Javeriano, 2004.

Ribes Iborra, Vicente. *Comerciantes, esclavos, y capital sin patria*. Valencia: Generalitat Valenciana, 1993.

Riedel, Oswaldo de Oliveira. *Perspectiva Antropológica do Escravo no Ceará*. Fortaleza: Universidade Federal do Ceará, 1988.

Riva-Agüero, José de la. *La emancipación y la república*. Vol. 7 of *Obras Completas de José de la Riva-Agüero*. Lima: Pontificia Universidad Católica del Peru, 1971.

Rodriguez, Jarbel. *Captives and their Saviors in the Medieval Crown of Aragon*. Washington, DC: Catholic University of America Press, 2007.

Rodriguez, Junius P., ed. *The Historical Encyclopedia of World Slavery*. Santa Barbara, CA: ABC-CLIO, 1997.

Rodríguez-Bobb, Arturo. *Historia del negro en el Caribe (Cartagena, Colombia): Políticas monárquicas, transgresiones, exclusión, estrategias, poderes, esclavitud, violencia y derechos suprimidos*. Berlin: WVB, Wissenschaftlicher Verlag Berlin, 2007.

Rojas, Reinaldo. *La rebelión del Negro Miguel y otros temas de africanía*. Barquisimeto, Venezuela: Fundación Buría, 2004.

Roncancio Parra, Andrés. *Índices de documentos de la Inquisición de Cartagena de Indias: Programa de recuperación, sistematización y divulgación de archivos*. Bogota: Instituto Colombiano de Cultura Hispánica, Ministerio de Cultura, 2000.

Roper, John Herbert, and Lolita G. Brockington. "Slave Revolt, Slave Debate: A Comparison." *Phylon* 45, no. 2 (1984): 98–110.

Rout, Leslie B. *The African Experience in Spanish America, 1502 to the Present Day*. New York: Cambridge University Press, 1976.

Rowlands, Alison. "Father Confessors and Clerical Intervention in Witch-Trials in Seventeenth-Century Lutheran Germany: The Case of Rothenburg, 1692." *The English Historical Review* 131, no. 552 (October 2016): 1010–42.

———. *Witchcraft Narratives in Germany: Rothenburg, 1561–1652*. Manchester, UK: Manchester University Press, 2003.

Rubenstein, Jennifer. "Accountability in an Unequal World." *The Journal of Politics* 69, no. 3 (2007): 616–32.

Ruiz Rivera, Julián Bautista. *Los indios de Cartagena bajo la administración española en el Siglo XVII*. Bogota: Archivo General de la Nación, 1996.

Rupert, Linda M. "Contraband Trade and the Shaping of Colonial Societies in Curaçao and Tierra Firme." *Itinerario* 30, no. 3 (2006): 35.

———. "Marronage, Manumission, and Maritime Trade in the Early Modern Caribbean." *Slavery & Abolition* 30, no. 3 (2009): 361–82.

Safford, Frank, and Marco Palacios. *Colombia: Fragmented Land, Divided Society*. New York: Oxford University Press, 2002.

Sandoval, Alonso de. *Treatise on Slavery: Selections from De Instauranda Aethiopum Salute*. Edited by Nicole von Germeten. Indianapolis: Hackett, 2008.

———. *Un tratado sobre la esclavitud*. Transcribed by Enriqueta Vila Vilar. Madrid: Alianza Universidad, 1987.

Schaposchnik, Ana E. *The Lima Inquisition: The Plight of Crypto-Jews in Seventeenth-Century Peru*. Madison: University of Wisconsin Press, 2015.

Scheele, Judith, Daniel Lord Smail, Bianca Premo, and Bhavani Raman. "Priorities of Law: A Conversation with Judith Scheele, Daniel Lord Smail, Bianca Premo, and Bhavani Raman." *Comparative Studies in Society and History* (January 8, 2018) https://cssh.lsa.umich.edu/2018/01/08/priorities-of-law/.

Schmidt Camacho, Alicia R. *Migrant Imaginaries: Latino Cultural Politics in the US-Mexico Borderlands*. New York: New York University Press, 2008.

Schmidt-Nowara, Christopher. *Slavery, Freedom, and Abolition in Latin America and the Atlantic World*. Albuquerque: University of New Mexico Press, 2011.

Schultz, Majken, Steve Maguire, Ann Langley, and Haridimos Tsoukas, eds. *Constructing Identity In and Around Organizations*. Volume 2. Oxford: Oxford University Press, 2012.

Schwaller, Robert C. "Defining Difference in Early New Spain." PhD diss., Pennsylvania State University, 2010.

Scott, Rebecca J. "Paper Thin: Freedom and Re-Enslavement in the Diaspora of the Haitian Revolution." *Law and History Review* 29, no. 4 (2011): 1061–87.

———. "Slavery and the Law in Atlantic Perspective: Jurisdiction, Jurisprudence, and Justice." *Law and History Review* 29, no. 4 (2011): 915–24.

Scott, Rebecca J., and Jean M. Hébrard. *Freedom Papers: An Atlantic Odyssey in the Age of Emancipation*. Cambridge, MA: Harvard University Press, 2014.

Seijas, Tatiana, and Pablo Miguel Sierra Silva. "The Persistence of the Slave Market in Seventeenth-Century Central Mexico." *Slavery & Abolition* 37, no. 2 (2016): 307–33.

Serulnikov, Sergio. *Subverting Colonial Authority: Challenges to Spanish Rule in Eighteenth-Century Southern Andes*. Durham: Duke University Press, 2003.

Sharp, William Frederick. *Slavery on the Spanish Frontier: The Colombian Chocó, 1680–1810*. Norman: University of Oklahoma Press, 1976.

Shiels, William Eugene. *King and Church: The Rise and Fall of the Patronato Real*. Chicago: Loyola University Press, 1961.

Singh, Nikhil Pal. *Race and America's Long War*. Berkeley: University of California Press, 2017.

Sinha, Manisha. *The Slave's Cause: A History of Abolition*. New Haven, CT: Yale University Press, 2016.

Skerritt Gardner, David. *Una dinámica rural: Movilidad, cultura y región en Veracruz*. Xalapa: Dirección Editorial, Universidad Veracruzana, 2008.

Smallwood, Stephanie E. *Saltwater Slavery: A Middle Passage from Africa to American Diaspora*. Cambridge, MA: Harvard University Press, 2007.

Souza, Laura de Mello E. *The Devil and the Land of the Holy Cross: Witchcraft, Slavery, and Popular Religion in Colonial Brazil*. Austin: University of Texas Press, 2003.

Starn, Raldolph. "Truths in the Archives." *Common Knowledge* 8, no. 2 (2002): 387.

Stearns, Justin. "Representing and Remembering Al-Andalus: Some Historical Considerations Regarding the End of Time and the Making of Nostalgia." *Medieval Encounters* 15, nos. 2–4 (2009): 355–74.

Stedman, John Gabriel. *Narrative of a Five Years Expedition against the Revolted Negroes of Surinam*. Edited by Richard Price and Sally Price. Baltimore: Johns Hopkins University Press, 1988.

Sublette, Ned, and Constance Sublette. *The American Slave Coast: A History of the Slave-Breeding Industry*. Chicago: Lawrence Hill Books, 2016.

Sued-Badillo, Jalil. "Facing Up to Caribbean History." *American Antiquity* 57, no. 4 (1992): 599–607.

Swanson, Robert. *The Twelfth-Century Renaissance*. Manchester, UK: Manchester University Press, 1999.

Sweet, James H. *Recreating Africa: Culture, Kinship, and Religion in the African-Portuguese World, 1441–1770*. Chapel Hill: University of North Carolina Press, 2003.

Swidler, Ann. "Culture in Action: Symbols and Strategies." *American Sociological Review* 51, no. 2 (1986): 273–86.

Swingen, Abigail Leslie. *Competing Visions of Empire: Labor, Slavery, and the Origins of the British Atlantic Empire*. New Haven, CT: Yale University Press, 2015.

Tannenbaum, Frank. *Slave and Citizen: The Negro in the Americas*. New York: Random House, 1963.

Tardieu, Jean-Pierre. "Un proyecto utópico de manumisión de los cimarrones del palenque de los montes de Cartagena en 1682." In *Afrodescendientes en las Américas: Trayectorias sociales e identitarias: 150 años de la abolición de la esclavitud en Colombia*, edited by Claudia Mosquera, Mauricio Pardo, and Odile Hoffmann, 169–80. Bogota: Universidad Nacional de Colombia, 2002, 169–80.

Tejado Fernández, Manuel. *Aspectos de la vida social en Cartagena de Indias durante el seiscientos*. Sevilla: Escuela de Estudios Hispano-Americanos, 1954.

Thornton, John K., and Linda M. Heywood. "'Canniball [sic] Negroes,' Atlantic Creoles, and the Identity of New England's Charter Generation African." *African Diaspora* 4, no.1 (2011): 76–94.

Tilly, Charles. "War Making and State Making as Organized Crime." In *Bringing the State Back In*, edited by Peter B. Evans, Dietrich Rueschemeyer, and Theda Skocpol. New York: Cambridge University Press, 1985.

Tovar Pinzón, Hermes. *La estación del miedo o la desolación dispersa: El Caribe colombiano en el siglo XVI*. Bogota: Editorial Ariel, 1997.

Twinam, Ann. "The Negotiation of Honor." In *The Faces of Honor: Sex, Shame, and Violence in Colonial Latin America*, edited by Lyman L. Johnson and Sonya Lipsett-Rivera, 68–102. Albuquerque: University of New Mexico Press, 1998.

———. *Public Lives, Private Secrets: Gender, Honor, Sexuality, and Illegitimacy in Colonial Spanish America*. Stanford: Stanford University Press, 1999.

Urban, William. *The Baltic Crusades*. DeKalb: Northern Illinois University Press, 1975.

Valencia Villa, Carlos Eduardo. *Alma en boca y huesos en costal: Una aproximación a los contrastes socio-económicos de la esclavitud - Santafé, Mariquita y Mompox, 1610–1660*. Bogota: Instituto Colombiano de Antropología e Historia, 2003.

Vega Franco, Marisa. *El tráfico de esclavos con América: Asientos de grillo y lomelín, 1663–1674*. Seville: Escuela de Estudios Hispano-Americanos de Sevilla, 1984.

Verges, Felipe. *Apuntes de derecho canónico*. Barcelona: Establecimiento Tipográfico de Jaime Jepús, 1867.

Vial, Theodore. *Modern Religion, Modern Race*. New York: Oxford University Press, 2016.

Victoria and Albert Museum. *Africans in Medieval & Renaissance Art: Duke Alessandro de Medici*. London, 2016. http://www.vam.ac.uk/content/articles/a/africans-in-medieval-and-renaissance-art-duke-alessandro-de-medici/

Vidal Ortega, Antonino, and Álvaro Baquero Montoya. *De las Indias remotas: Cartas del cabildo de Santa Marta, 1529–1640*. Barranquilla: Ediciones Uninorte, 2007.

Vila Vilar, Enriqueta. *Aspectos sociales en América colonial: De extranjeros, contrabando y esclavos*. Bogota: Instituto Caro y Cuervo; Universidad Jorge Tadeo Lozano, 2001.

———. *Hispanoamérica y el comercio de esclavos*. Seville: Escuela de Estudios Hispano-Americanos, 1977.

Villa-Flores, Javier. *Dangerous Speech: A Social History of Blasphemy in Colonial Mexico*. Tucson: University of Arizona Press, 2006.

Vinson, Ben, III, Sherwin K. Bryant, and Rachel Sarah O'Toole, eds. *Africans to Spanish America: Expanding the Diaspora*. Urbana: University of Illinois Press, 2012.

"Voyages: The Transatlantic Slave Trade Database," Emory University, 2013. http://www.slavevoyages.org/.

Wade, Peter. *Blackness and Race Mixture: The Dynamics of Racial Identity in Colombia*. Baltimore: Johns Hopkins University Press, 1995.

Warren, Wendy. *New England Bound: Slavery and Colonization in Early America*. New York: W. W. Norton & Company, 2016.

Watson, Alan. *Slave Law in the Americas*. Athens: University of Georgia Press, 1989.

Weissberger, Barbara F., ed. *Queen Isabel I of Castile: Power, Patronage, Persona*. Rochester, NY: Tamesis, 2008.

West, Robert Cooper. *Colonial Placer Mining in Colombia*. Baton Rouge: Louisiana State University Press, 1952.

Wheat, David. *Atlantic Africa and the Spanish Caribbean, 1570–1640*. Chapel Hill: University of North Carolina Press, 2016.

White, Heather Rachelle. "Between the Devil and the Inquisition: African Slaves and the Witchcraft Trials in Cartagena de Indies." *The North Star* 8, no. 2 (2005): 1–15.

Wickham, Chris. *Medieval Europe*. New Haven, CT: Yale University Press, 2016.

Williams, Eric. *Capitalism and Slavery*. Chapel Hill: University of North Carolina Press, 1944.

Wood, Stephanie. *Transcending Conquest: Nahua Views of Spanish Colonial Mexico*. Norman: University of Oklahoma Press, 2003.

Yaranga Valderrama, Abdón. "Las 'reducciones,' uno de los instrumentos del etnocidio." *Revista Complutense de Historia de América*, no. 21 (1995): 241–62.

Zavala, Silvio Arturo. *The Defense of Human Rights in Latin America: Sixteenth to Eighteenth Centuries*. Paris: UNESCO, 1964.

———. *La filosofía política en la Conquista de América*. Mexico City: Fondo de Cultura Económica, 1947.

———. *Servidumbre natural y libertad cristiana, según los tratadistas españoles de los siglos XVI y XVII*. Mexico City: Editorial Porrúa, 1975.

Zimring, Franklin E. *The Great American Crime Decline*. New York: Oxford University Press, 2007.

INDEX